'A compelling book... Candid, poignant, well-written and wonderfully life-affirming'
*Tatler*

'Brilliant... The book is so full of gems of description and honest insights into the realities of family relationships ... hard to put down... All in all, this is a must-read'
*Country Life*

'I loved *A House Full of Daughters*. I was initially intrigued, then gripped, and then when she began writing about herself, deeply moved and admiring of the way in which she charted her own journey. An illuminating book in which she charts the inevitability of family life and the damage and gifts that we inherit from the previous generations'
Esther Freud

'It combines history with memoir in a way that both historians and memoirists should envy'
Lady Antonia Fraser, *Observer*

'In prose that is lyrical and sometimes self-lacerating, she anatomises the failures of love and attention, none the less destructive for being inadvertent, from which these husbands, wives, parents and children, suffered so acutely... Lent grace by Nicolson's lustrous prose, and by the redemptive hope that love and forgiveness will free the latest generations from the baleful patterns of the past'
*Evening Standard*

'Juliet Nicolson is firing on all cylinders... She is able to write about powerful emotion in a way that is both heartfelt and unselfconscious... It makes the book perfectly personal as well as a fascinating history'
William Boyd

'Surprisingly affecting...impressively understated... remarkably sad'

'A marvellous ... ... ful eye for detail'
New York Times Book Review

# JULIET NICOLSON

Juliet Nicolson is the author of two works of history, *The Great Silence, 1918–1920: Living in the Shadow of the Great War* and *The Perfect Summer: Dancing into Shadow in 1911*, and a novel, *Abdication*. As the granddaughter of Vita Sackville-West and Harold Nicolson and the daughter of Nigel Nicolson she is part of a renowned and much scrutinised family and the latest in the family line of record-keepers of the past. She lives with her husband in East Sussex, not far from Sissinghurst, where she spent her childhood. She has two daughters, Clemmie and Flora, and one granddaughter, Imogen.

ALSO BY JULIET NICOLSON

JULIET NICOLSON

# A House Full of Daughters

VINTAGE

5 7 9 10 8 6

Vintage
20 Vauxhall Bridge Road,
London SW1V 2SA

Vintage is part of the Penguin Random House
group of companies whose addresses can be found at
global.penguinrandomhouse.com

Penguin
Random House
UK

First published in Vintage in 2017
First published in hardback by Chatto & Windus in 2016

Excerpt from 'Premonitions' from *The Bees* by Carol Ann Duffy.
Copyright © Carol Ann Duffy 2011. Reproduced by permission of the author
c/o Rogers, Coleridge & White Ltd., 20 Powis Mews, London W11 1JN

Photos: Clemmie with her daughter Imogen Flora, 2013, Copyright © Jenny
Lewis 2013; Victoria and Lionel, 1890, kindly lent by Robert Sackville-West;
Ice skating at Lady Walsingham's, 1940, kindly lent by Bronwen Tyler;
Philippa leap-frogging with friends, 1946, kindly lent by Jennifer, Lady Plunket.

penguin.co.uk/vintage

A CIP catalogue record for this book
is available from the British Library

ISBN 9780099598039

Printed and bound in Great Britain by Clays Ltd, St Ives plc

Penguin Random House is committed to a sustainable future
for our business, our readers and our planet. This book is made
from Forest Stewardship Council® certified paper.

MIX
Paper from
responsible sources
FSC
www.fsc.org    FSC® C018179

*For Clemmie and Flora and also for Imogen,
with all my love*

# Contents

# Seven generations, one family

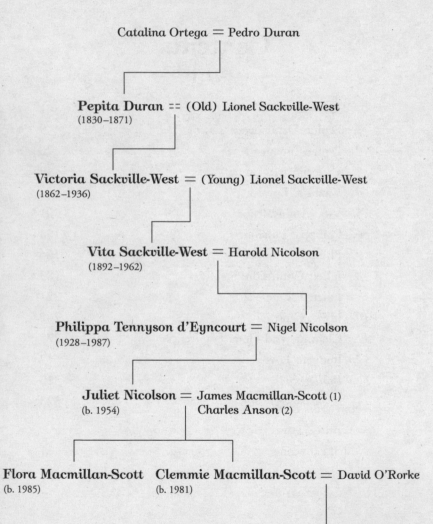

Catalina Ortega = Pedro Duran

**Pepita Duran** == (Old) Lionel Sackville-West
(1830–1871)

**Victoria Sackville-West** = (Young) Lionel Sackville-West
(1862–1936)

**Vita Sackville-West** = Harold Nicolson
(1892–1962)

**Philippa Tennyson d'Eyncourt** = Nigel Nicolson
(1928–1987)

**Juliet Nicolson** = James Macmillan-Scott (1)
(b. 1954)        Charles Anson (2)

**Flora Macmillan-Scott**    **Clemmie Macmillan-Scott** = David O'Rorke
(b. 1985)          (b. 1981)

**Imogen Flora O'Rorke**
(b. 2013)

◊

# Prologue

This is a book about seven generations of women in one family, my family. Beginning with the birth of my grandmother's grandmother in 1830, the story travels down the centuries until it reaches my two-year-old granddaughter in 2015. The historical span stretches from nineteenth-century southern Spain, through the diplomatic world of Washington DC at the end of the Civil War to England's Edwardian house parties, the wartime deprivation of the 1940s, London in the 1960s and Manhattan during the boom years of the 1980s before concluding in England in a new century. However, it is not really the historical context with which I am concerned, but rather the women who preceded me and who lived through those times.

The habit of writing down the story of our lives has long been a tradition in our family. My great-grandmother Victoria kept diaries and wrote a book of reminiscences; her daughter, my grandmother Vita, wrote several books about her predecessors including a joint biography of her mother and grandmother, within which she included memories of her own childhood and young adulthood. She also used her autobiographical experience (barely disguised) in her novels. My father devoted a large part of his professional life to writing and editing books by and about his parents, adding a portrait of his parents' marriage to an unpublished memoir by his mother. At times writing has assumed the role of unjudgemental family therapist, with each new version of an often repeated family story an attempt by the latest in the line of writers to be the most accurate, the most truthful.

Having reached a middle point in my life when I began to find it as tempting to look backwards as forwards, I too wanted to explore those generations that preceded me. There were stories I thought I knew well, assumptions I had made myself, or accounts that had been handed down by my parents which I had never bothered to question. But familiarity can render truth enigmatic. Just as it is possible to listen but not hear, so it is easy to look but not to see. This book is an attempt to hear and to see, to connect myself as truthfully as possible to a long line of women, and to hollow out some footholds into a generational path that is already crumbling with time and fading memory.

I wanted to look in chronological sequence at these women who were related to each other either genetically or through marriage, to see what conclusions I might draw from their collective stories. I wanted to try to understand them, be grateful to them where I should be, forgive them where I could, learn from their mistakes, find the courage to change when, perhaps, they had not been able to.

I also wanted to see how they would respond to the charge of privilege. In monetary terms all but one was born into a materially comfortable existence, even an aristocratic world rich with grand houses and centuries of ancestral culture behind them. Gleaming spoons shine from several of the mouths in this story. But I wondered if wealth and class always amounted to privilege in a broader sense. If a privileged child is one that enjoys a happy upbringing, with parents who love not only their children but each other, then some of these women could not claim that sort of advantage. And if privilege involves having a parent who encourages their daughter to succeed in the world then privilege was not always a feature in my family.

By considering the group of individuals who were responsible indirectly and directly for my existence, I thought a great deal about the one relationship that every woman has in common. We are all daughters. Whether you are a sister, an only child, adopted or orphaned, a mother, childless, married, divorced, single or widowed, all women are born and remain daughters. I began to see how daughterhood can trap as well as enhance lives. If there is any truth in the old saying that 'a daughter is a daughter for life, a son is a son until he takes a wife', parents have always had different expectations of their sons and daughters. There must be a reason why the word 'daughterhood' has no counterpart in sons. In our family sons have been encouraged to distinguish themselves and therefore become distinguished, distinctive, independent, free-standing from their parents. But daughters have at times struggled to leave dependence behind them and to embrace autonomy.

A daughter's attempt to break free from the parental bond can become an act of rebellion against an assumption that submission is not only expected but integral to the relationship. In our family one response to the feeling of entrapment was to run away, even if it meant abandoning young children. Another was to stand up to paternal authority and other male-dominated relationships by striking unspoken bargains involving money, sex or filial subservience. Although I had set out to write a book about the women in my family, as I moved from one generation to the next the role of fatherhood emerged as powerfully as that of mothers. I began to see that fathers not only played a hugely influential part but that in four of the seven generations, bargain or no bargain, fathers were the better, more loving, more engaged parent.

During the writing of the book repetitive patterns began to emerge with often surprising regularity. Sometimes these patterns were imposed by the circumstances of the time and by the slow-to-change prejudices and opportunities that women have encountered for centuries. And sometimes the patterns became blurred and eventually abandoned as equality for women edged ever nearer. But often the patterns were more personal and more disturbing. The story I slowly uncovered turned out to be riddled with secrets that parent kept from child and child from parent. Usually these secrets concerned romantic relationships. My great-great-grandmother concealed her love life from her mother; my grandmother went to great lengths to prevent her mother discovering the nature of her attachments to women; my mother conducted chunks of her life on the other side of locked doors and I found it impossible to confide my most important feelings to her.

Another pattern concerned parental, and particularly maternal, jealousy. This often occurred when a daughter established her personal and professional independence, especially when a new generation was able to benefit from new freedoms, both social and political, that had not been available to her mother. Sometimes the response to this jealousy was to sabotage a daughter's chances. At others it was to abandon her altogether.

Some of the women inherited a fear of intimacy, especially when the example set by their own parents proved lacking, through distrust or infidelity or simply the erosion of the original loving bond. Several of the women demonstrated their lack of self-worth and self-belief, slipping in middle age and later life into loneliness and isolation, numbing unhappiness in an addictive dependence on drink, money and sex. Only rarely did an individual, ensnared in this way, manage to break through the dependency.

The importance of place, sometimes in exchange for a human relationship, reoccurred in several generations. There are beautiful places in this story, Knole and Sissinghurst among them, two of the houses that several women in my family, including me, have at times loved above anything or anyone else. When relationships were at their most fragile, or had failed, a place, a house, a room of their own, even a pair of gates behind which to hide, offered the reassurance of security and uncritical continuity. And yet a sanctuary afforded by bricks and mortar rather than human comfort is open to its own peculiar vulnerability.

Not only does it encourage isolation and therefore loneliness but the quirks of inheritance laws, wills and financial difficulty can destroy such seemingly indestructible bonds.

A book that travels though generations moves to the rhythm of birth and death. Only with my parents' deaths did I consider mortality as something I too might one day experience. Penelope Lively has identified how with age 'the capricious nature of time' suddenly accelerates at a gallop, in contrast to the earlier amble of childhood. I now try to disguise that acceleration from my daughters, glossing over a painful arthritic thumb, vaulting a gate to show I still can, easing myself whenever possible out of daylight and into the softening glow of a candle whenever a camera is directed towards me. In part this book is an attempt to overcome the fugitive nature of time and, in many cases, the transitory nature of love.

My father loved to quote Virginia Woolf at me, from whom he had inherited his favourite refrain. When he was a schoolboy, lazy about homework and exhausted with the idea of keeping a diary, she had told him that 'nothing has really happened unless it is written down'. Despite the ubiquitous presence of Twitter and Instagram ensuring no single happening or fleeting thought goes unrecorded, this premise now seems crazy to me. It vaporises the concept of immediacy, even the existence of the moment for anyone who may be incapable or unwilling to commit their experience to paper or photographic documentation. The oral tradition has no place in this argument. But while my susceptibility to my father's caution has taken a long time to wane, I am growing increasingly sceptical. I wonder about the purpose of writing things down, of making records, of continuing to store the huge quantity of yellowing notebooks that have filled drawers and filing cabinets in passages and hallways all my life when most of it will mean little to later generations. At the very moment when I am adding to the clogged-up family cabinets, piling yet more words on top of a word mountain, part of me is rebelling. Just this once, but never again, I feel. The thing is, of course, things happen, people love and live and cry and laugh and die without a permanent record being made. Precious moments – the birth of a child, the death of a parent, the sun glinting on the sea – are more precious for their fleetingness in the mind than their dry durability in print. It is the fallibility of memory that gets in the way, plays tricks, distorts, blurs and causes an illusion that time has veiled the experience of life so effectively making it invisible to the mind's eye. Records can be useful, but only if one identifies the meaning within their jumble and attempts to find a buried narrative. With the flimsiest scraps of information – a photograph here, a letter there, a wisp of bridal lace, a dancing slipper, a glass obelisk, a hedge in a garden, the dedication in a book, the scent of lemony soap, a snatch of song, the glimpse of a once-familiar painting, the picking of home-grown raspberries, still dewy in the early-morning garden – it is possible, with thought and time, to discover what a mother and father were once like. Clues, both written and preserved through objects, can lead to discoveries about a long-dead grandparent, great-grandparent and even further distant ancestor, and invite an exploration of one's own relationship to them.

Once again it was Virginia Woolf who compared thinking to

fishing, 'the little tug – the sudden conglomeration of an idea at the end of one's line'. The act of remembering can often prompt this little tug, the 'Oh, *that* is what it was all about. *Now* I understand.' Of course this search for the illumination of mysteries carries with it the danger of uncovering things that were never meant to be shared; one can be left with uncomfortable secrets that cannot be unremembered. And yet it is often when those people who made us are no longer alive that we can reassess and be free of them and work out for ourselves exactly who we were and who we are.

# 1

# Pepita
## Dependence

Pepita, my great-great-grandmother, is responsible for the one-sixteenth of me that is proudly Spanish. Throughout my life I have been aware of the famous dancer, a spectacular beauty with what my grandmother Vita called her 'rapscallion background' who emerged from the backstreets of a southern Spanish town to conquer the stages of nineteenth-century Europe. My father always spoke her name with a deliberately exaggerated lilt, just as he pronounced 'Lolita' in the way Nabokov stipulated in the opening line of his novel. A framed drawing of Pepita wearing the tight-bodiced, sleeveless dancing dress that identified her as the 'Star of Andalusia' at the time my great-great-grandfather fell in love with her always hung on the sitting-room wall in our house. Pepita was a curious figure to me, foreign not only in look, but also in time and in culture. Hers was a sensibility wholly alien to an English upbringing in which teatime jam sandwiches had to be eaten before cake was allowed and children were more likely to learn the androgynous, cigarette-extinguishing footstep of the twist than the sexually charged strutting of the mid-nineteenth-century flamenco. My father was enchanted by the romance of Pepita's story, his mother having impressed it on him since his own childhood. He once gave me a Spanish doll made of hard pink plastic with a black lace mantilla over her face and highly rouged cheeks, and after a trip to Spain he brought me back a pair of wooden castanets with the word 'Malaga' in black ink painted over a pink hibiscus. Clueless what to do with them I was encouraged to be pleased by even the faintest hint of a Spanish heritage.

Pepita was born in 1830 in the throbbing, poverty-riddled city of Malaga. Her father, Pedro Duran, was a barber while the local glamour of her gypsy mother, Catalina Ortega, was enhanced by rumours that as a young girl she had earned money leaping though hoops at a circus. After the birth of her daughter, Catalina took in washing from neighbours and the local hotels, the clean sheets of Malaga's smarter districts hanging out to dry, suspended like huge truce flags, over Catalina's balcony. The family lived in Calle Puente, a small alley tucked away in a maze of slums not far from the river and where the heavy air, thick with southern heat, was impregnated with the smell of rancid olive oil, rotten fish, fresh manure and the combined scent of crushed cinnamon and chocolate. Calle Puente was choked with animal and human life. Neighbourhood chickens squawked for scraps on the earth floor and the jangle of bells alerted dawdling pedestrians to mules carrying vegetables in their panniers and luggage on their backs. Bumping their way along the alley, the animals paused only to raise their heads, stretch their necks and bray, an alarming, jarring, semi-human combination of sobs and sighs. Dozens of tiny naked children ran and played together in the sunshine, while the women swept rubbish from outside their doorways and gossiped, the men plotted and smoked cigars, and the exhausted faces of the very poor were just visible in the shadows, retreating from the harshness of the sun and of life.

On the morning I went to Calle Puente, determined to begin at the beginning and to find Pepita's birthplace, flowery house-coated women were scrubbing their front steps as skinny dogs ran circles around them. There was no sign of a donkey but families of cats and their kittens occupied the darkened street corners, licking and hissing, purring and scratching, tumbling and entwining and dozing in furry, sleepy heaps. A man in a blond wig with a five o'clock shadow and dressed in a silver miniskirt was making his unsteady way towards me on high heels while his companion, six inches smaller, trotted beside him, puffing on a cigar, a silky Pekinese tucked under his arm. The old 1830 houses of Pepita's day had crumbled away, but although the replacement buildings were new, a sense of deprivation and struggle lingered. A builder's van with its back doors open revealing a stack of tools was parked halfway down the street. The driver nodded a good morning and at the sound of our voices a couple of windows above us flew open. Two women, cigarettes hanging from their mouths, stared down at me. In hesitant Spanish and much backwards gesticulating with my thumb to indicate centuries past, I mentioned Pepita's name.

At once one of the women broke into a smile pointing with her finger in the direction of the river. 'Conservatorio Professional de Danza,' she said triumphantly, mimicking a little dance movement as she spoke. How was it possible that memories of a child who had danced as light as a bird in that tiny street in the southern sunshine had lingered for nearly two centuries? I did not question it. Maybe they had been handed from mother to daughter in the way that family memories should be.

In Pepita's day, Malaga was an ancient, bandit-riddled city, encircled by vine-clothed hills, a rough place to live, although foreigners were reassured that the Spanish knife was not as effective a weapon as the stiletto, the sharp instrument used by Italy's fiercest gangsters. The sunny, warm and dry climate attracted visitors looking for a cure from asthma and tuberculosis. The wide central thoroughfare was an aqueduct during the winter months, the murky water choked with rubbish and sewage, but during the summer it provided the parade ground for Malaga's best-dressed show-offs. Each week between twelve and fifteen thousand spectators would assemble in Malaga's bullring for the fight. Outside the arena, shouting above the great din of the crowd, pedlars hawked fans, paper parasols, cigars, oranges, slices of watermelon, phials of brandy, yeasty *churros* fried in oil and dipped in sugar, and iced barley to refresh the mouth. Inside the ring, the procession was headed by the picadors, secure on horseback, high above the sawdust, hands on hips, their lances carefully balanced, as was the custom, on the crook of one ankle. Next came the capeodores twirling their heavy violet-and-gold capes, followed by the banderilleros brandishing their icicle-sharp hooks, before finally the matador himself arrived, strutting into the ring in his brilliantly coloured silk-and-velvet costume, preening, proud, lethal. Women joined their men in the auditorium, flashing their sequin-spangled fans. Known for their impervious expression in the presence of the puddles of darkening gore that pooled across the bullring each week, the Malagueñas, the women of Malaga, wore their blood-scarlet mantillas especially high on their heads for the fight. Their distinctive red lace veiling, in contrast to the dour black of their counterparts in Madrid, was pinned in place onto their luxuriant loops of hair with a dried thorny cactus branch onto which sweet-smelling jasmine had been spiked. Richard Ford, travel writer and enchanted British onlooker, respected the haughty dignity of these women, aware that 'a Spanish woman's hair is the glory and the secret of her strength, a theft from Samson for her gender, while her fan is the index of her soul'. As the bullfight got under way to a backdrop of roaring spectators, each group of assassins took their turn in the murderous dance between man and beast, their lances and hooks progressively weakening the bull. When the final sword was plunged into the heart of the animal, the cacophony reached a crescendo and the huge beast fell to the ground.

Away from the flamboyance of the bullring, violence and criminality, prostitution and poverty, desperation and ruthlessness were endemic in the darkened corners of Pepita's city. Woe betide the visitor who wandered into the backstreets. By flipping a man's cape over his face from behind, a robber was free to stab him in the back while at the same time whipping his wallet from out of his pocket.

When Pepita was six years old her father, Pedro Duran, was

killed in a brawl during a street procession. His widow was left alone with their two children, Pepita and her brother Diego. Catalina began selling women's clothes, knocking on doors in alleys so narrow that it was possible to shake hands across the streets by leaning out of the protruding top windows. Diego was an independent child, wild, troublesome and determined to indulge in all the freedoms offered to an untamed and father-less son. At liberty to be out and about with his gang of friends, he joined the army at the first opportunity and left for Cuba, remaining abroad and out of touch throughout the early years of Pepita's childhood. Although their house was small and cramped and even their friends considered it 'old and bad', Catalina treated her daughter 'with great delicacy'. A fellow washerwoman was struck by the remarkable devotion Catalina showed to the child with the tiny waist, luminous olive skin and magnificent gold-brown hair that flowed down her back as far as the crook of her knees. As the other children of the Calle Puente ran freely around the streets, Catalina scarcely let Pepita out of her sight, sharing a bed with her, ceaselessly combing and dressing her daughter's magnificent hair and behaving with what the friend described as 'the fierce and possessive love which Latin women do often display towards their children'. While Pepita was Catalina's 'jewel, her treasure and her pride', the child's reciprocal devotion was interpreted by Catalina's disap-proving neighbours as 'excessive', the absence of any familial male presence exacerbating the exclusivity of the relationship.

Against all the odds, Pepita, a child born into poverty and hampered by the seemingly insuperable boundaries of her class and her sex, was inadvertently fortunate. Nineteenth-century

Spain, contained behind the barrier of the Pyrenees, slouched in comparison with the rest of Europe in its progress towards the emancipation of even the most privileged of women. Queen Isabella II nominally ruled the country but she was quite unlike Queen Victoria, her imperially powerful contemporary in Britain. Isabella was born in the same year as Pepita and acceded to the throne in 1833 aged three. She maintained her precarious hold as sovereign for thirty-five years even though it was continuously battered by challenges from male claimants. However, Isabella set no example for her sex and was never popular, described unkindly by an ex-patriot Englishwoman, Mrs William Pitt Byrne, as 'bulky rather than stately', possessing 'no dignity either in her face or figure'. Unlike the Queen of England, constitutional duties were never Isabella's priority. As the mother of a dozen children of varying paternity, she preferred instead to concentrate on keeping an impressively buoyant love life afloat. In contrast to the Spanish Queen, Pepita was blessed with what her neighbours called 'a face divine', but her greater, immediate advantage lay in being brought up by her widowed mother. Catalina, the hard-working saleswoman and washerwoman, was single-mindedly determined to overcome the restrictions of her circumstances and Spain's limited financial prospects for women.

Spain's all-powerful Catholic Church enforced women's accepted dual purposes as wife and mother, keeping academic and professional opportunities to the minimum. A working-class girl was instructed in the virtues of meekness and obedience and made to understand that a woman's body was under the direct control of her husband. While female adultery could result in imprisonment and even the death penalty, male infidelity was only punished if a mistress was actually caught in (or, equally culpably, beneath) the marital bed. Up until 1931 male marital supremacy was still so powerful that a wife could be sent to jail for between five and fifteen days if she went shopping without her husband's permission, or lost her temper and swore at him. If a woman owned any property prior to her marriage, the legal bond to a man required her to relinquish that ownership. The laws for a married woman were no different from those for the deaf, the dumb and the insane.

In contrast, the single Spanish woman of 150 years ago was entitled to a more liberal life than her married counterpart, with none of the obligations imposed by marital duties. Even so, until the age of twenty-five a woman still needed her father's permission to leave home and was barred from signing any commercial or legal contract without parental authority, including that of marriage. One way round the cat's-cradle of limitation was to be blessed with an indulgent or preferably dead father, or to marry and then leave your husband without annulling the marriage. However, if a gifted daughter was born into the poorest of circumstances, into a gyspy family, and if a parent encouraged her talent, then her opportunities to escape convention were far greater than if she had been born rich. Pepita was such a daughter.

The word 'flamenco' is arguably derived from the Arab '*felag*', meaning fugitive or escapee, and '*mengu*' meaning peasant. The flamenco dance had originated with the arrival in Spain of gypsies from countries as diverse as Morocco, Egypt and India, and as Arabian and Jewish refugees joined them, an oral tradition of dance and song grew up. Flamenco weaves together ancient stories of joy and desolation, loss and gain passed down by society's outsiders, refugees from oppression, and after the end of the Napoleonic Wars in the early part of the nineteenth century, the influence of the bullfight culture, its taming and conquering of the wild, began to merge with the inherent gypsy customs. Contemporary paintings show aristocratic Spanish men looking down from astride their horses with a combination of fascination and lust on the colourfully skirted and fringe-shawled Andalusian gypsies who inhabited backstreets like Calle Puente. The women, their hands on their hips, return the gaze with their chins tilted, their expressions provocative, fearless and knowing. These uninhibited women have a vulgarity and a physicality that might be intimidating not only to the delicate sensibilities of well-born girls but to the opposite sex, who appear mesmerised but also threatened by an unmistakable demonstration of female supremacy. Here was a matador in female clothing, capable of dominating and taming the machismo male bull with one sweep of her dress, one glance from her haughty, hypnotic eyes. With ivory castanets slipped over their knuckles and clasped within the palm of each hand, and gold embroidered ribbons streaming from their heavily embroidered skirts, they would arch their supple bodies into curves of such sensuality that as soon as they began to dance an electric current of desire ran through every onlooker.

Pepita learned to dance at the flamenco school near her house as soon as she learned to walk. She took at once to the lessons that her mother washed, haggled and worked so hard to pay for, performing with a lightness and delicacy that outshone the other students. Neighbours watched her drifting and floating down through the dust and mud of Calle Puente 'like a bird in the air'. Before she was twenty she had adapted the traditional Andalusian steps to suit her own style, merging the high leg kicks of *la Aragonesa*, the rhythmic *el jaleo de Jerez* and the encircled arms of the *la Madrilena*, working out for herself the choreography of an exhilarating performance. A stamp of a foot, a cleavage glistening with the energy of her movement and an expression both dismissive and alluring completed the composition of her *pièce de resistance*, the back-arching, leg-flaunting, spirit-rousing dance known as *el olé*. In one contemporary drawing Pepita is wearing her *vêtements de scene*, the dark blue velvet panels let into an ivory, breast-moulding top from which the shoulder ribbons slip provocatively, the outfit completed by a strikingly short ballet skirt of rose-red silk flounced at the edges with white and blue. In the picture Pepita's eyes flash and her lips are parted in a smile, and if you look carefully the shiny enamel of a perfect tooth is just visible between the parted lips. The demarcation between the dancers and those other women who lived in the sweaty, throbbing density of Calle Puente and the surrounding streets who earned money from the sale of their bodies was sometimes hard to identify.

One and a half centuries after Pepita had electrified her audiences I sought out the Spanish dancers for myself. In the plush upholstered atmosphere of a smart north London theatre I watched a restrained, controlled, almost sexless performance by a well-known visiting dancer. She was no less skilled than the younger members of the company who joined her in the chorus on the stage but at first I missed the haughty dangerous sexiness of youth and the heady atmosphere of liberation that I had read so much about. However, before long I was drawn to the subtle defiance of the limitations of the body and began to notice something else. Even when the dancer stood still and the music stopped there was a statement of dominance in that stillness, the dancer's supremacy needing no more acknowledgement. If the younger women demonstrated sexuality, this older woman exuded power, a balance of arrogance and assurance, before unleashing a seemingly unattainable sinuosity, standing her ground, entwining and releasing her arms and fingers with the dexterity of a world-class contortionist, lifting a skirt, flashing a thigh, wearing a red dress so tight and so revealing and yet so fluid that she appeared to be clothed in water.

In Malaga, dance is all around you, in the streets, in the cafes, in the cellars. In a small central square not far from the birthplace of Picasso, a young woman in a red-and-black body-skimming frock stood motionless in front of us, her audience, a scarlet hibiscus flower tucked into long black hair held off her face with black and red combs. Her neck was bare, her eyes dark and focused, her physical contact with the floor so secure that she seemed to have grown from the wooden boards beneath her feet. Slowly, teasingly, she tightened the leather threads of her castanets. Eventually she began to move, the seated guitarist beside her anticipating and reflecting as well as accompanying her every move. Alternating between a flirtatious combination of reserve and promise, she controlled an imagined beast. It was an astonishing display of female matadorial dominance acted out through the *sevillanas*, the dance taught by Andalusian mothers to their daughters. As she finished her performance an older woman took her place. Unlike the dancer in London this woman substituted coarseness for fineness, crudity for subtlety, vulgarity for classiness, her movements simulating a total lack of sexual inhibition. Whispers of disapproval ran through some of the onlookers. Others marvelled. But at the climax of the dance even the uneasiest members of the audience found themselves cheering.

Late one evening we took the small lift down to a cellar where long tables had been laid for a supper of cheese, spicy sausage and beans, and sweet honey cakes. A buxom woman dressed in purple stood in front of us, embarking on a long song, a lament of loss, the struggle audible in the notes and visible on the genuine anguish in her face alternating with a wild piercing cry of joy. The verses were interspersed with rhythmic bursts of hand-clapping and apparently random shouts of '*olé*' and only at the very end of an hour-long performance of song did the woman kick off her shoes and burst into spontaneous dance. My fellow diners, a group of flamenco devotees, explained to us the concept of *el duende*, 'the spirit of evocation', the sensation aroused by a deep response to an artistic performance and which has an unforgettable effect on those watching and listening. When we emerged into the busy streets of Malaga, I felt as if I had participated in a seance and that *El duende* had taken me closer to the reality of Pepita's world.

In 1849, when Pepita was nineteen, her dancing having mesmerised local audiences in the Theatre Principal in Malaga since childhood, Catalina knew her daughter was ready to make the next professional step. Together they travelled to Madrid where they rented a room in a basement apartment near the capital's main theatre, the newly revamped Teatro del Principe. Catalina, whose determination to get her way was often hard to resist, persuaded a reluctant Antonio Ruiz, the director of ballet, to give Pepita an audition. The management of the great Spanish theatres of the mid nineteenth century, like the Teatro del Principe, associated such raw, uninhibited movement as Pepita's with the servant and peasant class, and preferred to offer their sensitive audiences the more reserved steps of classical ballet.

Ruiz was bemused not only by this excitable, overbearing mother but also by Manuel Lopez, Catalina's vulgar, self-important escort with his unappealing goggle eyes. Catalina had taken a lover soon after her husband's death but Manuel Lopez was no substitute for paternal authority. A reformed bandit, smuggler and dealer in charcoal who more recently had worked as a cobbler, Lopez was a comic character, flashy and opportunistic, unscrupulously on the make in his broad-brimmed and high-crowned hat with silken tassels. Despite the dubious nature of her two chaperones, Ruiz overcame his prejudice against Pepita's companions and her extrovert style of dancing. Enchanted by Catalina's lovely daughter he decided to try and mould her to the theatre's own dancing standards and agreed to arrange lessons for her. But the lessons were not a success and Ruiz cancelled them with baffling speed. An angry Catalina blamed his decision on his failure to recognise Pepita's own version of 'excellence', even though it was so at odds with the Teatro's more conventional tastes.

Catalina remained convinced that her daughter was as gifted as any of the greatest Spanish dancers, her ambitions for Pepita as determined as ever. During their visit to the capital mother and daughter had met a young ballet teacher, a year older than Pepita but the same height, with attractive, sloping eyes, a fine long nose and an impressive physique. Juan Antonio Gabriel de la Oliva was an experienced dancer accustomed to the stages of Madrid, although his family of harness makers and tailors meant his background was much like Pepita's. Being a Spaniard of hot blood and ardent feelings, he accepted Catalina's invitation to give Pepita dancing lessons and within the time it took to perfect a stretch of the foot and an arch of the arm he had fallen in love with his pupil. He was not the first to be taken by Pepita with her astonishing hair, lithe body, dimpled chin, her graceful walk and tantalisingly black eyes, remarkable for their distinctive almond shape, or *rasgado*, which in Spanish also means 'outspoken' and 'generous'. But Oliva had an advantage over his rivals. Oliva pledged to forgo his fee for the dancing lessons in return for Catalina's approval of their courtship, promising to conduct his suit with every propriety. Under his tuition Pepita began to shine, her reputation growing with every performance and beginning to spread throughout Spain. Two years later, Pepita persuaded herself that she had fallen in love with her dancing teacher. Catalina gave their betrothal her blessing, satisfied that Oliva had a secure future as a teacher and that she had negotiated a decent marriage contract that included the continuation of the dancing lessons. However, Catalina did not consider the impact that this arrangement might have on her own relationship with her daughter. The bargain she was making on her daughter's behalf included the assumption that Pepita's daughterly loyalty and devotion to her mother would remain unthreatened and intact.

On Friday 10 January 1851 at eight in the morning, the engaged pair walked together through the crowded, boisterous streets of Madrid to be married in the local church of San Milan. On saints' days and at weekends, religious processions regularly weave their way through the alleys that surround the church, the cymbals clashing, the trumpets blowing, the noise from the column of drums beaten by alternating pairs of hazy-moustached schoolboys and burly men reverberating around the old city. At the heart of these processions a huge bier sways at shoulder height, cigars smouldering in the free hands of the bearers, their marching feet crushing bunches of rosemary strewn on the path in handfuls as the procession approaches, releasing the sudden pine-like smell that competes with the sweetness of incense. On the day I visited a pickpocket was caught working the dense crowd, a warning shout went up as the thief, his face white, his nose bloody, was apprehended by the mingling police and marched off to jail.

On her wedding day, Pepita chose to wear black lace in the Andalusian marital tradition. After the ceremony the protracted celebrations began with coffee and chocolate in the popular Café Suizo, followed by a family dinner in the fashionable Fonda de Europa restaurant where a feast of Andalusian dishes – salty, deep-fried anchovies, tangy-sweet orange, cod and potato salad, and delicious cinnamony almond milk – went on long into the night. And still the celebrations continued at a riotous party where the guests danced polkas, waltzes and quadrilles, and the groom held his beautiful bride swaying in his arms as they threw themselves 'with zest', as one fellow reveller noticed, 'into every dance'. It had been a full day and night of unforgettable gaiety.

However, not long afterwards it all went wrong. Catalina began to whisper to whoever would listen that Oliva was turning out to be an unfit husband for such an exceptional child. She implied that the new groom felt uncomfortable at being outclassed on the dancing stage by his pupil. But the friends and neighbours who had witnessed the stifling dependency between Catalina and her daughter suspected the real truth behind Catalina's sudden disapproval of the man she had appointed as her son-in-law. The predictable emotional backlash had hit the possessive Catalina as the consequences of her matchmaking became clear. Catalina suspected that her son-in-law had usurped her position as the most important person in her daughter's life.

Unprepared for the sense of loneliness and jealousy that followed her daughter's marriage to the lowly dancing teacher, Catalina panicked. Incapable of preventing her throttling maternal love from sabotaging Pepita's own happiness, Catalina had fallen into a paradoxical parental trap by simultaneously wanting the best for a daughter while being disinclined to lose her. Only three months after the wedding Catalina suggested to Pepita that Oliva had already been unfaithful to her. Allowing her shocked daughter Pepita to absorb the news of Oliva's treachery, Catalina then took Oliva to one side and informed him that his wife had betrayed him with another man. Astonishingly, despite a complete lack of evidence both Pepita and Oliva believed her. Catalina's meddling had momentarily paid off as the shaken pair began to live apart But Catalina had forgotten how well she had taught her daughter the importance of ambition. As Pepita's reputation and popularity grew she emerged, not only from her wrecked marriage but from under the thumb of the wrecker.

## 2

# Pepita
## Independence

As Pepita got richer, so she became grander. Her fame and wealth as a dancer prompted an unpredictable swing between indulgence and neglect of the intrusive, possessive but devoted Catalina. During a short stay in Granada Catalina and Manuel Lopez left the city, alarmed by the lethal presence of cholera which riddled the congested streets and which in one particularly bad epidemic in 1845 had resulted in the deaths of over a quarter of a million Spaniards. For safety Pepita, the still dutiful, if often absent, daughter, moved her mother and quasi stepfather to a substantial new house in the central square of Albolote, a small country town a few miles from Granada.

Catalina celebrated her splendid social and financial elevation by arriving at the Casa Blanca in a suitably 'fantastic equipage' led by a unicorn. Delighted by the amazement that her account of such fabulous transport inspired in anyone who would listen to her, Catalina would eventually give way and explain that 'unicorn' referred to the horn shape formed by two horses led by another. However, Catalina's developing taste for the extravagance funded by her newly rich daughter was real enough and continued to swell as she indulged herself in a new taste for lovely clothes, beautiful linens, a personal maid and elegant furniture. Each Sunday before Mass, a pair of large, matching velvet armchairs would be carried with some ceremony by Catalina's servants into Albolote's church and placed at the head of the congregation at the high altar to ensure that the villagers were aware of the hierarchical order of things. As the congregation glared, and Lopez consulted his splendid new gold watch, his fingers laden with rings, Sunday mornings in Albolote began to resemble a night out at the theatre rather than a morning spent in devotion. Eventually the priest put his foot down. He banned the chairs and the affronted Catalina never entered the church again. But while Catalina was all too visible in Albolote, the provider of all these riches, Pepita herself, was usually nowhere to be seen.

Dancing continued to supply the passport that lifted Pepita out of the confines of maternal control and across the barrier of the Pyrenees. She began to accept bookings in theatres all over Europe, causing a sensation wherever she went. Audiences clamoured for the newly established 'Star of Andalusia' to prove that her hair, her implausibly magnificent crowning glory, was not fake. To a roar of approval, one by one she pulled out the pins that held the much-admired locks in place, allowing them to fall in a waterfall to her knees as she enchanted sell-out auditoriums in Bordeaux, Copenhagen, Frankfurt, Berlin,

Stuttgart, Vienna, Budapest, Prague and then triumphantly in Paris and at Her Majesty's Theatre in London. Cartoonists showed men whipping fresh flowers from the garlanded headdresses of their exasperated wives and hurling them with uninhibited enthusiasm in the direction of the stage, aiming for Pepita's outstretched arms. I treasure the much-thumbed, four-page programme of piano sheet music for *la Madrilena* that Pepita once gave to a pianist in Vienna in 1853 so that he could provide her with her favourite performance music. The cover drawing shows Pepita in her dancing costume, her hair streaming down her back, castanets in her upraised hands. She is a terrifically impressive sight.

Abandoned and frustrated in Spain, with only the self-aggrandising Lopez and the curious neighbours for company, Catalina found herself edged into the margins of her daughter's life. Explaining to the villagers that her daughter was away 'triumphing in Europe', Catalina ensured that her outward pride remained undimmed, boasting 'in confidence' to her new friends in Albolote of her daughter's financial generosity and of the distinguished suitors that competed with one another for the chance to court the lovely dancer. Several of the residents of Albolote remained gratifyingly impressed, at least for a while, by Catalina's increasingly elaborate anecdotes and were left in no doubt that '*la estrella de Andalusia*' was intimately acquainted with some of the most distinguished members of European society. Sumptuous dinners at the Casa Blanca would be interrupted the moment that Pepita's frustratingly unrevealing letters arrived. The cursory news would be read aloud and every detail, however scant, savoured as the letter was passed from hand to hand. Some villagers were led to suspect a close association with royalty, although they understood that discretion prevented Catalina from divulging identities. Rumours involving the Emperor of Germany were not denied, despite the fact that no such person existed. Perspicacious villagers stated years later that they had privately congratulated themselves in detecting 'traces of an inferior origin', in the garrulous Catalina, the gypsy turned 'bourgeoisie' for whom nothing but an emperor would suffice as escort for her daughter.

Expensive telegrams had been delivered to theatres all over Europe containing appeals from mother to daughter to visit the splendours of Casa Blanca but it was a year before Pepita came home. The drama and pomp surrounding the arrival of the twenty-five-year-old star in the summer of 1855 formed a lifelong memory for those small children who lived nearby. The brass band from the adjoining village set up their enormous drum on Catalina's terrace and the boisterous welcoming party, complete with a lavish banquet that concluded with 'chocolates, sweets and liquors', went on until the break of dawn. Never had a mother made her pride in her daughter more obvious. Pepita rose to the occasion, playing her part as the embodiment of feminine charm and seduction, taking the hand of one especially shy young villager and leading him onto the floor for the dance of his lifetime. With one flounce of her gorgeous gown of rose-coloured silk raised at the front to display an elegant leg to best advantage, her delicate pointed toe slippered in gold brocaded velvet, four or five extravagant rings on her left hand, two more on her right, she taught him to dance a waltz. Not bothering to temper the extravagant passion that she displayed onstage to anything more suitably restrained for a parlour in a small Spanish town, and aware that every eye was on her, she moved with the assurance of a predatory jackal. With the glitter from the diamonds in her ears reflected in the eyes of her awestruck dancing partner, he told his friends later that he thought he 'should have died of ecstasy'.

Pepita stayed with her mother for two months, laughing, dancing, calling on the neighbours, admiring their gardens, delighting in their little fish ponds and showing off to her many female visitors her lovely jewels, including an emerald brooch in the shape of a lizard. Before they left they would be rewarded with a little memento, a signed portrait of herself. By the end of Pepita's stay most of Albolote's well-appointed drawing-room walls boasted a lithograph of their local star. She made friends with all the children who lived nearby, and caused the local lads who found her 'dangerously' attractive to swoon that 'her *tout ensemble* took away sleep'. She paid her mother's bills, smiled with teeth 'as white as ivory', enchanted everyone she met and above all made Catalina happy. When Pepita occasionally withdrew into her own room the glitter dimmed and a sense of solemnity, even sadness, would shroud the house before it was time to dance once more. Her sombre moods were as mysterious to her mother as was the recipient of the long letters Pepita wrote in the privacy of her room. Alert to her mother's compulsive romantic plotting although never quite clear what part Catalina had played in the break-up of her marriage to Oliva, Pepita concealed the details of her romantic life from Catalina. Unknown to Catalina, Pepita had fallen in love.

*

Lionel Sackville-West was a twenty-five-year-old attaché in the British Legation in Germany. A reserved young man with a substantial beard, impressive sideburns, and a battalion of intimidating, aristocratic relations at home, he was on holiday in Paris in October 1852 when one night at the theatre he spotted Pepita sitting in the stalls. Already aware of her fame, Lionel was stunned, even hypnotised, by the sight of her. Her voluptuous mouth, her oval eyes bright beneath the curve of her eyebrows and the 'love-lock', as Vita described the curl of dark hair that rested on her cheek, were not the only assets to attract his attention. Her figure was set off by graceful shoulders, dimpled arms and small delicate hands. She combined the agility and slimness of a top dancer with an endearing womanly round-ness. He persuaded a friend who knew where Pepita was staying to take him to the Hotel de Bade for an introduction, not, as Lionel later recalled, 'to a fast woman, but to an artiste and a lady and a danseuse'.

That night Lionel's virginal reserve vanished and he later admitted, in respectfully oblique terms, that he had indeed visited Pepita 'with the intention of its leading up to that object', although he also swore that 'the actual fact came about at her solicitation'. For the next seven days and nights the door to Pepita's hotel room remained closed and locked from the inside. And for the next four years, with Pepita's career at its height, Lionel and Pepita stayed in hotels all over Europe under their own names, mutually untroubled that their indifference to gossip might affect Lionel's public position as a young diplomat with prospects. When challenged later about his lack of caution he admitted: 'I cannot tell you whether it was known in the hotels that I was passing the night with her; there was no secrecy about it whatever. I gave my name at the hotels.' Friends and colleagues thought privately that he had lost his mind. Pepita, on the other hand, had landed once again on her feet.

Lionel was the fifth son of the fifth Earl De La Warr, younger brother of, and more importantly heir to, the childless Lord Sackville, owner of Knole, one of Britain's grandest and largest stately houses. The financial security and the material privilege that Lionel brought Pepita was a world away from free dancing lessons. But they could not formalise their relationship. In Britain, the Matrimonial Causes Act of 1857 allowed women to divorce on the grounds of adultery but in Spain the right for women to divorce and remarry was not legalised until 1932. As Lionel followed his lover from capital to capital to see her dance and to share her bed, an ever widening circle of concierges and room-service waiters in Europe's grandest hotels knew about the intimate relationship between the British aristocrat and the Spanish dancer. But Lionel kept his romantic life a secret from his family while Pepita ensured that Catalina remained equally unenlightened. Three years after the door to her suite in the Hotel de Bade had shut behind them, and two years since her last visit home, Pepita wrote to tell her mother that she would be coming to stay, this time for an extended visit.

Catalina had moved once again. After the difficulty with the armchairs in the church, the disapproval of the priest and the waning of the community's indulgence of the unpredictable couple, Catalina and Lopez had pronounced themselves disenchanted with Albolote and had set out to find a new property on the outskirts of Granada. Buena Vista, also known as the

House of the Royal Peacocks for its indigenous collections of the exotic beasts, was even grander than Casa Blanca. Surrounded by two vineyards, and beautifully kept lawns, Buena Vista sat at the heart of its own substantial estate. The house faced onto a courtyard where a fountain played cheerfully and from which a bronze statue of Pepita dancing *el olé* emerged soaking wet but triumphant from the splashing water. In contrast to the drama of her last visit, the explanation for the quietness of Pepita's arrival, and the absence of drums and clashing cymbals was soon apparent. On 20 May 1858 Pepita's first child, a son, was born, and Catalina's smothering motherly spirit was once again allowed to flourish. When Pepita had difficulties with breastfeeding, Catalina was the embodiment of maternal concern, arranging for the baby to be suckled for the first nineteen days of his life by her own maid who had herself just given birth to her eleventh child. The birth certificate credited Pepita's husband Oliva with the child's paternity despite the common knowledge that he and Pepita had been separated for six years. Pepita did not dismiss her mother's hopeful enquiries about whether the baby was in fact the child of the fictional Emperor of Germany. She allowed Catalina to speculate that a secret, albeit illicit, marriage might already have taken place despite Pepita's still legal connection to the long-departed Oliva.

The baby was christened Maximiliano and known in the family as Max, although his middle name was Leon, the shortened Spanish version of Lionel. As Pepita had been heard boasting that her best jewels were a gift from a prince of Bavaria, and when the 'sponsor' of the child was officially recorded as 'Duke Maximilian of Bavaria', a cousin of the ruling family of that country, the obvious conclusion was tempting. But Pepita refused to confirm her mother's suspicions, staying at Buena Vista for six more months until Catalina's old jealousy inevitably returned. Frustrated by the way motherhood occupied Pepita's time and by her own inability to discover the identity of her grandson's father, Catalina quarrelled violently with her daughter and Pepita left at once.

The neighbours continued to sniff scandal as the loquacious Catalina, stung at her exclusion from her daughter's confidence, tried to bluff her way through Pepita's sudden departure by explaining that Max was now 'short-coated' as opposed to being confined to baby dresses and was therefore old enough to accompany his mother abroad as she returned to the stage. Neither the neighbours nor Catalina knew that Pepita had gone straight to join Lionel in Germany, but in retaliation for her rejection, Catalina persuaded a friend of Oliva's to attempt a reconciliation between her daughter and son-in-law. As soon as Pepita was told of the proposal she suspected Catalina's meddling, though in order to maintain her mother's ignorance about Lionel she wrote her a letter announcing that she would be coming to Paris and that maybe a meeting with Oliva would be possible. On receipt of the letter Catalina changed tactic, unable suddenly to resist the possibility of an emperor as a replacement son-in-law. The only inconvenience was Oliva. He must be disposed of. And Catalina knew an ideal potential assassin. She was surprised and also a little hurt when her son Diego, recently returned from abroad, proved as uncooperative as his sister and refused Catalina's lucrative commission to carry out Oliva's murder.

All Catalina's best efforts either to derail or to promote her daughter's romantic life had failed and the secret affair between Pepita and Lionel continued to deepen. Lionel remained publicly reticent, even taciturn, but in private he was unrestrainedly sexually passionate and undeniably sexually potent. Over the next few summers he either bought or rented a series of sumptuous villas for his mistress and their son at Heidelberg, Turin, Lake Como, Arona, Genoa and Lake Maggiore. Eventually Pepita gave way, confident by now of the security of her relationship with Lionel, and allowed Catalina to meet and be impressed by 'the tall fair good-looking and handsome man, of a distinguished appearance' with whom her daughter lived. On 23 September 1862 Catalina and Manuel joined Lionel at his splendid apartment in Paris near the Arc de Triomphe where Lionel and Pepita's second child, a daughter, Victoria Josefa Dolores Catalina, was born. The baby herself was often known by her mother as Pepita, the Spanish diminutive for Josephine, and an indication of how close Pepita felt to her daughter.

For two more years her career remained Pepita's priority. But as her energy for dancing began to fade so the relish and physical stamina with which she addressed herself to caring for her children gathered momentum. She discovered that motherhood fulfilled her and her indulgence of the children was rewarded by their devotion, especially that of Victoria who slept in her mother's bed, just as Pepita had slept with Catalina when she was a child. The family expanded with speed as four more children appeared in quick succession in the nursery of Max and Victoria. Eliza, born in 1865, did not survive childbirth, but the others did, Flora arriving in November 1866, Amalia fifteen months later in 1868 and finally Henri sixteen months after that in 1869. And with the expanding family came a further shrinking of Pepita's need for Catalina. She no longer travelled across Europe, or made visits to Spain, and in the summer of 1866 Lionel bought her a house at Arcachon, near Bordeaux, in the south-west of France. The town was near enough to Madrid where Lionel was now First Secretary at the British Legation, a train ride from his apartment in Paris and above all a place where Pepita and her five illegitimate children could live in healthy and discreet contentment.

The train journey from Bordeaux to Arcachon is about thirty-five miles and, allowing for the many stops en route, and the intersections across country lanes, it takes city dwellers today a little over an hour to reach the seaside town, just as it did when the railway was built in 1857. The landscape outside the window alters with every bend in the track as the train winds through the once swampy wasteland of the Landes, huge pine forests and extensive woods of oak, poplar and chestnut cultivated over the past few centuries through which wild boar used to snout before being shot by hunters out for sport on frosty autumn mornings. Nearer the coast vast acres of bright green vineyards producing some of the most delicious wine in the country alternate with buttercup-speckled meadows, small villages of beamed houses, ancient churches and isolated farmhouses. In the winter months when Pepita lived in Arcachon, shepherds tending their flock and dressed in leather jerkins would stand on stilts to prevent themselves from sinking into the treacherous mudflats, seeking out from their commanding height any sheep that had became lost and entangled in the marshy bushes. On arrival at Arcachon railway station I discovered that it is still necessary as it was in Pepita's time to cross the track before stepping up onto the platform where nowadays a bus instead of the old horse-drawn cabs waits to take passengers and their luggage the short distance into the centre.

Arcachon is a town of two parts. The Ville d'Hiver occupies the upper sloping streets that abut the hills covered with pine trees, gorse, heather and ferns. The lower section, the Ville d'Eté, is built along an extensive sandy beach where the sea is not really the sea at all but an enormous saltwater lake, sixty-eight miles round, a fertile bed for growing oysters. It is an idyllic stretch of water for sailing and fishing, connected to the open ocean in the Bay of Biscay by one very narrow opening. Pepita had grown up with Malaga's combined benefits of sunshine and dry air, and she was once again living in a place viewed by the sick (and hypochondriacs) as a huge free pharmacy. Nowadays Arcachon is a magnetic seaside town both for families and sailors. In Pepita's day it was a haven for the consumptive, the air impregnated with the resin of the pine trees, while sea bathing and saline water, assumed to be good for the lungs, counteracted the worst effects of tuberculosis. An English doctor, James Henry Bennet, visited the resort in the early summer of 1868 while writing a guidebook to healthy climates for the tubercular patient. But Bennet's attention was soon diverted by the activities at the beach, struck by the emancipated attitude the French took to bathing. The doctor was fascinated by the accomplished confidence with which novice swimmers of all ages took to the water, at first using 'corks or gourds tied under their arms', while the more experienced 'discard all such aid'.

'Ladies and gentleman,' Dr Bennet observed, 'put on their costumes in the privacy of special elevated cabins that were placed at some distance from the shoreline.' Emerging from the cabins they added 'broad brimmed straw hats and wide waterproof capes' which would be taken off by the bathing attendant at the water's edge. 'This costume,' he remarked, 'like all picturesque costumes makes the young and the pretty look younger and prettier but certainly does not set off to the same degree the more matronly of the lady bathers.' Men dressed in their own multicoloured sailor-like costumes spoke freely with their fellow lady bathers in their semi-disguise of 'black woollen drawers that descend to the ankles and a black blouse or tunic descending below the knees and fastened at the waist by a leathern girdle'. At first Dr Bennet found this 'aquatic mingling' of the sexes to be 'an infringement of the laws of propriety and decorum' but quickly came to believe that British sea bathers, for whom segregated swimming was rigorously enforced up and down the English coast, could learn something from their relaxed French counterparts.

This quiet fishing town, as well as becoming a pharmaceutical and touristic haven, was still unobtrusive enough a retreat for members of the rich elite to conveniently house their inconvenient mistresses. Pepita's house, the Villa Pepa in the Ville d'Eté, sat in one of the most desirable positions in the centre of Arcachon, straddling the land between the sea and the long inner road, the Boulevard de la Plage. Pepita advertised her superior social standing as 'Countess West' in the magnificent twelve-foot gates that she placed within the railings that ran the length of the large garden. Two white-painted letters, S and W, were proudly entwined at the top of the curly ironwork. But the locked gates not only suggested wealth and position but imprisonment. It was a long way from the simple freedom of the Calle Puente. Monsieur Desombre, the local builder, was commissioned to make the grand railings and the matching coroneted and monogrammed gates on both the beach and street sides of the property, and to add another two floors to the house. The whole thing was finished off with a handsome Chinese pagoda. Desombre also built a gardener's cottage, a stable and two bathing huts on the perimeter of the garden on the beach side. But the lavishness of the property neither fooled Pepita's Roman Catholic, lip-curling neighbours nor endeared them to her. They had learned of the dubious marital arrangement of the new occupant of the Villa Pepa and they did not approve.

Each morning Pepita, tiny but haughty, would glide past the disapproving locals, the long train of her black lace-ruffled dress stretching out behind her like the black wake of a small boat. Running beside her, the younger children struggled to keep up, while Victoria held her mother's long plaits high to prevent them from dragging in the dusty streets. Not willing to trust many with her money, even the town's bank manager, Pepita walked with a noticeable limp as her purse, stuffed with gold coins and banknotes and strapped to her thigh, banged against her knee beneath her long skirts, giving her the security of knowing that her fortune was safe. On warm summer days the family would emerge from behind the gates to play on the beach. Max and Victoria, dressed in navy-and-white sailor hats, the ribbons floating down their backs, would sit beside their mother as she trickled sand through the silky drawers of the smaller children, laughing with them as the fine grains tickled their toes.

Lionel came to spend time with his young family four or five times a year or as often as he could leave his work at the Legation in Madrid and then at the embassy in Paris. His visits were anticipated with huge excitement as Pepita, singing her favourite song, 'Plaisir d'Amour', instructed her children to tie cherries onto the branches of the trees of their garden and, still agile, dressed up in her old lacy dancing clothes and kicked up her legs to reveal tiny black satin ballet slippers, her expression reflecting that sexy imperiousness with which the packed theatres of her youth had been so familiar. Lionel could not refuse Pepita anything. His initials were on her gate, his surname was on her visiting cards, and finally he even agreed to put his name on the birth certificates of the last three children Pepita bore him. But he was defying the law. Divorce remained as out of the question for a Catholic in France as it was in Spain, and despite Catalina's best efforts a few years earlier to annul the marriage, Oliva was still dancing, still breathing, still Pepita's husband.

However, during Lionel's long absences life became more difficult for his mistress as she became exposed to the full force of the disapproval of smart Arcachon society. The sort of small-town introspection that inspired Balzac in his 1832 novella, *Le Curé de Tours*, was here directed at a woman who seemed to flaunt her adulterous state as her crocodile of children born of '*père inconnu*' followed her down the street. The British chaplain who lived opposite the Villa Pepa reluctantly acknowledged that on the rare occasions he permitted himself to look in Pepita's direction he could see 'the remains of former beauty' but could not ignore the impression that 'she was at that time stout and rather coarse looking'. On most days if he saw the coroneted gates swing open he would cross over to the other side of the boulevard with a slight shudder and walk on.

Photographs taken only ten years after Pepita had danced like 'a bird in the air' show her wearing a floor-length cream dress, a substantial expanse of fleshy embonpoint exposed, and provide some justification for the chaplain's assessment of her expanding figure. The shuttered windows and defensive iron railings of the Villa Pepa added to the isolation and notoriety of the 'Countess West' entourage. Although she tried to make friends with the British community, respectability continued to elude her. The monogrammed visiting cards lay rejected and unused between their fine dividing layers of yellowing India paper. Speculation of every variety fizzed around her, from non-payment of bills and wages to inappropriate relationships with members of the lower orders. There were suggestions that she drank too much, alcohol emerging for the first time in this family story as the unreliable companion and perfidious comforter of all lonely people, and that she even allowed four-year-old Flora to wash her hair in the leftover dregs of champagne.

The only people who would speak willingly to Pepita were her servants and the hungry poor who were often welcomed in an act of charity into the Villa Pepa for a meal. Victoria later boasted that her mother's 'kindness and gracious manners made her generally beloved', as she gathered people around her who she believed would not judge her. During Lionel's long absences from Arcachon, neighbours talked. The notoriety of Villa Pepa always threw up something new about which to speculate. News spread that Monsieur Desombre regularly accompanied the countess on outings in her carriage, was entertained at Villa Pepa, invited to look at her photograph albums, to stay for dinner and to smoke his daily cigar in her company. And her suspiciously dependent friendship with Monsieur Henri de Béon, the solicitous assistant stationmaster at Bordeaux railway station, only intensified the chatter. Soon there were rumours that Béon did more than advise the countess on railway time-tables and provide a courteous helping hand when Pepita and her children were boarding the train. The rumours amplified when Monsieur Béon was appointed as Pepita's personal 'super-intendent' and often stayed the night at Villa Pepa. The curtain of trees in the garden was not quite thick enough to disguise the sight of Pepita wandering about in the morning '*en negligée*', and prompted neighbourly support for the absent British aris-tocrat and the conviction that he would have every right to throw Béon into the deepest part of the Bay of Biscay.

If the stigma of her adulterous state was humiliating for Pepita, it was baffling for her children. A low wall divided the Villa Pepa from the Johnstons at Villa Mogador. The Johnstons were wealthy wine merchants, one of sixteen English families living in Arcachon who would have nothing to do with the phoney countess. Minna and Bella, the little Johnston girls, were under instruction not to communicate in any way with the children from Villa Pepa, despite surreptitious whisperings over the wall. Victoria was well aware of the rule, if confused about the reason behind it. A little further along the beach the crenellated casino was approached by a red-carpeted staircase, the building splendidly decorated in imperial colours of purple, scarlet and gold. One day Pepita defied the stares and took Victoria to the casino's children's ball. Nervous in her best frock, Victoria climbed the grand staircase holding her mother's hand, but once inside not a single person spoke to her or danced with her and 'we felt very much out of it', the shame of the experience remaining with her all her life. A joint photograph of Pepita when Victoria was about six shows the firm-jawed determination of the elder and the dependent sweetness and affection of the younger, a portrait of a mother and daughter in isolation, reaching out to one another for protection and companionship.

Pepita's sense of alienation deepened still further when the town's Catholic priests refused her the twin comforts of absolution and communion. Eventually the priest at Notre-Dame d'Arcachon took pity on her and told her of a place where she might find spiritual reassurance. Pepita would set out in her carriage with Victoria to the tiny village of Le Moulleau. The dramatic red-brick Notre-Dame du Moulleau stands on top of a small rise and looks out to the sea. It is known as the sailors' church. Before embarking on a long journey and knowing they might not see their homeland for a long time, sailors would spend their last hours in this place then look back at the building from the ocean in the hope of one last blessing before losing sight of land. At the back of the church a little path leaves the bright sunlight behind and pushes into the shadows. Soon the noise of traffic recedes, and the visitor is engulfed in birdsong. When I visited this beautiful place recently I found a sense of peacefulness there that I was quite unprepared for. No wonder it became Pepita's secret asylum from the painful ostracism of the Arcachon elite. Here she could be left alone to pray. It seemed to me a place where, if only briefly, she might have been truly happy.

But at no point during her time in Arcachon did Pepita send for her own mother, their once powerful alliance and 'excessive' love having dwindled away, at first with Pepita's full-blown independence and then her commitment to her growing family. There was no coming together later in the way that a grandmother might have hoped. The relationship between Catalina and her grandchildren was non-existent. Perhaps Pepita and her mother had quarrelled again? Perhaps Pepita had allowed herself to forget about Catalina? Or perhaps Pepita feared that her mother's impulsive, unrefined, madcap presence in Arcachon, and her habitual attempts to derail her daughter's life, would only deepen the dubious reputation of the inhabitants of the Villa Pepa? Perhaps she suspected that the joint presence of Catalina and Pepita would have given Arcachon society a wonderful excuse to make their exclusion of the West family complete? Perhaps Pepita felt that her mother's exuberant, excitable vulgarity would show up her daughter's humble origins and erode her own precarious reputation still further? Whatever the reasons, without any documented or eyewitness evidence, it is difficult to explain fully the collapse of this intense relationship and the apparent harshness with which Pepita rejected her devoted mother. However strong the family compulsion to analyse our history and draw conclusions about generational patterns, no explanation for the rupture of the relationship between Pepita and her mother is given in any of Victoria's later written and oral reminiscences. And Victoria's own daughter Vita (whose biography of Pepita and Victoria was inspired in part by innumerable conversations with Victoria) did not include any reason for Catalina's failure to visit Arcachon.

Although Pepita continued to speak affectionately about Oliva to her children, she did not receive or invite a visit from her husband either, the split engineered by Catalina proving irrevocable emotionally if not legally. From time to time Pepita would send Oliva money for which he wrote to thank her. But he remained in Spain, having helped himself to the contents of the abandoned Casa Blanca, growing overweight but continuing to dance and to teach the young ballerinas of Andalusia, until the tragic news reached Arcachon that cancer had ravaged his tongue. The silence that had been growing between Pepita and the country of her birth and the most important figures of her young life was now complete.

During the summer months when the climate brought warmth if not social acceptance, it was easier to ignore discomfort, but during the icy Arcachon winters when boredom was pervasive and the wind swirled across the beach, life for the West family was less enjoyable. Even the indigenous invalids felt the monotony, drugged by the sedative emitted from the resinous fir trees, listless through gazing at the evergreen trees, trapped by the muddy roads. Sometimes Pepita would escape the claustrophobic atmosphere and take the children to visit Lionel in Paris but he had at last been forced to make the demarcation clear between his growing professional responsibilities and his complicated private life. Despite Pepita's pleas, Lionel refused to take her to a fête at the Tuilleries, denying her the excitement of being presented to the Empress Eugenie. The children were forbidden from visiting Lionel at the embassy, or from making friends with local children playing in the Champs Élysées for fear of compromising their father by advertising their existence. Paris could present even more of a social trap than Arcachon.

But in February 1871 Lionel spent a happy few days at Villa Pepa, looking forward to the birth of another child. Three weeks later, on 6 March, three telegrams from Stationmaster Béon reached Paris at short intervals containing ever more desperate bulletins. The baby boy, Frédéric, had not survived. Pepita herself was dangerously unwell. Lionel rushed from Paris to Arcachon. On 11 March Pepita's bedroom was in near darkness when Lionel came through the door too late, and saw the mother of his children lying on her bed, a crucifix clasped between her fingers, the embalmed waxy figure made young again, beautiful but unreal, by the local chemist. The body of the baby had been placed beside her, confirmation that his arrival had been the cause of her death. Sitting in the gloom of the shuttered house, barely able to understand what had happened, was Pepita's confused and frightened eldest daughter. Lionel knelt beside Victoria, shattered by the shock of losing the woman who had died with his name on her lips, paralysed by guilt that as the father of this dead baby he was responsible for Pepita's death, and distraught that he had not arrived in time to say goodbye to the woman whose death certificate stated she was his wife.

Having given instructions to Pepita's loyal friend, the builder Desombre, to make a coffin 'for a lady who enjoyed the position of my wife', and to fulfil her request by digging her grave in the garden by Villa Pepa's small chapel, Lionel left the town. But he had unwittingly abandoned her to the town's unforgiving authorities who dealt with all women of ill repute in the same way. Pepita enjoyed no privileges in her position as the mistress of a British diplomat. Lionel's request for her burial at home was declined by the church and the city officials. An application for an exception to be made reached the offices of the Pope himself but was also rejected. So Pepita was buried on an unusually cold and snowy day, denied a headstone to mark her place, in the vast, identity-smothering city cemetery.

No record exists of any arrangements that had been made by Pepita for Catalina's old age. With the lack of communication between them Pepita's financial generosity had also come to an end. While she was helping out the poor of Arcachon she had ignored the needs of her own mother. A few years after Pepita's death a distressing report reached Lionel. An elderly couple had been spotted selling groceries from a room in the backstreets of Malaga. Catalina and Lopez had apparently shrunk away, leaving behind the splendid House of the Royal Peacocks (had Pepita reclaimed the house as her own and sold it?) and returning to the hardship of a long-ago life, but one that no longer held its original gaiety and optimism. Later still, Catalina was reported as being observed in 'an old furniture shop, greatly changed and simply clad', managing once again the sale of old clothes and an array of second-hand junk. The bright, maternal presence of Catalina, the 'zest' behind her daughter's triumphant career, had returned to extreme poverty, her demeanour, in the words of Catalina's cousin, a man who sold fruit from the back of a donkey, 'crestfallen' and 'decayed'. Catalina died alone and disappointed, deprived of a relationship with her grandchildren and many years after losing all contact with Pepita, the daughter whom she had adored.

Pepita's eldest daughter Victoria was eight years old. I was the same age when my own grandmother died and I remember well the confusion, mystery and impossibility of it all. I remember seeing my own father weep and experiencing that first, faint insight into what the world-altering nature of the death of a parent might feel like.

3

# Victoria
## Bargaining

The years that followed the sudden death of Victoria's mother and her near-abandonment by her father were desperately lonely ones. All gaiety and indulgence vanished in 1871 together with Pepita's long black maternal skirts under which Victoria and her brothers and sisters had so often taken refuge from the hostile adult world. Illegitimate, motherless and with a father suddenly thousands of miles away, Victoria West had effectively been orphaned overnight.

In my family parents always seem to be escaping when their children need them most. Lionel had accepted a diplomatic posting to Buenos Aires, the remoteness of South America an antidote to his life in Europe where he would otherwise be reminded of Pepita and his responsibilities towards his sons and daughters. At first Pepita's grieving children remained at Arcachon in the care of the assiduously helpful Monsieur Béon and his mother, but after two years the Béons and the children moved to Paris on Lionel's instruction. The eldest child Max was sent away to school in Bordeaux while Victoria went to board at the Parisian convent of St Joseph in rue Monceau. Now eleven years old, almost illiterate and wholly unaccustomed to domestic rules, she was no longer known by her family nickname 'Pepita' but as Mademoiselle Quarante-Deux, the number marked in ink on her black uniform. Nuns taught her the names of French rivers and the geography of French principal towns, while the Béons were paid handsomely by Lionel to look after the three younger children. During the holidays when Victoria and Max joined the others, Victoria willingly assumed the parental role that her absent father imposed on her. 'You are a big girl now,' he wrote to her from Argentina, 'and I greatly count on you, my dear daughter, to take care of the family.'

Victoria had learned from her mother's example how to look after her sisters and brothers, her resilient temperament preventing her from accusing Lionel of abandonment. She responded cheerfully to the letters he sent her from Argentina, full of implausible stories about the lions and tigers he had stalked and shot on his adventures and of promises that one day he would teach her to ride. She expressed such faith in his eventual return that Lionel grew increasingly fond of her in his absence. But he came rarely to Paris, making just two visits during the seven years Victoria was at St Joseph's. Although she disguised her disappointment and unhappiness well, the rigours of a Paris convent could freeze the soul. Years later Victoria would describe her painful memories of the nuns' constant supervision, the discipline and the lack of human kindness. She missed Arcachon, she missed the warmth of the sun, the comfort of laughter, the company of her brothers and sisters, and she missed her mother. As Victoria reached puberty she had to confront alone the mysteries and terrors of adolescence. Fainting from the coldness of the convent and reduced to whispered prayers imploring God to supply some warmth, the pupils' complaints were harshly rewarded with extra lessons, compulsory early-morning church services and rigorous walks. During the holidays the Béons issued sinister warnings. There were secrets she was better off not knowing. Victoria was not to mention her mother's name. She was not allowed to play with any of the children of the Béons' friends who came to the house. She was not allowed to stray into the streets alone, as a Spanish dancer called Oliva might be waiting there to kidnap her, claiming her as his own daughter. And there were unexplained complications to do with her irregular birth certificate that delayed her confirmation and caused the Roman Catholic-raised Victoria much distress. From the earliest age she had followed the example of her mother that faith mattered, even if the practice sometimes proved elusive.

When the elderly Madame Béon died Amalia and Flora joined their sister at the convent, Max was sent to learn farming in South Africa and Henri, the youngest child, was enrolled in a *lycée*. But nine years after Pepita's death an unlikely Mary Poppins appeared. The kindly, clever and gutsy Marion Mulhall, married to the Irish editor of South America's English-language newspaper, had travelled with her husband extensively across that continent, unruffled by torrential rain, disease, dead horses floating in rivers, the British slaughter of tigers and the capture of live alligators for sport. Mrs Mulhall was the distinguished author of two books, *From Europe to Paraguay and Matto-Grosso* and *Ten Years of a Lady's Travels in the Pampas*, and had befriended Lionel in Buenos Aires. She was robust but also sympathetic to his circumstances and offered her help.

In the summer of 1880 Mrs Mulhall arrived in France with her husband and Lionel. They gathered up the three girls and Henri and took them all across the Channel to the Mulhalls' house in West Sussex. Lionel breathed a sigh of relief. The children spoke only French and Spanish, but Mrs Mulhall contrived in a jumbled mixture of foreign languages and hand gesticulations to get Victoria on her own during the Channel crossing where she spilled the beans about the girl's unconventional parentage. Up until that moment no one had told Victoria that her parents weren't married. 'This was a great shock and surprise to me,' Victoria wrote in her diary and for a while she kept the news from Max and her sisters. But in order to protect her adored little brother Henri from discovering his parents' secret from the boys at Stonyhurst, his new English Jesuit boarding school in Lancashire, she thought it kinder to give him the shocking facts herself. The news of the illegitimacy got out at once and Henri's life at school as a strange child who did not fit in was made relentlessly miserable. And Victoria was not there to look after him.

Gradually a collection of previously unknown English aunts and uncles variously rejected or embraced their new nieces and nephews. Lionel's brother, the Earl De La Warr, lived near

Grasslands, the Mulhalls' house in Sussex, and welcomed the children to his own home at Buckhurst while their Knole uncle, Lord Sackville, refused to have anything to do with them. On Mrs Mulhall's advice Victoria was sent to a school in Highgate to learn English, and while she was in London she met her father's two formidable sisters. The inquisitive, powerful but friendly Countess of Derby was the first to call. She quickly became appreciated as their protective Aunt Mary. Years later Victoria told her daughter Vita that during those uncertain days Aunt Mary 'seemed the best disposed to us of the world' but when tea was over at Derby House and the butler announced the arrival of Aunt Mary's ferocious sister, Bessie, the Duchess of Bedford, the children were whisked from the room. Unlike her disapproving sister, Aunt Mary continued to watch Victoria carefully and was pleased with what she saw. The shy young girl was becoming a delightful and rather beautiful young woman, conducting herself with dignity and charm and all the other complimentary embellishments that were desirable in a Victorian lady.

In June 1881, a decade after Pepita's death, Lionel, whose good reputation had been rising steadily within the diplomatic profession, was made the British Minister to the Legation in Washington DC. Political power and influence was controlled by Congress and by the hugely rich senators, their walking sticks twirling in front of them, their dandy frock-coats swinging out behind, their superiority evident in the gracious manner with which they received respectful nods thrown in their direction by passers-by. The increasing significance of diplomacy depended on establishing relationships, either through what one contemporary called 'the cardboard exchange' of printed cards with credentials or through social intercourse. The foreign offices of Europe still considered a posting to Washington to be a second-rank appointment and 'a hardship post', but although not yet equal to his counterparts in Paris and Berlin the role was gathering significance. Lionel was expected to be the host at influential receptions and parties and a new minister who had shown no inclination to marry was in need of a hostess. Aunt Mary knew at once how to help her wifeless brother out of his social dilemma and approached the matter by starting right at the top.

When Queen Victoria was consulted about the prospect of a young, half-Spanish, illegitimate daughter becoming the chatelaine of the British Legation in Washington she was not only amused but instantly sympathetic to the idea. Victoria West had been lucky. Since leaving Paris she had not only fallen into the hands of a well-connected aunt but those of the British sovereign with whom she shared a name. Now young Victoria's character and potential social standing in America's capital faced the even more rigorous inspection of the arbiters of Washington society, a four-strong committee of the wives of the President, the Secretary of State, the Undersecretary of State and the leading Republican senator. Aunt Mary had done her work well. Victoria West's impeccable references came from impeccable sources. No committee could ignore the recommendation of a British queen. The nineteen-year-old girl was given the go-ahead to cross the Atlantic in December 1881 and join her father at the legation in time for Christmas.

In 1792 General Washington had decided that the city to which he gave his name should become the country's capital and had invited Pierre L'Enfant, a young French civil engineer, to lay out a grand street plan. There had been little money to maintain L'Enfant's splendid parks and the impressive but costly canal that had taken more than two decades to complete, but five years after the end of the Civil War in 1865, Washington embarked on a decade-long facelift. However, according to the social historian Patricia O'Toole, the city still 'oscillated between the pretentious and the primitive'. Squalid areas of poverty, crime and prostitution were juxtaposed with streets on which well-off inhabitants drove, walked and strolled and which had been widened, paved and lined with thousands of leafy, shady sycamore trees, bringing distinction and elegance to the city. Carriages manned by uniformed footmen rumbled through the streets of Georgetown above the eighty miles of sewers that had been built with great speed and little skill between 1871 and 1874. Plumbing remained basic and in the summer heat the place stank. As a sign that things were changing, the most infamous brothel of the Civil War, Mary Ann Hall's establishment round the corner from the Capitol building and facing Maryland Avenue, had been turned into a women's health clinic, although the indefatigable Mary Ann continued to trade until 1886. Her obituary in the *Evening Star* lamented her departure as one 'who knew her sterling worth'. The smallpox and typhoid epidemics that had raged through the population during the war had still not been totally eradicated. President Arthur found potential staff wary of coming to the city for fear of malaria. The late President Garfield's son caught the disease, and in

March 1882 Lord George Francis Montague, the Third Secretary at the British Legation, keeled over from diphtheria at the age of twenty-seven. There had been talk of moving the entire capital to less swampy, less dangerous ground at St Louis, Missouri.

Twenty years after the end of the Civil War, the city had begun to hum if not yet to buzz with social life. In July 1881 President James A. Garfield had been assassinated four months into his first term of office by a delusional voter, but by the time Lionel arrived in November, Chester Arthur's new administration was well under way. Lionel moved straight into 1300 Connecticut Avenue, the British Legation's new red-brick building on the corner of Connecticut Avenue and North Street, only a few minutes by carriage from the White House. Ten days later the wife of a former Secretary of State and an unignorable social pace-setter, Mrs James Blaine, pulled out all the stops and gave a magnificent dinner party with Lionel and the new president as joint guests of honour. Carriages were not called until midnight and the evening was considered a terrific success. When Victoria disembarked in New York from Cunard's SS *Bothnia* a month later and joined her father in Washington, Mrs Blaine was the first person Lionel took her to meet.

The newly vamped and liberal-minded city impressed the writer Henry James, who had just completed his novel *Portrait of a Lady* and had returned after six years travelling to find the place 'informal, familiar, heterogeneous, good-natured, essentially social and conversational, enormously big and yet extremely provincial, indefinably ridiculous and yet eminently agreeable'. In 1863 Washington DC had passed its own law to abolish slavery three years before the rest of the Southern states gave way, such iniquity still seen by some as sanctioned by God and as the backbone of the nation's economy. During the 1870s and 1880s Washington was as advanced in its view of women's place in society as Spain was backward. In 1872 Victoria Woodhull, a thirty-four-year-old spiritualist, Wall Street financier and founder of a newspaper, had stood as the first female candidate for president of the United States, campaigning for women's freedom to marry, divorce, have children and to establish equality without restriction by law. But just before the election she was arrested and charged with obscenity. Her account of the adultery of a senior political minister had pushed the tolerance of the government too far. The electoral count revealed that she had apparently received no votes at all, but the total absence of support prompted speculation that the result was a fix. The possibility of a woman assuming the highest office had at least been suggested and many considered and some hoped that it would not be many years before a female candidate won. Washington was a good place for a woman to make her mark in the late nineteenth century, and it was her womanhood that propelled Victoria West into a position of recognition and power.

The fascination in Victoria's birth, class and upbringing was in sharp contrast to the prejudice that had confronted Pepita in the stuffy backwater of Arcachon. While Washington society could also be snobbish and judgemental, there was a consensual agreement that energy, manners and above all the good looks of a young woman qualified her for acceptance.

And if that sort of young woman had made some sort of alliance with a well-placed older man there was nothing to prevent her from becoming the more formidable of the pair. Henry James understood the phenomenon. 'Young men of this class never do anything for themselves that they can get other people to do for them,' he said, 'and it is the infatuation, the devotion, the superstition of others that keeps them going. These others in ninety-nine cases out of a hundred are women.'

As the scrutiny directed towards the minister's daughter turned swiftly to approval, Washington should not have had to look hard for the reasons behind the inexperienced Victoria's surprising sophistication and self-assurance. She was the daughter of a woman who had always risen to the occasion, whether convincing the theatres of Europe to employ her, or mustering some dignity with which to challenge the spite and prejudice that characterised Arcachon society. But Victoria was admired foremost for the loyalty and support she demonstrated towards her father. She had been her mother's daughter; now she was her father's, basking in the reassuring security of '*filia-philia*', the unique bond that comprises father–daughter love. Retaining her innocence and a childlike quality, Victoria also displayed the dignity of a much older and more experienced woman. But by manipulating the restraints imposed on her by the ostensibly subservient roles of daughterhood and femininity, she benefited from the arrangement that she had, in effect, negotiated with her father. Just as Pepita had profited financially and, in part, socially from her association with her powerful lover, so Victoria began to derive her public authority, whether consciously or not from apparently surrendering it to her father. Mother and daughter had both made a patriarchal bargain, agreements that were to remain fundamental to the practical and emotional structures of their lives. For most of my life I regarded this arrangement with suspicion. It is only recently that I have begun to realise that it is not perhaps an arrangement from which other women, myself included, are immune.

Outside the legation, Victoria managed her acceptance into Washington's smartest dining rooms with a knowing intelligence, beginning not with the powerful men, but with their wives. Her initial reserve appeased the competitive instinct that thrived between Washington's most influential women. Shyness was considered a commendable quality in one so young. Precocity would have threatened the position of those who did not have youth and beauty on their side. And she had one further asset. Washington was a city not only shot through with feminism but with Anglophilia. In America the popularity of a well-born Briton had been rising ever higher since 1860 when five thousand eager people gathered outside the Prince of Wales's Chicago hotel, anxious for a glimpse of the bulky regal silhouette through the bedroom window blinds. The language of the British upper class was imitated in person and in print. A character in Edith Wharton's *House of Mirth* pronounced that it was 'a deuced bold thing to show herself in that get-up'. The British propensity for taking exercise, for relaxing, for enjoying life, for simply 'watching a bumble bee blunder in and out of the flowers', as one popular social commentator remarked, was the subject of envy as well as curiosity.

The eccentricity and glamour of the nation's capital appealed at once to the newly arrived Victoria and she shone. Within weeks she had managed to overcome any disapproval of what she called 'the blot' of the illegal circumstances of her birth. The press loved her and she loved them loving her. She has 'beauty, charm, modesty, grace, clothes and taste', they wrote as Victoria began a lifelong habit of pasting flattering comments into her scrapbook, highlighting her favourite lines in red-penned exclamation marks. One journalist thrilled her by writing that 'her style of beauty is more Castilian than Anglo-Saxon' as did another's discreet reference to her unorthodox parentage. 'Miss West's harsh English angles are rounded off by the graces of her Spanish mother.'

A day or two after meeting Mrs Blaine, Victoria and her father dined at the socially intimidating home of the historian Henry Adams and his wife, along with their ubiquitous friend Henry James. Despite their powerful position in society the Adamses were refreshingly unstuffy, preferring their guests to tap on the window with an umbrella than announce themselves at the front door, and delighted when a visitor called by unan-nounced for a cup of tea. Although Victoria had little formal conversational experience, the Adamses loved her 'charming foreign accent, so pretty and so elegant'. Eliza Dolittle-like, she had scored another hit. But there was one more hurdle to clear.

The White House was famous within society for its shabby interiors and revolting food. Mrs Adams had barely survived the dreary teetotal administration that had preceded President Arthur. She had been poisoned by the Potomac water served to the guests instead of champagne and appalled by the pretentious presidential china, declaring that 'to eat one's soup calmly with a coyote springing at you from a pine tree is intimidating and ice cream plates disguised as Indian snow-shoes would be aesthetic but makes one yearn for Mongolian simplicity'. But everything was changing under the new regime. Chester Arthur, the tall, elegantly dressed, newly elected, recently widowed president, had turned not to a daughter but to his sister Mary to act as his social hostess, and Henry Adams reported that the new president was possessed of 'social charms we now understand to be most extraordinary'.

There was something both stylish and romantic about Arthur as he invited the fashionable jewellers Tiffany & Co. to help with the redecoration of the fusty, cockroach-infested White House rooms. The multicoloured glass screen that Tiffany designed for the entrance hall was a sensation. Everyone agreed that Arthur had demonstrated impeccable taste when he instructed the Green Room to be adorned with exotic plaster birds and installed silver walls imprinted with golden flowers and a shimmering sky-blue ceiling in his own 'sleeping chamber' as the press described the presidential bedroom. The White House cellar was stocked with the finest of fine wines and the kitchen was presided over by a first-class French chef. Those who previously would have done anything to get out of a social summons to the White House would now do anything to receive an invitation to dine there.

On New Year's Day 1882, two weeks after her arrival in Washington, Victoria and her father attended a reception at the newly decorated mansion. Wearing a deep-green day dress and a matching hat, her long hair held up loosely with combs, her waist the slimmest in town, her eyes the darkest blue, her lashes the longest, Victoria walked up the steps to the White House on the arm of her father, splendid in his diplomatic uniform of blue tail coat and gold lace cuffs. The other sober-suited and conservatively dressed guests, already assembled in the velvet-curtained Red Room and unable to compete with such a combination of youth and glamour, could only stare. The press were enchanted all over again. A year later Victoria was invited with her father to return to the presidential mansion for a state dinner. The sixteen-stone wife of a senator who was shown to a sturdy chair on the left of the president was disconcerted to see that the illegitimate daughter of the British minister had been seated on his right. Upright, slim and elegant, Victoria took her place with confidence, and with the sort of smile that could soften the hardest of hearts, she turned to greet the president. Arthur's heart dissolved. The senator's wife sat silent and ignored, counting the carnations in the huge arrangement on the table in front of her as the president devoted his attention to his young companion. Dinner was barely over before he could contain himself no longer. Would Miss West do him the honour of becoming his First Lady? Finding it impossible to respond with the solemnity that the president clearly expected, Victoria burst out laughing. 'Mr President,' she replied as soon as she had composed herself, 'you have a son older than me and you are as old as my father!' But the proposal was genuine, making its way into the carefully enumerated list of suitors in Victoria's book of reminiscences, and serious enough to alarm the government into issuing a denial on 23 February 1883 under the headline 'The President NOT to get married: Special report to the world.' The official statement continued: 'The story that the President is engaged to Miss West is absurd and without foundation'. But the denial only confirmed that Victoria had made her way to the top of Washington society.

During her first year in Washington, Victoria turned the British Legation into one of the most sought-after places to be seen in. She was a natural hostess, respectful to the distinguished and solicitous to those shy guests who came to the legation expecting to be ignored. Her vivacity and warmth contrasted with her father whose colleagues concurred 'had an unusual power of silence', regarding him as aloof and, even worse, dull. Victoria ran the large house and its squadron of servants with the efficiency, authority and leadership of a hospital matron. The flower arrangements were exquisite and the meals delicious. Each day Victoria would visit the Central Market on Pennsylvania Avenue that provided rich and poor alike with Chesapeake Bay crab and terrapin while the surrounding woods and farmlands ensured that the stalls were loaded with wild duck and turkey, pheasant and partridge, asparagus and tomatoes. America was the land not only of the free but also of the plentiful, at least in Washington. Victoria was given guidance by her new friend Mrs Blaine whose menus included 'oysters on the shell, mock turtle soup, broiled chicken and fried potatoes, sweetbreads and peas, asparagus, Roman punch, partridge and salad. Ices, charlottes, jellies, sweetmeats.' Invitations to a Legation Ball, each attended by five hundred guests, were passports to social success. At one of them the always popular Henry James, greeted by his hostess in a dress of pale pink tulle over pale pink satin and sashed with pink silk, exclaimed, 'You see in what a roseate vision Washington appears to me!'

Two years after Victoria's arrival, her sisters, Flora aged seventeen and Amalia fifteen, were at last allowed to leave the hated convent in Paris and join their father. As each sister came of age, Victoria threw them a coming-out party. No one forgot the Highland Fling Ball because Victoria had arranged reeling lessons in advance for all those who did not already know the steps. No one forgot the evening when departing guests were presented with a going-home gift of a tiny ribboned nest of hummingbirds. Ravenously hungry young men fell in love with Miss West when, ignoring Washington protocol, she directed them straight to the dining room instead of the ballroom. Wilting wallflowers never forgot their grat-itude for her tactful coaxing from the corners of the ladies' room before being fixed up by their hostess with a dashing dancing partner. Victoria's popularity soared not only among Washington's plainer debutantes but also with the 'mightily grateful' less affluent young men when she banned the prac-tice of sending bouquets *during* a ball. This expensive habit had become so excessive that while the popular girls tied the flowers round their waists, entering the ballroom according to Victoria 'looking like a maypole or a Christmas tree', the also-rans sat dejected, conspicuous by their lack of floral embellishment. Victoria began to assert her growing influence as a trendsetter more forcefully. No one objected when she stopped admitting being 'at home' to the tiresome Washington habit of indiscriminate dropper-inners who would arrive at teatime unannounced to trap the bored hostess behind her teapot. Her aversion to those strangers who insisted on the intimacy of a handshake was shared by many, so she started the fashion for wearing gloves or carrying parcels to avoid such contact. Soon the number of unexpected and unwelcome visitors across town began to dwindle and a doffing of the hat replaced the hated handshake.

The years Victoria spent in Washington offered her a better sort of finishing school than any mother could have arranged and she knew it. A long time later she told her grandson Nigel that those seven years were 'the greatest triumph' of her life, when everything was full of hope and nothing was tarnished and her innocence had not been tainted by cynicism. And yet for all her beauty and dash, originality and sense of fun, she did not succumb once to romance during those seven years. It was not for lack of candidates. According to her *Book of Reminiscences*, thirteen besotted hopefuls other than the President had presented themselves for marital consideration. Several Wall Street hotshots visiting the capital from New York were on Victoria's 'Romantic Proposals' list of *'Ceux qui m'ont demandé en marriage jusqu'à juillet 1890'* ('Those who had proposed marriage to me up until July 1890'), as was an obsessed Russian diplomat and an infatuated French cheese-maker. Phra Darun Raksu, a member of the Siamese royal household, did not even make the list, but only because Victoria never gave the besotted diplomat an opportunity to ask her the question. One similarly lovesick admirer regretted that his advanced age put him out of the running. In his seventy-seventh year the spurned poet Robert Browning wrote Victoria a wistful card. '*Miss West. J'ai vu trop tard la parfaite beauté.*' He had encountered her beauty too late. Cecil Spring Rice, known as Springy and a junior secretary at the legation, who years later wrote the words to the hymn 'I Vow to Thee My Country', was in despair at the failure of his youthful pursuit of Victoria. 'You have one great fault that I can neither forgive nor forget,' he wrote. 'It is simply that you like other people better than me.' He could do nothing to alter the flippancy with which she treated his love for her. 'You play with it and manage it like a seagull the winds; on which he floats but which never carries him away.'

The newspapers hinted that Victoria was 'no longer a bud' but they were wrong. She convinced herself that her responsibilities as a daughter prevented her from falling in love, writing to her elder brother Max that 'I am so happy with Papa and help him in so many ways that I prefer to stay with him and take care of him'. She also claimed in her diary she had not been tempted by any of the men who 'laid siege' to her because 'I can't trust any man enough. They are always so spoiled by Society and club life.' Baron Carl Bildt, the chargé d'affaires at the Swedish Legation, was the only one who came close to breaking her resolve. He would whisk her in his buggy 'with great dash and speed and chic along the flowering avenues of Washington'. She enjoyed the outings so much that she nicknamed him 'Buggy'. But when she realised that he wanted more than a gay companion, she backed away. Sex had been responsible for her mother's social ostracism and the consequences of sex had been responsible for her mother's death. Sex alarmed Victoria. Although she could be a skilled and ruthless manipulator of men's feelings, she was content for now to have her flirtatiousness reciprocated but without any commitment on either side. She had been put off all thoughts of physicality by Eugénie Louet, her official 'companion' and unofficial lady-in-waiting. Eugénie, known as Bonny, had begun working for the West girls in England and had become Victoria's closest confidante. She brimmed with French wisdom about the ways of the world and was happy to fulfil a quasi-maternal role. But her honest and full-blooded explanation of the facts of life confirmed Victoria's resolve never to get involved with a man on such a horrifying basis.

When Lionel was not needed at his office, he travelled across the country with Victoria, father and daughter chaperoning each other. In Virginia they visited the church at Jamestown where in 1613 Pocahontas, the daughter of an Indian chief who married an English tobacco planter, had been baptised. Victoria was so enthralled by the romance of the story that she prised loose a brick from the church wall and turned it into a cherished paperweight. In Baltimore they stayed at Cylburn, a Victorian mansion owned by Jesse Tyson, a fifty-five-year-old, wispy-moustached Quaker, the hugely rich owner of chromium, copper and iron mines, pig breeder and teetotaller who kept champagne in his medicine chest with which he dosed all visitors who 'showed the slightest sign of fatigue'. His tireless but unsuccessful pursuit of Victoria lasted six years although his lavish silver ornaments for her dressing table were gracefully accepted. Lionel and Victoria went sleighing and tobogganing in Ottawa, where Victoria wrapped herself against the cold in a sealskin jacket and matching hat. They joined a large party of international diplomatic, royal and financial guests on a train owned by Henry Villard, the president of the Northern Pacific Railroad. Queen Victoria sent her regrets that she would not be spending six weeks travelling to the edge of America's final frontier, or to watch an Indian war dance in Montana where one of the inebriated face-painted dancers pointed to the lovely English girl as she prepared to leave and suggested, 'You go? Me go.' He had to be restrained from climbing aboard Victoria's carriage in his attempt to accompany her on the rest of her journey.

The Wests rode the Northern Pacific Railroad to Seattle where an ox was roasted in their honour. In Vancouver the British fleet greeted their arrival with a welcoming cannonade. They camped in Yellowstone Park, pitching their tents around an enormous campfire where Victoria persuaded their German companions to sing the famous patriotic rousing song 'Die Wacht am Rheim', before the expedition culminated in the excitement of seeing a climactic eruption of the geyser Old Faithful. Even the natural world seemed irrepressible in Victoria's presence.

In 1884 Chester Arthur announced he would not stand for re-election due to ill health. His successor was the Democrat Grover Cleveland and the British minister was seen to switch allegiance seamlessly from one president to the next, as he was professionally required to do. But Lionel's charmed life and that of his three illegitimate daughters was suddenly jeopardised by Lionel himself. A farmer living in California, a naturalised American of British descent named Charles F. Murchison, wrote to Lionel out of the blue for advice about how he might vote when Cleveland stood for re-election in 1888. Murchison was eager to know which presidential candidate would best represent England's interest in the Anglo-American dispute over Canadian fishing rights. Victoria cautioned her father to have nothing to do with the letter and managed three times to talk him out of sending a reply. But one day when Victoria was out of town Lionel defied her advice and posted the letter. Murchison's sweet-talking words, flattering the British minister as the 'fountainhead of knowledge', proved to be the saccharine lining of a trap. Murchison was revealed to be a fake, in truth a Republican trickster called George Osgoodby. With his ill-judged letter to the fictitious Mr Murchison giving his own private, biased views on Grover Cleveland and the Democratic candidate's likely pro-British policy, Lionel had broken the cast-iron rule of a professional diplomat's political neutrality. The British press led on the story, with huge capital-letter headlines.

THE BRITISH LION'S PAW THRUST INTO
AMERICAN POLITICS.
THE FOREIGN OFFICE ASTONISHED
THE SCREECH OF THE EAGLE
SACKVILLE SACKED

A man whose mild manner and discretion had endeared him to many, even those who, according to his granddaughter Vita, considered him 'as tightly shut as an oyster', had suddenly lost his job through saying too much. But Lionel and Victoria were once again in luck. A month after the scandal hit the headlines Lionel's childless brother died, leaving the Sackville title and Knole, his huge house in Kent, to Lionel, making it diplomatically convenient for Lionel to make plans to return to England with his daughters.

At first the Sackville-West family spent an indulgent six months in Cannes where a fellow holidaymaker, the Prince of Wales, took such a shine to Victoria that he invited her to sit beside him in the casino and to dance with him at the Monte Carlo club. Eventually the family boarded a ship for England. As July gave way to the heat of August Victoria was invited to stay with a relation of her De La Warr cousins at their house near Southampton, overlooking the Isle of Wight. As she sat down for lunch on the Capabilty Brown-designed lawn, wearing a tight-fitting bodice and a skirt of a pale yellow-striped satin, Victoria felt pleased with her appearance. 'Yellow suited me being rather dark,' she explained matter-of-factly in her memoir. 'And I had in my hair a wreath of ears of wheat a la Cères.' And then a young man with beguilingly hooded eyes appeared in front of her on the lawn. He was twenty-two years old and his name was Lionel Sackville-West, exactly the same as her father's. But this Lionel was her first cousin. At dinner that evening, under the seductive gaze of his steady conker-coloured eyes and 'his charmingly gentle smile', Victoria recognised the unmistakable glint of desire. 'I felt much disturbed,' she wrote nearly forty years later in the memoir, as for the first time in her life she momentarily forgot about being a hostess, a proxy-mother, and even a daughter.

## 4

# Victoria
### Loyalty

If Pepita's celebrity was emphasised to me as a child, it was her daughter's beauty that I envied. At home we have two drawings of Victoria. An observer invited to guess her age in the more finished of the two is usually a decade out. Perhaps the fashionable French Edwardian artist Paul Helleu succumbed to her coquettish manner, his eye distorted and dazzled by her appearance. Or perhaps he was simply working out his commission with characteristic tact, a painter chosen by all society ladies of a certain age for the charming manner in which Helleu consistently allowed them a young and flawless complexion. But his likeness of Victoria is not wholly hagiographic. Her face was famously unlined, desirably velvety, the envy of her contemporaries and a source of pride to Victoria herself. Throughout her life she felt no need to wear make-up and boasted of the unmarked delicacy of her skin. She was diligent in ensuring that her image would be remembered and not only in photographs and on canvas. Among the fads of the rich Victorian determined to preserve a record for future generations were obelisks carved from glass that reproduced a face in profile. Victoria was especially proud of this likeness – the smooth-lined nose, graceful neck and expressive lips reproduced in the intricate column of meticulously carved crystal that glitters on my desk. A life-size cast of an exquisitely fine-boned hand always lay on a table in the sitting room at Sissinghurst and in the Musée Rodin in Paris a marble sculpture of her head, inclined to one side, shows a woman in no doubt of the seductive power that resulted in those thirteen or so proposals of marriage during her years in Washington. Even her favourite white heliotrope perfume was rumoured to be laced with an elusive essence of hypnotic desirability.

At the age of twenty-seven Victoria had probably never been lovelier but she did not encourage the attentions of the young man who had tried to remove her yellow dress with his eyes at the Hampshire dinner table. Nor did she respond to Lionel's deluge of increasingly intoxicated letters. He was five years younger than Victoria, a Protestant and a first cousin. As a husband he was out of the question. Putting him from her mind she chose instead to concentrate on her filial duty, reminding herself that her father was her priority, especially now he carried the responsibility of a title and its attendant demands. Conveniently, she was able to explain to Cousin Lionel, thereafter known as Young Lionel in order to differentiate him from his uncle, Old Lionel, that she was already committed elsewhere, but the truth was that the prospect of going to bed with a man scared her frigid. With the hip-length hair, cheek-stroking eyelashes and remarkable beauty of her mother, and a maturity and capability that outdid most other young women of her age, Victoria had neither the time nor the inclination for an intimate relationship with any man except her father, who gave her everything she needed. An alliance that had begun between two virtual strangers, a young woman with no adult experience of life and a solitary unmarried man, still mourning the only woman he had ever loved, had grown into a partnership and a mutual dependence that Victoria and Old Lionel had no wish to alter. If Washington had been an extended trial run for living together, then the move to England provided them with the nearest thing a father and daughter can achieve to a marriage, with the obvious exception.

The next suitor to claim Victoria was not a person but a place. Knole has been the Sackville family home for centuries. The calendar house is famous for its show-off statistics, incorporating 365 rooms, fifty-two staircases, seven courtyards and thousands of windows, and is reached by a long drive leading directly off Sevenoaks High Street. The early part of the house was built in the middle of the fifteenth century by Thomas Bourchier, the Archbishop of Canterbury, and was then given 'voluntarily' by another archbishop, Thomas Cranmer, to Henry VIII in 1538 before Thomas Sackville, Elizabeth I's Lord Treasurer (the position equivalent to today's chancellor), became the owner. The house was completed during a hundred years of almost continuous construction from the end of the fifteenth century to the beginning of the seventeenth. The eventual agglomeration of buildings was huge. Even Vita, who knew

Knole better than anyone, never stopped having to work out the quickest way from one part of the house to another. An Edwardian scullery maid admitted on her retirement that she had only seen the dining room twice in four years, while a hall boy did not realise that the bearded man in shirtsleeves who chopped down bushes in the undergrowth was not the under gardener at all, having never in several months of service been introduced to his employer.

When the Sackville-West family first arrived from Washington, exhausted by the parties and balls of the South of France, the horse-drawn carriage containing Lionel and his daughters Victoria and Amalia made its way through the thousand-acre park, up Knole's long and sinuous drive. More than a century later the experience of arriving at Knole at dusk, just as the winter sun is setting, remains identical as you pass the rounded backs of grazing deer, tame enough to lift their heads only briefly at the sound of the car before lowering them once again to the grass. Like waiting for the first glimpse of the sea over the brow of a hill, I have always loved that feeling of anticipation, before the house appears. It remains hidden until the last moment when suddenly a mass of asymmetrical courtyards rises up from the low dip ahead, looming like a small village against the sky.

Victoria's first and muted impression was not of the house itself but of the housekeeper Mrs Knox, who was 'very nice and obliging'. But soon a sense of awe and privilege that seduces anyone who has been lucky enough to spend even one night at Knole merged with Victoria's realisation that she was not any old visitor: she belonged to the place and the place to her. The advantages for a young chatelaine at Knole were undeniable. As well as the fun of having the Sackville jewels to dress up in for dinner in the grandeur of a bedroom which had once belonged to Archbishop Cranmer, finding an unknown Gainsborough in the attic, opening cupboards that were jammed with ancient treasures as well as years of junk, befriending two cranes christened Romeo and Juliet who stalked the garden and, snob that she was, enjoying the 'bowing and scraping' of the servants, Victoria set about the practical task of making a previously dust-sheeted and cobwebbed Knole comfortable.

'Ai kip ha-oose,' she would say, boasting in her distinctive French-accented English that 'keeping house' continued to be her chief role, as she applied to Knole those skills that she had learned in Washington. She found herself in charge of a place where the rooms were named after archbishops, a Venetian ambassador, a king and other eminent residents and visitors from preceding centuries. The walls were hung with paintings by Van Dyck, Reynolds, Gainsborough and Hoppner, the wooden floors covered in precious carpets, furnished with faded velvet chairs and sofas including the famous drop-sided 'Knole settee'. The peculiar 'old house' scent of centuries impregnated the rooms, described by Vita in her history of Knole as 'a mixture of woodwork, pot-pourri, tapestry, and the little camphor bags that keep away the moth'. That potpourri recipe had been handed down the years from 'a prim looking' Lady Betty Germaine, a Sackville family friend during the reigns of George I and II, much as a family portrait or the story of a dancer might make its way through successive generations.

Victoria began to electrify Knole, not only with her presence but also by installing light at the flick of a gold embossed switch. Old Lionel, no longer employed by the government and dependent on the limited family funds, could scarcely afford the enormous bills Victoria incurred as Knole gradually became equipped with all the modern tricks and conveniences. Central heating was fitted as well as plentiful plumbed-in bathrooms, making obsolete the procession of maids who until then had carried heavy jugs of hot water the long distances from kitchen to bedroom. Victoria oversaw every detail of the renovations of the bedrooms and bathrooms, even joining in on the redecoration. Stamps had long held a particular fascination, perhaps since the eagerly awaited letters that she would receive at the convent in Paris from her father in exotic countries. Extravagant but also budget-conscious, and evidently ingenious with scissors, she papered an entire bedroom herself in used stamps, and although it was unforgivably painted over in the 1960s, two of her framed collages survive, the bowls of flowers of all colours made entirely out of stamps eased off their envelopes and cut into shapes forming the most delicate of leaves and foliage. Each one must have taken her weeks. Some of Knole's most treasured paintings, among them portraits by Reynolds and Gainsborough, were sold to pay for the upkeep of a house that acquired a reputation for being one of the most comfortable in England. The Prince of Wales came to stay, as did his close friend Mrs Keppel. The Astors came, John Singer Sargent came. Corridor creepers were no longer anxious about repeating a famously unfortunate incident when a man, mistaking the Bishop of Chester's room for that of his mistress, shouted 'cock-a-doodle-doo' as he leapt on top of the distinguished cleric. Little face-saving panels with changing slips of paper had since been built into the doors identifying the occupant. Victoria was not only the most generous but also the most tactful of hosts.

When the gleaming Maudslay with doors at the back and passenger seats facing each another as in a bus, drew up at the front of the house, Victoria boasted that Knole was the second private residence, after the royal palaces, to have its own car. In April 1891 Victoria recorded in her diary that a telephone handset had been installed in Lionel's bedroom to 'our great amusement'. The connection was thrilling but unpredictable, the Knole line finding itself at times accidentally linked up to a number where Lord Salisbury, the prime minister, could be heard testing the clarity of the connection by reciting 'Hey Diddle Diddle, the Cat and the Fiddle'.

Both Lionel and Victoria continued to miss Pepita. Both were capable of bursting into tears at the mention of her name decades after her death and both were anxious not to allow that name to fade. Not long ago I opened a drawer in a chest at Knole to find a collection of her painted fans, their delicate ivory spindles packed away in tissue paper, unused but, at least at the time of storing, not forgotten. And there were times of family despondency, when even Victoria's exuberant personality could not raise her own or her father's spirits, the added shame at his disgraced exit from Washington still hanging over him. Eddy Sackville-West, a young cousin, remembered many uncomfortable, wintery dinners in the family dining room with his Uncle Lionel. In the oak-lined Poets' Parlour, named after the portraits of Dryden, Pope and other late-seventeenth- and eighteenth-century writers bankrolled by the 6th Earl of Dorset that stared down from the walls, the diners ate in a silence alleviated only by Victoria's faltering attempts at chatter, the hush articulating her father's melancholy better than any words could do. Victoria's efforts at small talk competed only with the ticking of clocks as the ferocious winds blew down the large chimney and Eddy felt the whole room contracting and expanding irregularly 'like the heart of a dying man'. But if mealtimes remained challenging, Victoria could at least remember how as a small child in Arcachon her father's gloom had lifted at the sound of her mother's singing, and she made sure the long corridors at Knole were filled with the unaccustomed sound of music as she sang her mother's favourite song, 'Plaisir d'Amour', and 'Anges purs, anges radieux' from Gounod's *Faust* at the top of her clear voice. There was nothing she would not do to make her lugubrious father happy. In order to ease his lumbago she insisted on mixing the water for his daily bath herself to make sure the temperature was right. She had supper with him every night and afterwards they played Halma, a new form of draughts that had been all the rage in America.

As well as concentrating on the welfare of her father and their guests, Victoria oversaw the twenty-five indoor servants. Presided over by the housekeeper Mrs Knox and Hicks the butler, the staff included footmen, housemaids and laundry maids who collectively ensured that spending a Saturday to Monday at Knole was a covetable invitation. Meals prepared by the irascible, saucepan-flinging French chef were delicious, if elaborate, his speciality an ortolan within a quail, a truffle within the ortolan and pâté de fois gras within the truffle. The wood for the numerous fireplaces throughout the house was cut in the estate woodshop and planed smooth so that guests putting a log on the fire would not get splinters. Looking down from an upper window in the staterooms, one can still see, grouped around the Queen's Court, the now abandoned and nettle-throttled buildings that were occupied by the services required for the smooth running of the Big House. There is the carpenter's shop, the brick builder's shop, the forge that employed four full-time resident blacksmiths, the laundry and, a little distance away, the ice house. When the brewhouse ceased production in the 1920s, a compensatory beer ration was allocated to all the resident staff both within and without the house. All these staff looked after three full-time residents. Flora West had married a Frenchman and lived in Paris, and Victoria's brothers Max and Henri were both farming in South Africa, while Amalia remained at Knole with her father and sister, accepting for the moment, if a little sulkily, Victoria's dominant role.

There were two other competitors for Victoria's attention. She had indicated that she would consider the suit of the Marquis de Loys Chandieu, a temptingly rich Frenchman, who she had met the preceding winter in Cannes. 'Abroad' as Chandieu was known because he lived there and because stating the obvious was a sort of in-joke in the family, was frequently invited to stay at Knole, and despite his Protestant family's unease at Victoria's Roman Catholicism, he was determined to overcome Victoria entrenched resistance to romance. Meanwhile, Young Lionel had fallen heart, soul, mind and, above all, body for his yellow-outfitted cousin. He bombarded her with letters and indulged in explicit, tortuous conjecture that Abroad would eventually claim her hand. While Victoria may have been falling romantically in love with the marquis she was not impervious to her smooth-talking cousin. Sensing both vulnerability and hesitation beneath Victoria's confident exterior, Lionel seized his advantage.

'I am raving MAD for love of you,' he wrote in his careful script, while Victoria replied in slapdash, smudged, black-ink sentences that follow the edges of the page in a tight circle so I have found it necessary to turn the sheet round and upside down in order to establish the sense of it all. But the reckless-ness of her handwriting was in contrast to the reservations she expressed. While Lionel was away, working for his Foreign Office exams in Germany, he stayed in touch by writing to Victoria every day. 'I was nearly asleep in church today when I was woken up by hearing the fellow praying lustily for our lady Queen Victoria. That dear name makes me start whenever I hear it. I am sure, darling, if the prayers of a fellow like me are any good, you ought to be happy as you are MY lady queen.'

An elaborate double bluff formed part of his extensive seduc-tion repertoire: he lavished flattery on Abroad. 'He can give you everything to make you happy and comfortable and you would be able to do so much for your sisters and brothers and I can give you nothing,' he wrote disingenuously, well aware of Victoria's love for Knole and therefore that as next in line to inherit the house, he would eventually have a huge advan-tage over the inconvenient Abroad. Three months after their first meeting Young Lionel returned from Germany. After dinner he walked with Victoria through the staterooms, heady with the ever-present scent of her white heliotrope perfume with its enticing combination of marzipan, vanilla and cherry pie that lingered in a room long after she had left. Putting aside his customary ploy of self-deprecation, Young Lionel led Victoria along the beautiful Cartoon Gallery to the King's Bedroom where, finding the light of a full moon emblazoning the magnificent silver furniture, he was unable to contain his emotion any longer. 'God help me, V. I love you so,' he blurted out. His boldness remained undaunted three months later when, just before Christmas, with the moonlight glinting cooperatively once again on the silver mirrors, silver chairs, silver snuffboxes and silver sconces, Lionel asked Victoria to marry him.

Ever-conscious of her obligations towards her father, Victoria remained unsure of the advantages and drawbacks offered by each of her suitors. '*Je serais ou marquise ou pairesse*,' she wrote, acknowledging that the second title was marginally more attractive, at least to Victoria, a peeress in England having more cachet than a French marchioness, though in truth she wasn't really eager to make a commitment to either man. However, although persistence is flattering, even to the most committed spinster, what Victoria liked best was a hidden bargain, whether it was a reusable stamp or a cousin who offered something no money could buy. Young Lionel's conclusive advantage lay not in the eloquence of his love letters, nor in his caressing, undressing eyes, but the three-for-one benefit that a marriage to him would bring: a respectable legal contract with an English aristocrat; the legitimate right to stay in the house she now adored; and guaranteed cohabitation with her father, the man to whom she had always felt most loyalty and with whom her sense of identity was bound up.

She confided her decision to accept Young Lionel's proposal first to her Aunt Mary who supported her niece wholeheartedly, giving 'a hundred thousand advantages to set against objections that might be raised'. Next Victoria wrote to her brother Max, giving him the news of her engagement. Anxious to dispel any accusations that she might be abandoning their only parent, she insisted for the umpteenth time how 'formerly I could not make up my mind ever to marry, as I felt it my duty to stay with dear Papa and take care of him in his old age'. Marriage to Young Lionel ensured that she would remain a devoted daughter because it meant she would never leave him behind at Knole.

On 26 January 1890 Young Lionel and Victoria announced their engagement. And at the age of twenty-seven, although she had not quite fallen *in* love with Lionel, she began to discover that *making* love was rather wonderful. Shortly after her arrival at Knole the local Sevenoaks photographer had recorded the presence of the new mistress of the house. Some of the relentlessly stiff portraits show her posed rather incongruously at a spinning wheel in the staterooms, while in others she is clearly *not* lost in the pages of the book she holds on her knee. In an official photograph taken a few months later to celebrate the engagement, Lionel is standing looking one way while Victoria is seated looking the other, a good yard of air between them. They appear never to have met before, as they deploy all the reticence, even indifference, that Edwardians considered appropriate between members of the opposite sex when posing for the camera in public.

But in the library at Knole I came across another photograph that had not been pasted into the official record book which confirmed not only that Young Lionel had finally persuaded Victoria to give in but that she was not regretting the decision. The newly engaged pair are oblivious to the cameraman, suddenly unmistakably tactile, Lionel's arm enfolding Victoria close while she rests her head on his shoulder in a gesture of complete physical intimacy.

Lionel released all Victoria's long-held inhibitions. She had finally found a man to lift her out of the dependence of daughterhood and into her long-delayed physical maturity. It was as if a stabled racehorse had suddenly been set free into open pasture. Victoria's diary tells the story of the accelerating daring with which she allowed Lionel a first glimpse of her bare foot, and then a proper kiss in a blush-concealing tunnel on the train. Lionel stepped up his postal artillery from Germany in accordance with their mutually mounting passion as he marked his letters in numerical order from the day of their engagement until reaching number twelve when he wrote: 'It is a month ago today since I told you in the KB [King's Bedroom] and tomorrow it will be four weeks since I first kissed you on the lips and when I first taught you that you were a little more passionate than you thought – how gradually it all came about and how we used to learn something new every day till the grand climax that evening in the armchair in your room . . . but there is still something better to come than—' and then one apparently incriminating word has been heavily crossed out by Victoria before the sentence ends 'on the dear old seat in the garden'. If you hold the paper up to the light you can just make out beneath the looped, black-inked barbed-wire fence that the word, rather disappointingly, is 'spoonings'.

The news of the engagement went down surprisingly well with the family. Young Lionel's immediate relations were pleased that Victoria had agreed to bring up any children of the marriage as Protestants and Old Lionel was as happy as he had ever managed to be, knowing that while he was gaining a son-in-law he was nevertheless keeping his favourite daughter. The wedding presents were carefully noted down on receipt by the bride and groom in separate lists, Lionel's far longer than Victoria's, and were displayed for the guests to marvel at in the drawing room. The Chinese minister in Washington sent a cloak of Tibetan goat, the Prince of Wales gave Victoria a pearl-and-diamond horseshoe brooch, Flora presented her with a gold quill pen with diamonds, Amalia a silver pepper grinder, and from Old Lionel there was an exquisite diamond tiara.

The wedding took place on 17 June 1890. Huge arrangements of lilies decorated the bridal route that ran along the passages, through the galleries and the halls, from Victoria's bedroom. Eventually the bride, dressed in white satin and wreathed in old lace, arrived at the small private chapel where John Donne, the seventeenth-century metaphysical poet, had often preached during the twenty-five years that he was a vicar in Sevenoaks. The town baker had made a spectacular two-foot-high wedding cake, intended to be an exact model of the house in sponge. No one was tactless enough to point out that it looked nothing at all like the house. Sevenoaks High Street was decked out in bunting and the local schoolchildren threw roses at the nuptial carriage as the newly-weds went off to France on honeymoon. I choose to think, or at least to hope, that the sexy few weeks preceding her wedding day meant that Victoria eventually married out of happiness and that she treasured the memories of the day. Not long ago I found a cardboard box at the bottom of a forgotten metal filing cabinet in the attic at Sissinghurst. On the lid was Victoria's signature in her large handwriting. Carefully wrapped inside pages of old newspaper was the spray of orange blossom that she had worn pinned to the sleeve of her wedding dress. The blooms were now paper-fragile and colourless, dusty and scentless, but preserved by Victoria just like her mother's precious fans. However, the existence of the box may have been nothing more than Victoria's habit of keeping markers of moments, an extension of the family compulsion to record events. The cupboards and drawers and attics of my life have always been crammed with notebooks, childhood drawings, photographs, paintings, Christmas cards, and all manner of mouldering hats and wedding veils. We seem powerless to resist the urge to make an archive, even if it means the occasional tendency to tip over into cluttered sentimentality.

In France the newly-weds discovered the best thing about married life: a mutual exhilaration for uninterrupted sex. Victoria could not get enough of it. Overcompensating for many years of self-imposed denial, she described in her diary

The 'Star of Andalusia', Pepita in 1853

The Villa Pepa, Arcachon, 1870

Pepita and Victoria, 1867

Top left: Victoria brushing her amazing hair,
Washington DC, 1880

Top right: Formally engaged,
Victoria and Lionel, Knole, 1890

Bottom left: Informally smitten,
Victoria and Lionel, Knole, 1890

Bottom right: Victoria with Vita, 1892

Top left: Vita with 'Boysy', 'Dorothy' and 'Mary of New York', 1897

Top right: Vita as a basket of wisteria, 1900

Bottom left: Victoria and Vita out for a drive, 1899

Bottom right: Vita and Lionel, Knole, 1903

Top: Vita's wedding, with her bridesmaid Rosamond Grosvenor
angrily censored by Victoria's pencil, 1913

Bottom left: Vita with her boys Ben and Nigel, Long Barn, 1923

Bottom right: Vita and Hadji at the South Cottage, Sissinghurst, 1960

Ice skating at Lady Walsingham's, Norfolk, 1940

Above left: A happy Philippa (middle) leap-frogging with friends, 1946
Above right: Nigel signalling his approval of his young fiancée, 1953

Pamela and Gervaise, St Margaret's,
Westminster, 1926

Philippa and Nigel, St Margaret's,
Westminster, 1953

A wary quartet of in-laws leaves St Margaret's: Vita, Pamela, Harold, Gervaise, 1953

Philippa in tubercular isolation,
Woods Corner, 1955

Philippa, an apprehensive new mother,
with Juliet, Shirley House, 1954

Juliet and Romeo with Philippa and Nigel, Shirley House, 1956

how she threw herself into a life of delayed sexual abandonment. She could hardly believe her luck when she realised that no one could prevent Lionel coming into her bedroom anytime she or he liked. Without intending any puns, she described in her diary how he spent hours 'filling me with such intense pleasure I would not have cared if the ceiling had fallen down'. The cultural highlights of the chateaux of the Loire all but passed them by as they travelled in a state of rapture from hotel bed to hotel bed barely seeing the light of day, let alone any architectural wonders. Victoria's only distraction from Lionel's attentions came during her visit to the Villa Pepa at Arcachon as she walked through the rooms where her mother had once sung in French of the pleasures of love, saw Pepita's portrait still hanging on the walls and, as she confessed to her brother Max afterwards, was 'overcome by emotion'.

When the honeymooners returned their new-found enthusiasm continued to run riot. They were insatiable, grabbing any time of the day or night in which to indulge themselves. Mrs Knox the housekeeper was required to turn a blind eye to a previously reliable mistress who now could not bring herself to leave the helter-skelter of the marital sheets and was sometimes late for an appointment by forty minutes. Nowhere on the estate, inside or out, proved a deterrent to lovemaking. They would escape to the outside benches, the enclosing walls of the vegetable garden, the romantic part of the garden known as the 'Wilderness' where there were any number of old beech and chestnut trees to hide behind, miniature apple orchards beneath which they found a camouflage of iris, snapdragon and larkspur. They disappeared into honeysuckled thickets and ducked behind the old interior brick walls. It was possible to avoid the twenty gardeners who cared for the pleasure gardens as well as the conservatories that supplied the house with peaches and grapes, but there was no escape from dozens of silent spying witnesses, the ceremonial stone Sackville leopards that stood on every corner of every part of the building. Inside the house the temptations of their feather-mattressed bed, the four posts reaching as high as the ceiling, were challenged by the number of alternative pieces of furniture and rooms on and in which to make love, including sofas, baths and even in the locked storeroom where the Knole fire engine was kept. In their own bedroom Victoria would rub her bare feet along a black sheepskin rug that made her skin give off sparks at the merest touch. Predictably, 'the electric game was a delight to Lionel', while an occasional night in a London hotel with modern beds was exciting 'a *cause* de spring mattress'. Lionel's 'Baby', Victoria's nickname for her husband's valiant penis, rarely flagged under the demands imposed upon it. Victoria integrated this time-consuming activity into her life with impressive ingenuity, managing to sit on the lawn in front of the house embroidering a fire screen of the Chateau de Blois, one of the few buildings they had actually managed to see on honeymoon, while concealing from any passing gardener that she was simultaneously playing with 'Baby' who from excessive overuse, was in 'chronic condition'. Lionel employed every superlative when boasting to his brother Charlie of the 'dream of beauty' that joined him in this lust fest, leaving Charlie no imaginative challenge in visualising Victoria's incredible physique.

She has the most lovely drawers and nightgowns and to see her undress and display all her charms is enough to make me mad. She is most beautifully made – has the most lovely olive skin and superb hair. Her breasts are too delicious for words, round, firm and soft with two darling little buttons which I adore kissing. She has the most magnificent hips and legs with the most ravishing little lock of hair between them which is as silky and soft as possible. Farther I must tell you she is the very incarnation of passionate love. We go to bed awfully early and I often undress her – I unbutton her dress at the same time caressing her under her stays – I lift up her skirt over her head taking good care to feel her on the way.

Inevitably, there was little time for study, but when Young Lionel failed his Foreign Office exams no one seemed to mind much, especially Victoria and her husband. It meant there would be no posting abroad and also they would have more time to spend in bed now that the pressure to do any work had been lifted. Although all of society was keen to invite the newly married couple to balls and parties, and although Victoria felt obliged to take part in the dancing and shooting programme that was part of the upper-class way of life, she infinitely preferred spending time at Knole engaged in whichever occupation suited her best, whether 'walking and sticking stamps on, reading, playing the piano, and making love'.

With the emphasis of life firmly on the physical rather than the cerebral, Victoria occasionally missed the intellectual energy that had fizzed at the legation in Washington. A few months after her wedding she wrote in her diary, 'L. says that I talk a lot and I do as I am always trying to keep the conversation going at meals, which I dread. I think there is so little small talk in England.' For a while, however, the euphoria of the passionate early days of marriage, running the house and fulfilling her wish to be an exemplary wife made her happier than she had ever been before. But as Victoria's role as a wife consumed her, she began to fail the pledge she had made to Max to continue to devote time to their father. As Old Lionel's naturally reserved nature deepened, he withdrew first from playing gooseberry to his daughter and son-in-law and then from all but essential social contact.

Later that year Victoria was not surprised to discover that she was pregnant. Throughout the following months she was convinced that the baby would be a girl and announced she would give the unborn child her own name, because although she herself had been christened Victoria, she had loved her mother's habit of calling her Pepita. Having witnessed the early stages of Pepita's fatal struggle with childbirth at first hand, Victoria had rewritten her will and had taken the precaution of writing Lionel a loving letter to say goodbye. But she was unprepared for the agony that built during her twenty-hour labour. When the actual moment of birth eventually approached the torture was almost intolerable and she could not prevent herself from yelling at poor Lionel as he desperately struggled to ease a reluctant cork out of the bottle of sweet-smelling chloroform. The physical endurance of having a baby was so traumatic, sending her '*affolée*', or momentarily insane, that Victoria was convinced she would die. Eventually, on 9 March

1892, a daughter, Victoria Mary, was born. The name was shortened at once to Vita so that the mother and daughter could be told apart. Victoria knew at once that she would never put herself through such a dreadful experience again, risk repeating the fate of her own mother, allow her beautiful figure to become distorted once more by pregnancy or succumb to the double-chinned, middle-aged appearance of Pepita. She was fearful of the way children age their mothers. Her friend Daisy Warwick, a one-time mistress of the Prince of Wales and mother of two, agreed. 'We were good mothers in those days,' she said, 'but preferred to keep our children young, for the younger generation would date us and time was the one thing we could not control.'

However, when Victoria had recovered from what she referred to as 'the horrors', and from her surprise and relief at surviving the shattering experience of childbirth, she fell in love with her baby. As Victoria concentrated her attention on the child she felt such 'intense happiness' that when Victoria was sixty she viewed Vita's babyhood as 'one of my happiest recollections'. She was captivated by her little hands, her tiny sneezes, thinking of Vita as a 'live doll', relishing her absolute dependence on Victoria, finding her enormously entertaining, and astonished when she said 'Dada' at only six months old. Enchanted, she watched her child totter through the Green Court followed by a pair of male attendants, a footman in powdered wig and her grandfather, both poised to catch the little girl should she fall.

Vita's birth re-enforced the change in relationships in the house as Victoria's transition from wife to mother further eroded the time she had formerly reserved for her father. For the first time she began to behave selfishly towards the man who had relied on her so heavily since the day she had arrived in Washington as his hostess and support. Old Lionel's reclusiveness became even more marked with the birth of Vita. He developed a fierce antipathy towards all visitors. As soon as a telegram arrived alerting the household that guests were on their way from London, Old Lionel would rush to Sevenoaks station and take the next train in the opposite direction. His beard grew ever more biblical as he hid away in a study that contained little more than a wasps' nest preserved under glass and a battered chair, reflecting on his youth, on his professional work as a diplomat in legations around the world, on his happiness as the lover of a famous dancer, and trying to forget his shame at his expulsion from Washington. At times his love for Pepita returned with a new vigour. One day he saw the tiny Vita hanging off Victoria's long, unpinned plaits, just as Victoria had once clung to her own mother's famous hair, and he shouted at his daughter: 'Never let me see that child do that again!' his voice combining anger with pain. But despite the evident desolation of her father, Victoria frequently lost her patience with a man she now found to be 'contrary in every way'. Plaintively, Old Lionel would ask 'What do I do?' as Victoria made obvious her irritation with him. In her memoir of her mother, Vita described the little 'flick' in Victoria's voice that betrayed impatience and Victoria herself confessed to her diary that 'Papa gets on my nerves terribly and rubs me the wrong way all the time. He can't help it poor man, as there is not an atom of sympathy in his nature.' As a witness to these scenes, Old Lionel's distress 'burnt' into Vita's mind. And as Victoria became ever busier running the house, the estate and caring for her own daughter, Young Lionel, who shared none of these roles, also began to feel marginalised.

Since Vita's birth there had been no more high jinks on the Knole furniture or behind the garden walls. Memories of the trauma of childbirth, and the fear of joining the statistical one in ten women who made up the average maternal mortality rate during childbirth, had not evaporated. Victoria remained terrified of becoming pregnant again despite her determination not to. Although she and Lionel continued to make love for the next year or two, the frequency diminished with Victoria's failure to trust the sickly smelling cocoa butter, the slimy sponges soaked in quinine, the glutinous spermicidal jellies or any of the other new but reliably unreliable choices of contraceptive methods. Nor had she forgotten Lionel's ungainly struggle with the chloroform bottle, the only painkiller available to counteract such agony. Victoria consulted her cooperative doctor and it was with a sense of mourning for the exhilaration of the past as well as secret relief for the present that Victoria broke the news of the doctor's advice to Lionel. They must abstain from sexual relations. The risk of conception without total abstinence was too great. And another pregnancy was out of the question, Victoria explained, because the doctor had diagnosed 'my circulation as extremely low and my nervous system out of order'.

Where were Victoria's friends when she needed them? Where were the aunts, her brothers, who might have warned her of the implications of this decision? One of her sisters, Flora, was married and living in Paris and she had grown apart from the other, Amalia, who although she had continued to live at

Knole for a while after Victoria's marriage had become resentful of Victoria's dominant role in the house and the sisters had fallen out badly. Victoria even kept a list of all Amalia's irritating habits, including telling lies, being ungrateful, being extravagant and gossiping. During the time when Victoria's relationship with Young Lionel had excluded all others, she had neglected to preserve other intimate relationships, either with siblings or with women friends. Now, when she needed advice about such a personal matter, there was no one to turn to other than the doctor who told her whatever she wanted to hear. The inevitable consequences of the absence of physical companionship, an essential part of most marriages, were set in motion.

Victoria's sexual desertion of Young Lionel prompted his desertion of her. Lionel was six years younger than his wife and with his highly charged sex drive he began to look for diversions. During the 1890s a series of titled and married women volunteered to become Lionel's partner in bridge and tennis. An opera singer called Olive Rubens had become a favourite and she and her husband Walter were invited to take up residence in the Old Laundry building at Knole which Lionel converted into a comfortable apartment. Soon Olive began to drive Victoria mad by practising her out-of-tune arias loudly and at great length outside in the Pheasant Court beneath Victoria's bedroom window. And as Lionel retreated still further into the impressively deep cleft of Mrs Rubens' embrace, early-middle age began to erode Victoria's fragile self-confidence, the physical changes falling severely on a woman whose beauty had been celebrated for twenty years. Just as her mother had never fully lost the extra weight she had gained with each pregnancy, so Victoria's figure thickened as she aged.

In the face of Olive Rubens' growing influence, Victoria herself began to feel lonely. She had begun to dine alone, indulging a new passion for fresh air and insisting on eating outside, even in the middle of winter, a tray on her knees, half submerged beneath snowflakes. Lionel remained inside in the warmth with Olive. In order to distract herself Victoria embarked on a commercial adventure, a stationery and knick-knack shop in London's Mayfair called Spealls. Although her zeal for salesmanship would have made her Spanish grandmother proud, Victoria's new-found preoccupation with her upmarket shop in South Audley Street brought its own problems. There were constant rows with the Spealls staff, customers and suppliers. Lionel tried not to show his exasperation with this new obsession. He was accustomed to her exulting in stealing writing paper and envelopes from hotels and country houses where she was a guest and pretended to share her excitement that the lavatory paper she pocketed from the Harrods Ladies room absorbed ink beautifully. He had not criticised her preoccupation with used stamps (many of which continue to flutter from the bottom of the grey tin trunks stacked in the attics at Sissinghurst that contain some of her most precious papers). He feigned interest in the bookplates she commissioned for book titles of every conceivable category: the one with the illustration of sundials for sticking into books about sundials; the drawing of Chenonceau intended for all books on the chateaux of the Loire. But there were limits. Lionel refused to become involved with the recycled Christmas cards, the sprigs of holly, parcel-packed sleighs, frosty robins, baby Jesuses in cribs that Victoria meticulously cut out and pasted into albums. Vita tried to please her mother by joining in the cutting and pasting exercise, but when she proved to be a failure at home craft agreed to compose mottoes to stick onto the base of ashtrays that proved popular sellers in the shop. Occasionally Vita's tolerance would also give way as she swore that she couldn't 'hear the word Spealls once again without screaming'.

But the shop did not put a stop to Victoria's loneliness. Increasingly, she started to look for something or preferably someone who might distract her, protect her, love her. Sir John Murray Scott, the son of a Scottish doctor, known to the Sackville family as Seery, was the perfect individual to combine the two roles. A weighty six-foot-four figure with white whiskers, blue eyes and rosy cheeks, Seery first filled Victoria's depleted emotional needs and then her financial requirements.

Although Seery owned properties in London and Scotland, most of the Wallace Collection treasures, left to him by the childless Sir Richard Wallace for whom Seery had worked as secretary, were kept in Wallace's enormous gold-fretted-balconied house, just down the road from L'Opéra in Paris. I recently stood outside the huge door, now an entrance to the head office of a French bank, and looked directly up to the icing-sugared pinnacles of Sacré-Coeur sitting on top of the hill of Montmartre. But the interior is no longer intact. During Seery's day a sequence of lovely rooms housed the astonishing Wallace Collection. The modern world had not yet invaded this time capsule, with its numerous ticking clocks, chiming the quarter-hours in unison.

No telephone bells rang here, no electric light competed with the candlelit sconces that illuminated the eighteenth-century treasure house, its 'silent and sumptuous' furniture displaying the decorative masterpieces of successive French reigns.

Where Lionel was always leaving, bounding up from the breakfast table to go to a committee meeting, not even able to spare half an hour to have a row, Seery always had time for Victoria, even time to analyse their own disagreements. As Lionel became more and more inaccessible, Victoria relied more and more on Seery's unconditional devotion. His sudden death in 1912 from a heart attack just as Victoria was waiting for him to arrive for lunch crushed her, although the shock was mitigated in part by the extreme generosity of his will. During his lifetime Seery had given Victoria £84,000 as well as a house in Mayfair, and left her a further £150,000 in his will plus the exquisite contents of his house in Paris, the bulk of the treasures of the Wallace Collection. His will was contested by Seery's two brothers and two sisters who accused Victoria of using undue influence on their brother. Although she won the case, by the end of it she was still broken-hearted but also practical, selling almost the entire Wallace Collection in order to help boost the Knole bank account. She kept back only a few things, among them a circular marble ormolu table with the letters of the alphabet engraved on each of its drawers and two grey urns decorated with sphinxes, scallop shells and lion masks that Victoria gave as a much treasured present to Vita. When I visited Seery's country house outside Paris the empty plinths in the garden confirmed that the urns were never replaced.

With Seery's death, Victoria's sense of herself started to

disappear, the props of her life beginning to crumble and, like the urns, difficult to replace. She had always found her own existence unpredictable and thrilling, never failing to comment in her diary and in letters to Vita on the hardship, the adventure, the blessings, the unfairness, the drama of it all, exclaiming with non-ironic regularity '*Quelle roman est ma vie!*' Throughout the drama of the court case with Seery's siblings she had maintained an impressive dignity. But her temper in tandem with her self-pity meant her behaviour grew ever more erratic. For a while she struggled on. 'I am very 1792,' she would announce to puzzled friends, intending to clarify that she shared her resilient sensibility with all French aristocrats who had somehow survived the revolution.

Many years later my father would tell us stories about Victoria's eccentricity in her old age. As children he and his brother would be driven to 'Grannyma's' for lunch at her solitary windswept home, perched like a uncertain gull on the blustery cliff near Brighton, which the eminent architect Sir Edwin Lutyens had doubled in size and 'improved' for her. My father and uncle would be made to sit for hours on the all-weather balcony 'huddled in her fur coats and with hot water bottles on our knees, waiting for lunch at five p.m. when it would be served by the under gardener, the cook having given notice that morning'. Victoria was so frequently in debt to her servants that her house was known in the family as the Writs Hotel. Because there were often financial rewards attached, Ben and Nigel tolerated the visits, even their grandmother's insistence that they stroke the underside of her forearm to feel its softness of which she was most proud. Grannyma gained her grandsons' reluctant loyalty through bribes of food packages sent to school and with cheques rewarding them for accepting her invitations to lunch. My father remembered how they would be 'smothered with flattery or scorched by reproaches'. He always spoke of his grandmother with a mixture of reverence and horror. Throughout his life her powerful personality remained vivid to him, a woman of capricious eccentricity, of generosity, absurdity, capability, gullibility, manipulation, flirtatiousness, sexiness, charm and waywardness. In 1933 a letter to sixteen-year-old Nigel that begins 'What a delightful surprise it was to hear from you. I thought I had become absolutely nothing to everybody', is followed by an offer to send him a weekly supply of fresh salmon and pay for the installation of a private bathroom for his own use. A few months later another letter announces that a 'hamperette' from the Army & Navy containing 'cold tongue in slices, biscuits, cakes' is on its way to him at boarding school, and wonders if 'You would like some Kia-ora the week after?' while reminding him 'that you are a very naughty boy, in neglecting your Grannyma in that unseemly fashion. I don't want long letters but I like a little word of appreciation and remembrance once a fortnight.' The letter is signed 'Grannyma on the balcony', her passion for fresh air still undimmed.

But I now understand that the decline of Victoria's mental stability was a tragedy not only for her but also for Vita. The self-pity of Victoria in old age is at heartbreaking odds with the youthful woman who managed two grand residences in two countries with celebrated style and capability and who seemed to have half the world's men at her feet.

After Seery there had been other admirers; the wealthy American financier and newspaper proprietor William Waldorf Astor, the French sculptor Auguste Rodin and her architect Edwin Lutyens among them. Just as Pepita chose each provider for what he could give her at the time, so Victoria had learned to chart her way from one financial and emotional prop to the next. Pepita's mother, Catalina, had been the first to support her daughter, followed by Oliva, who was in turn replaced by Old Lionel. Victoria mirrored Pepita's search for refuge at first with her father, then with her cousin, and then with a sequence of useful and paternalistic men of whom Seery was the largest in every way. Only rarely has a woman in the past few generations of my family broken out of this particular pattern of bargain-making with men. Vita was one of them.

## 5

# Vita
## Ambivalence

When Vita was born in 1892 the influence of the socially buttoned-up Victorian age was at last beginning to wane. Immersed within the late-flowering, self-conscious, hedonistic romanticism of her class, she grew up first as a child confined to an almost archaic household, and then as young woman on the cusp of great social change. During the very early years of her childhood her mother was the dazzle at the centre of her life. 'If ever the phrase "turn one's heart to water" meant anything it meant when my mother looked at you and smiled,' Vita was to write later of her mother. Victoria and Vita were barely out of each other's presence as Vita's unpleasing hair was ringletted to Victoria's satisfaction and Vita became willingly enslaved to her memerising mother, in the same way that Pepita had once adored Catalina. 'My love for her mounted higher and higher,' Vita wrote, even when her mother generously forgave her for minor transgressions that she had not committed. There were times when Vita would 'have died for her, would have murdered anyone that breathed a word against her.'

In her novel *The Edwardians*, using fiction as a transparent disguise for autobiography, Vita describes watching Victoria dressing for dinner. As her mother was strapped into her corset, 'the silk laces and their tags would fly out under the maid's deft fingers with the flick of a skilled worker mending a net' and Vita would help herself to the chocolates that Victoria kept in her dressing-table drawer and follow Victoria's reflection in the looking glass as her mother placed the family diamonds around her neck. When Victoria had completed her toilette, and glittered her way downstairs to greet her dinner guests, Vita would return to the nursery with a nanny who was under maternal instruction to humour Vita's aversion to rice pudding.

But soon Victoria made life difficult for Vita. Or maybe it was the other way round. 'She loved me as a baby,' Vita remembered, 'but I don't think she cared for me much as a child. I don't mean to imply that my mother neglected me but simply that she figured more as a restraint than anything else in my existence.' And Vita was right. Gradually Vita's independence began to irritate Victoria and her own centre of interest moved from her child to herself. As Victoria's pleasure in her growing daughter diminished so her power over her slackened and paradoxically pushed Vita further from her. Vita did not conform in a satisfactory way to Victoria's conventional expectations. A photograph of a furious four-year-old Vita indicates her mood when made to pose surrounded by dolls. At the age of five she was demonstrating an unusual taste for wearing khaki uniform. She appeared at lunch with, at her own admission, her 'painfully frizzled' hair inadequately combed. Her appetite for chocolate was excessive. She was growing fat. She was so ugly and unkempt it hurt Victoria to look at her. Other mothers voiced complaints about the way Vita teased their children on the rare occasion outsiders were invited for tea or during the dancing class introduced by Victoria as a weekly feature in Vita's curriculum. Warnings were issued as the often unintentional but irreversibly damaging process of undermining the self-esteem of a child rolled on, the consequences of suffocating love alternating with disproportionate levels of control. The shift from Victoria's long-held position of power in which Old Lionel and Young Lionel had indulged her behaviour in any way she wished was now challenged by her self-contained child. And Victoria did not like it. Her growing conventionality was threatened by Vita's refusal to conform to her notion of an ideal daughter. The child was *difficult*.

As Vita took those first infant steps down the straight path that bisects the Green Court at Knole followed by that anxious but obsequious footman and her doting, ageing and forlorn grandfather, an awareness of her own importance as the only child of the house was inevitable. 'I am an incredible egoist,' she wrote later, 'that's the long and short of it.' The Sackville-Wests had always celebrated their relevance within the wider world. The walls of Knole were covered with portraits of Vita's ancestors, most of them men, most of them proud, indulged, powerful individuals for whom the concept of self-promotion if not always self-love was integral to their lives. But surrounded by a group of self-absorbed individuals whose attention to her solitary progress along the paths and corridors of her upbringing was intermittent, Vita had to shout louder and work harder if she was to attract attention.

Regulation, criticism and restraint inevitably prompted rebellion. The three-foot-high wooden doorstop in the form of Shakespeare that Victoria had given to Vita 'because I think you like poetry' propped open her bedroom door rather than closed her in. As soon as Vita was able to run through the Green Court and out of the small central door in the main gate, the Outer Wicket, she vanished into the park. And here her desire for a secret existence began to develop. 'Secrecy was my passion,' she acknowledged. 'It's a trait I inherit from my family so I won't blame myself excessively for it.' Here in the park she found freedom from her mother's authority with the children of a local family with whom she made friends. Four of the five Battiscombe children were girls. Ralph, the only boy, was Vita's ally and best friend. They dressed up as Boer generals in miniature army uniforms and together shoved putty up the Boers' (played by Ralph's sisters) noses, bound their mouths with handkerchiefs, tied them to trees and beat their captive legs with nettles. According to Vita the girls enjoyed it just as much as she and Ralph did, confident they would not sneak to their mother because sisters do not betray brothers.

As Vita's mother became ever odder, so a daughterly affection for her father grew. Together they maintained a teasing conspiracy that while Victoria's increasingly dotty habits were infuriating, they were also idiosyncratically endearing. They tolerated the contrast between her wild extravagance and extreme parsimony. They were amused by the paper obsession that spilled over from the professional demands of Spealls into all other areas of her life. Husband and daughter indulged wife and mother with an excess of patience that encouraged her worst excesses. As Lionel and Victoria's involvement with Olive and Seery reduced the companionship of marriage to discussions of daily practicalities, Vita realised that her parents were 'ludicrously ill matched'. The adolescent Vita rejected the wary and cynical grown-up environment and withdrew into her own private existence as often as she could. But she valued her father's gentle ways, his shy attempts to advise her, and felt it her filial duty to protect him from his wife's criticism.

Their intimacy grew in part from Vita's own guilt at not being a boy, depriving her father not only of an heir but a son with whom he could do things that fathers liked to do with sons. 'Dadda used to take me for terribly long walks,' she wrote in her confessional memoir that formed part of *Portrait of a Marriage*, 'and talk to me about science (principally Darwin) and I liked him a great deal better than mother of whose quick temper I was frightened. I don't even remember thinking her pretty which she must have been.' The contrasting manner of her father, with his dull personality, and his lack of originality, 'at heart requiring nothing of life but that it should be peaceful at home', was something of a relief to Vita.

Two additional parental figures played an influential part in Vita's upbringing, both old men who lived in the house and who, in their differing but consistent, uncritical ways, offered the child more stability than either of her parents. Her grandfather, Old Lionel, welcomed the companionship of his granddaughter with her childlike acceptance of his 'funny ways', and redirected his dwindling resources of affection towards her. He would save the choicest hot-house peaches, cherries and plums from the silver bowls in the dining room, filling his pockets with the delicate fruit, before concealing it in his desk in 'Vita's drawer' and inviting his compliant granddaughter to play a well-rehearsed game of hunting for the hidden treasure. Vita applauded his enjoyment of whittling lids of cigar boxes into paper-knives, and admired his biannual habit of reading the whole of Edward Gibbon's six-volume study of the collapse of the Roman Empire. Although Vita used to 'scream in agonised protest' she did not object to Old Lionel's extraordinary habit of squirting orange juice directly into her eyes, as he explained that Spanish mothers swore it made their babies' eyes more beautiful. His evident distress on the day she had swung on Victoria's braided hair, just as Victoria had once done with Pepita, enhanced Vita's understanding of her grandfather's great romance, long buried but retrievable at the flick of a plait.

Old Lionel died in September 1908, aged eighty-one. He had been suffering for several months from prostate cancer. Sixteen-year-old Vita had been sent away to stay at Seery's house in Scotland to be protected from the trauma of death while Victoria sat with Old Lionel, his hand in hers, his mind veering along the uneven passage between consciousness and unconsciousness. Although Victoria had been in the same house when her mother died she had never seen anyone during the last moments of life. Afterwards she told Vita that as her father's breathing finally stopped she had been thankful for the peacefulness that accompanied the ending and for the knowledge that she had forgiven him 'for all the harshness and unfairness he had often shown me'. She knew that Old Lionel had given her much more than harshness. From the age of nineteen he had provided her with her major role in life and her sense of who she was.

For Vita, the twenty-five-stone Sir John Murray Scott, with his round pink face like a baby, and 'white mutton-chop hair', was her mother's most devoted protector and never-quite-lover. 'His generosity and hospitality were unbounded, and proceeded from no love of ostentation for he was essentially simple – but from the inherent warmth and open handedness of his nature,' she wrote.

Seery was in love with Victoria but he also adored Vita, treating her, Victoria noted in her diary, 'like a daughter', while in return Vita thought of him as the perfect fairy godfather. She loved him at once for being 'exceedingly charming and exceedingly stout'. Soon after their first meeting he gave her a longed for cricket set and she responded in the most appreciative way she knew, by including him in her 1901 handwritten will, bequeathing him her claret jug, her whip and her treasured khaki uniform. 'Of all human beings he was the most kindly, the most genial, the most lovable and the most grand-seigneur,' she wrote years later.

Every spring Vita went with Victoria to spend two months in rue Lafitte. As a child Vita felt she was entering an 'enchanted refuge', a way of life left behind long ago where knives for sharpening quill pens lay on writing tables next to the sand sifters that dried and blotted the ink. She had only to pull on a thick silk tassel for one of the male servants, in their wasp-like yellow-and-black-striped waistcoats, to arrive at once and fulfil her every whim. In the dining room where a huge silver bowl 'the size of a foot bath' spilled over with a conservatory's profusion of lilacs, roses, irises, tulips, carnations and lilies, cobweb-laced bottles of exquisite wine were brought from the cellar and poured with the respect worthy of a High Mass. When her mother left to shop with Seery's money in the show-rooms of Paris's great couturiers, Vita was left alone in this extraordinary place to commandeer an ancient wheelchair and spin herself through the silk-hung rooms that became as familiar to her 'as bread, milk, water, butter'.

When the city became too hot in the oppressive summer heat, Seery and his companions would travel the few horse-drawn miles and escape to the sixty acres of the Bois de Boulogne. The tiny pink-and-white chateau of Bagatelle, with its huge garden in the centre of the park where French kings had once hunted bears, formed another part of Seery's Wallace Collection inheritance. The house had originally been built in a three-month twinkling in 1777 for Marie Antoinette and provided Vita and her mother with the ideal place for a lavish picnic. As Seery 'rolled and billowed along on disproportionately tiny feet' and kept the flies away by flapping his large silk handkerchief, Vita kicked off her shoes and ran barefoot through the grass of Bagatelle's lovely garden.

But her mother always had the greater claim on Seery, and with the precarious assembling, dismantling and rebuilding of all these relationships, Vita grew to rely on the undemanding stability that she found in a fifth but inanimate presence. From the earliest age Vita felt herself to be the daughter of Knole. The area within the stone walls that enclosed the deer park made up the landscape she loved best and to which she belonged. As an adult she described the sense of enthralment she felt on arriving at the house. She wrote of her continuing happiness on moonlit evenings and in the autumn mist at seeing the buildings 'emerging partially from the trails of vapour', and hearing 'the lonely roar of the red deer roaming under the walls'. Knole would capture the heart of any child with its portraits framed in gold and topped with coronets, its silver furniture, and its heraldic leopards that stare down imperiously on the courtyards from their elevated position on the huge leaded expanse of roof. It certainly captured mine when, for a few months, when I was seven years old, we were lent a small house within the park. The vast attics with their ornate ceilings and the planked floors made from entire bisected tree trunks had provided an opportunity for exercise on wet days for centuries of silk-skirted women. The attics were now crammed with long-discarded paintings, clothes, furniture and treasures like the spotty rocking horse that had been the plaything of the 4th Duke of Dorset a hundred years before. The glorious tapestries with their medieval hunting scenes inspired the stories and plays and full-length novels that came to absorb so much of Vita's time. From the age of twelve she would hide away in the wooden summer house that overlooked the Looking Glass Pond in the garden and write.

Indulged in her 'only child' role, Vita was accepted, welcomed and loved as integral to the place by all those who worked there. The hierarchical protocol that discouraged all but essential mingling of upstairs with downstairs was abandoned for Vita who tasted cake mixture in the kitchen, watched the gamekeeper skinning a deer for the chef, helped the Knole painter mix paint, chatted with the under maids, became girl-confessor to the anxious carpenter whose son was leaving the family trade to become a chauffeur. She spent long hours hanging around with Hicks the butler who could bring a still-life painting of fruit and oysters to life by plucking a grape from the canvas and then unclenching his fist to pop the real thing into the child's mouth. Only once did a genuine oyster slither into the palm of his hand, a magic trick that left such a trail of slime in his grasp that Hicks swore he would never repeat it.

Later, and increasingly fancifully, Vita personified Knole, categorising it as the longest relationship of her life and the one of which she was most proud and most protective. In adulthood she thought of Knole in terms of a guardian rather than a lover, because unlike any of her lovers, Knole remained indispensable. It inspired her, rooted her and nourished her, its ancientness fundamental to her sense of self in what felt like an increasingly 'uneasy century'. Knole was a source of continuity, a dependable parental presence, reassuring her about where she belonged. In her undated and unpublished 'Book of Dreams' she admitted to a puzzling nightmare that recurred throughout her life during which Knole caught fire. 'I have never dreamt about Sissinghurst catching fire; only Knole,' she wrote, the destruction of that place her greatest fear. She was in no doubt that her relationship with Knole 'transcended her love for any human being'.

However, an invisible guillotine lurked, waiting to sever Vita from her visceral connection to the great house. Vita had been born a girl. And primogeniture, the ancient law largely affecting the aristocracy, dictated that the inheritance of a title and its associated property could only be handed down the male line. As a privileged, isolated daughter, 'without a brother or sister to knock the corners off me', she was the victim of a deceptively inconsequential 'defect of birth'. Vita had always known of the inevitability of her enforced rupture from Knole, and it was made all the more painful by the knowledge that it would simultaneously accompany the death of her beloved father. By allowing herself to fall in love with Knole she knew that ultimately and inevitably when the ownership zigzagged to her male cousin her heart would be broken. But she took the risk, considering it worthwhile. Inhibited by society's restrictions on their gender, Pepita, Victoria and Vita all developed ways to control a world whose structures attempted to deny them that control. Pepita achieved it through her dancing and her alliance with Old Lionel. Victoria managed, led by the example of her mother, by allying herself to strong men. But Vita's intentions were established from the earliest age. She would seize the controlling power for herself. She would ally herself to Knole for as long as possible. She would immerse herself in the knowledge of its ancient stone and in its history. She would identify herself with the place. And even when she would one day be forced to leave it, she would never compromise her independence with another human being. She would take instruction from no one. She would remain as self-contained as Knole itself.

*

But for the first two decades of her life, at least outwardly, she conformed to the expectations of her class. Following the conventions of her social position she was educated initially at home partly by governesses but more comprehensively by herself in Knole's splendid library where all of English literature and English history opened itself up to her curious mind. She was sent for a while to Miss Woolff's day school in London where she made friends with two of the other pupils, Rosamund Grosvenor and Violet Keppel. In 1909 Vita came out as one of the years most prominent and surprisingly unreluctant debutantes. Although as a child she had fought for equality among her playmates, a feminist within her rarefied world, Vita's was an existence in which only men were encouraged to distinguish themselves, and even if they failed to do so, were forgiven. It was a world full of prejudice and restriction in which women were not expected to excel in anything much beyond the twin necessities of beauty and fecundity. But society's expectations of daughters were changing, even within Vita's class, as women's growing determination for public influence was voiced by educated female writers, activists, reformers and politicians. Vita's deep-seated confusion, her sliding out from definition, was derived from her concurrent pride, participation and revulsion for the fading society that had begun to crumble before the First World War. Virginia Woolf identified 1910 as a pivotal year, a time when 'human character changed', when the bourgeois certainties of the nineteenth century were collapsing in the ascendant onslaught of modernism and the attendant power of the ego. In 1910 Edward VII died and Manet's and Gauguin's paintings in the post-Impressionist exhibition in London caused old ladies to faint in horror. But despite Vita's partial attempts to separate herself from convention, neither she nor her parents held any expectations that she would follow a professional career.

After her regular 'slumming' expeditions to London's East End in 1910, where she joined her well-born peers in ladling out soup to the poor, Vita would return home to Knole by carriage to dine off Georgian family silver, eating meals prepared by the family chef and served by the family butler. There were dinners at the Ritz and opulent balls in the private ballrooms of London's grandest houses, and for a while Vita found herself having fun while secretly admitting her enjoyment to be shaming. '*N'est-ce pas dégoûtant d'être snob,*' she wrote in her diary before dressing for an evening at Blenheim. Even so, Vita was an aloof oddity among her suitors, 'the little dancing things', the young men of noble birth and heir to Britain's statelies that her parents hoped hopelessly might make a match with her. She was an intimidating figure, partly because her shyness was interpreted as disapproval, and partly because, at the heart of her, the disapproval was itself genuine. These characteristics were as obvious to a grandchild (me) fifty years later as they must have been to anyone hoping to capture the love of this imperious but eligible young woman in 1910.

Vita was not yet ready to abandon youthful dependence entirely. During the course of the next five years two dramatic and draining legal cases almost shattered Victoria's physical and emotional stability and required all of Vita's daughterly compassion and patience. Both cases concerned brothers and sisters. One was Victoria's successful bid to uphold Seery's will. But the other caused her the deeper pain and was also of greater concern to Vita.

The 'Inheritance trial' came to court in February 1910, a year and a half after Old Lionel's death, and centred on the legitimacy of Victoria's brothers and sisters. If Max as potential male heir could prove his father had married Pepita, Knole would belong to him and not to Young Lionel. If Victoria defended her husband's right to retain Knole she would necessarily be drawing attention to her adored mother's amorality. She had to decide whether her loyalty lay with her dead mother or her husband. Did her desire to retain her deep attachment to Knole outweigh the shaming option of publicly confirming her own illegitimacy along with that of her brothers and sisters? Would a decision to support her husband's claim to Knole outweigh her protective love of her mother? Guilt lurked whichever way she turned. Young Lionel was not sympathetic. He did not understand her dilema or care 'how much I mind my poor mother being made out an impropriety', as Victoria put it, 'or how I want everything to be done to stop throwing mud at her'.

Eventually Victoria decided to fight for her husband's inheritance and the right for herself, Young Lionel and Vita to continue to live at Knole. During the trial, even though she was never called to take the stand, newspapers were once again captivated by Pepita's daughter. They were enchanted by 'her deep sapphire eyes, her soft dark brown and wavy hair and her well proportioned figure which falls into harmonious curves'. They also fell for Vita, the only child of the house. Vita at first faced the publicity with reluctance, feeling like a coconut at a coconut shy, but was soon surprised to find herself enjoying the attention, 'like royalty – only without the disadvantage of royalty whose functions go on day after day, year after year'.

After six days the case was won by Young Lionel, the illegitimacy of Victoria and her siblings confirmed. The carriage transporting the victorious Sackville-West family was filled with bouquets of orchids and lilies, divested of its smart pair of cobs and, accompanied by cheering crowds, pulled on ropes by the brawny firemen of Sevenoaks. Bond, the family coachman, remained in the driving seat, his top hat at its familiar jaunty angle but his whip and indeed his own role redundant, the horses absent from the end of his reins, his expression betraying how foolish he felt. When they turned the final bend of Knole's long driveway, the Sevenoaks Horticultural and Floral Society presented Vita with a bouquet of lily of the valley, and the coachman's wife gave her a box of chocolates. Vita had become so famous that an envelope bearing an American stamp and sparingly addressed to 'Kidlet, England', the name Seery and subsequently the press had affectionately given her, was delivered to Knole unerringly by the postman. As Vita sat with her parents in the horseless coach she shared in the celebratory reprieve, profoundly happy that Knole was to remain her home for a while longer. Just like her mother before her, she continued to reject all enticements to marry, among them proposals from a British lord (Lascelles, the owner of the magnificent Harewood House in Yorkshire) and an Italian marchese (Orazio Pucci, whose Florentine origins, red roses and romantic invitations to the opera proved fleetingly persuasive), in favour of retaining her position as daughter of the house. But then she met Harold.

\*

Harold Nicolson was a brilliant young diplomat, born a Victorian and belonging firmly within that world of certainties, a man who believed in hard work and optimism. Unlike her father's courtship of her mother, Harold's pursuit was intellectual rather than sexual, and therefore, to Vita, much more enticing. 'Some men seem born to be lovers,' she wrote, 'others to be husbands. He belongs to the second category.' But just as Victoria herself had been indecisive about accepting Lionel so Vita was battered with conflicting arguments and emotions about her acceptance of Harold's proposal. In 1913 Victoria's influence over her daughter resumed its power. The prospect of Vita moving out of Knole reignited her maternal possessiveness and a manipulative scheming that would have made Catalina proud. Not only was she disappointed in Harold's lack of money and title but, as her father's daughter, she became obsessively anxious that marriage to a diplomat would entail Vita moving abroad. For the next six months, while Harold was working at the embassy in Constantinople, Lady Sackville-West imposed a ban on all expressions of endearment in their letters to one another. Perhaps she remembered the passion in Lionel's courtship letters to her and hoped any romantic feelings between Vita and Harold would not develop if they were not written down. She was wrong. Things do still happen even when they are not written down. Even, or especially, in his absence, Harold was irresistible. Young Lionel wrote to his daughter on the news of her engagement in his quiet understated and yet generous way: 'You know how bad I am about saying things but I am glad to see you so happy, and it is rather nice being fond of someone isn't it? And I have never minded in the least his not being a Duke.'

But although Vita was engaged to be married, she was not obeying the fidelity rules. For much of her early life Vita changed her allegiances as frequently as she changed her style. She used clothes to symbolise her shifting identities. Acting her way through the changing parts of her life, she dressed alternately as a wisteria aged eight, Alice in Wonderland aged ten, a debutante aged eighteen, a wounded male French soldier aged thirty, and eventually in the wartime breeches and pearls of the land girls which became the permanent uniform of her later adult years. Absorbed in a lifelong debate about her own defining personality, she used what she called her 'duality of nature' as a private justification for unregulated behaviour and as an inexhaustible source for her writing. With the contrast of the dark complexion of her Spanish grandmother and the heavy eyelids of her father's British antecedents, nothing fascinated Vita as much as herself. Proud of what she saw as her ambivalent nature, she was self-knowing enough to recognise the elements of her own moral inventory. Authoritative and yet irresponsible, passionately loyal and compulsively unfaithful, generous and selfish, briefly sociable and latterly reclusive, she was a woman riddled with the contradicting afflictions of a movie star – ego, self-doubt and neediness. And even as she accepted Harold's proposal she was simultaneously allowing her affair with Rosamund Grosvenor to sizzle behind the backs of her parents and her fiancé.

Shortly after her twenty-first birthday, at exactly the age that Pepita had fallen in love with Lionel, Vita set out with Rosamund on a sexually charged visit to Spain, a country which felt partially her own. The trip was an affirmation of Vita's gypsy spirit and the greater lure for the adventure was not in fact Rosamund but Pepita. Vita was not too late to find people who remembered her grandmother. Old men spoke of how Pepita had mesmerised every onlooker as she walked down the street, the curl of hair – her *sortijilla* – coiled high on her cheek, stroking the edge of her ear. Vita had inherited from her mother a dizzying infatuation for the dancer and recognised in herself a mirror image of Pepita's tendency to tenderness and ruthlessness, commitment and inconstancy. One weekend Vita escaped from Rosamund and accepted an invitation to a party in the private courtyard of a house in Seville where flamenco dancers had been invited to perform.

The evening began with an enormous woman, sitting on a chair and singing what seemed like an interminable requiem, wailing and wringing her hands in a voice like a trombone. And then the gypsy dancers themselves arrived with the 'bony architecture of their features and the tragic dignity of their sunken eyes' displaying the wisdom of experience. Entranced by 'the strangely undulating and sinuous figures dancing with a curious intensity in which there was no thought of anything but rhythm and dancing', it was the dancers closest to her own age who thrilled her most, those creatures who were 'divinely young, elusively adolescent'. One very young couple particularly magnetised her, 'as fine and graceful as a pair of antelopes . . . tawny and beautiful', as they clung to one another, waiting their turn to dance, 'suspicious and alert as though the outside world threatened the affinity between them'. When they eventually took to the floor, 'an undercurrent of truth running with a snarl between them', their performance reeked of a sexuality stripped down to a fundamental simplicity, the heightened concentration of such undiluted passion transcending anything trivial or lustful, and infused with 'purity and beauty'. This sense of freedom was infectious, absorbed at a deep level by Vita herself, apprehensive of the potentially restricting consequences, both emotional and physical, of the impending legal contract with Harold.

On her return, Knole rather than Harold deepened its hold on her. Vita began to feel that with marriage she would be losing more than she would gain and took to her bed with depression. She had not done enough living to give up her freedom; she was in love with and often in bed with a woman; the prospect of marriage was beginning to feel like a trap. Her mother's intrusive self-pity at Vita's impending departure was both infuriating and a factor in her struggle to make the right decision. Victoria was always hard to ignore. 'Mother used to come to my room holding a little green bottle of disinfectant to her nose and saying that there were three hundred steps between her room and mine and what a bore it was feeling one had to go and see someone who was ill.' And then circumstances tilted Vita back further in her mother's direction.

During the summer of 1913, with the engagement still just in place, Vita was overcome with admiration and pride for the courage and bravado with which her mother defended herself in the witness box during the trial over Seery's will and developed 'a new worship for Mother'. Victoria, recently and hugely rich thanks to Seery and the courts, seized her opportunity and took Vita shopping in Paris, buying her a daughter's ransom's worth of diamonds and emeralds hoping she could still somehow retain her power over Vita. Victoria held a controlling advantage over her daughter that Catalina had lacked. She had money. Seery's money. Having suffered the deaths of a father and a surrogate father, and having lost the love of her husband to Olive Rubens, Victoria tried to keep Vita with her for as long as possible, wheedling the loyalty out of her with a diamond necklace, cluttering up further Vita's indecision about whether she belonged more to her parents, her home, or the young man she was due to marry on 1 October. In *The Edwardians*, Vita's own conflicting behaviour emerges in the mind of her alter ego Sebastian. 'He had, apparently, no opinions but only moods – moods whose sweeping intensity was equalled only by the rapidity of their change.'

Two weeks before the wedding Harold remained deeply worried about Vita's fluctuating feelings for him, although he was unequivocal about his for her. Echoing Lionel's double-bluffing technique to a once ambivalent Victoria, Harold wrote to his fiancée: 'You do not care nearly as much for me . . . I don't mind really, as all I want is for you to let me adore you.' His simple request unravelled the cat's cradle of anxieties and arguments that were driving Vita to distraction and although she wept for an entire hour the night before the wedding 'thinking of Knole' and the impending loss of her liberty, the following morning the storm of uncertainty over her marriage had passed, at least for now.

Wearing gold brocade and a long veil of Irish lace, Vita was married by the Bishop of Rochester in the chapel at Knole just as her parents had been twenty-three years earlier. The brides-maids were Harold's sister Gwen and a distraught Rosamund

Grosvenor, Vita's ex-girlfriend, jilted by Vita only days earlier. Walter Rubens played the organ as accompaniment to his wife, Lionel's mistress, Olive Rubens. Olive had been practising for days, horribly audibly and increasingly shrilly in the Pheasant Court, and on the big day she dressed in a gown of chestnut-red velvet edged with skunk and sung an aria by Gounod, Victoria's own favourite composer. As Victoria sulked upstairs in bed, Olive warbled and Rosamund wept, Vita wrote that the bridal couple's eyes met as if to say 'that this was the most tremendous lark out of which they must get the most fun possible'. Afterwards there was a huge party with four duchesses and all the jurors from the Seery trial. The newly-weds took a train to lovely Coker Court in Somerset which had been lent to them for the first night of their honeymoon, and Vita wrote in her diary that the wedding had been 'a great success'.

Victoria recovered in time to instruct the official press photographer to delete the figure of Rosamund entirely from the wedding pictures and write in pencil at the bottom 'Can't be published without being <u>much</u> altered especially the nose', a slashing pencil mark running right across Vita's offending protuberance. Mothers of daughters with Sackville blood are famously sensitive about the disfiguring effect of the large hereditary nose. But there was more of an explanation to Victoria's angry behaviour than dissatisfaction with Vita's appearance. Three months after the end of the Wallace Collection trial Victoria had lost the companionship of her only child. As Vita embarked on her own adult life, independent of her parents, Victoria felt bereft.

Not long after Vita's wedding, Victoria went to Paris to sit for the sculptor Auguste Rodin. Her diary describes the pain of the realisation that her daughter was no longer hers. 'R was so kind to me today when I broke down talking about Vita. When he saw my eyes full of tears he got up and came to me with his hands full of terre glaise [clay] and knelt in front of me and said "pauvre amie, comme vous souffrez de son absence car vous l'avez faite et fabriquer a votre gre mais c'est naturel qu'elle doit quitter car elle aime son mari"* and the old dear was looking up with so much sympathy and kissing my hands so respectfully.'

On 6 August 1914, three days after the outbreak of war, the ominous sound of the trains at Sevenoaks station taking hundreds of young men across the Channel could be heard across the park. That evening at Knole Vita gave birth to a son. Childbirth was nearly as hazardous in 1914 as it had been twenty years earlier, and especially so, it felt to Vita, within her own family. Not only had the experience traumatised her mother but it had been responsible for the death of her grandmother. As Vita went into labour at ten o'clock that night Victoria took up her position in a chair outside the closed bedroom door. Not until seven the following evening did Vita allow her to come in. The feeling of hurt and exclusion was inevitable. There was a fight between mother and daughter about the baby's name, with Victoria insisting on Lionel, and Vita on Benedict. Victoria sulked, screamed and threatened. 'If Vita prefers the name Benedict to her mother's love she is welcome to it' was

---

* *poor friend, you suffer in her absence because you have made her and shaped her to your own liking, but it is inevitable that she must go because she loves her husband*

the message delivered to the new mother. 'I think she is crazy,' an exhausted Vita said to Harold. Just one year later Vita was apprehensive but excited at the prospect of the birth of a second child, 'certain of a sister' for Ben. The baby was due at the end of September but by the end of October, nearly five weeks late, there was still no sign that the baby was ready to arrive. Eventually, on 1 November, Vita was put under anaesthetic for five hours and the nine-pound baby was delivered. The little boy, a second son, had died before there had been a chance of life.

Physically Vita was left black and blue from the ordeal. Emotionally she was desperately shaken, her need for Harold never greater. 'It isn't so much that I grudge all the long time or the beastly end as everybody thinks,' she wrote a month later to Harold in London. 'I mind him being dead because he is such a person . . . I can't bear to hear of people with two children. Oh Harold darling why did he die? Why, why why did he? Oh Harold I wish you were here.' In January 1917 a third son, a survivor, my father, was born in London, but Vita's ability to make sons felt particularly poignant both to Victoria and to Vita. Ben and Nigel had both arrived in the wrong generation, too late to inherit. If sons had been born to Victoria, the ownership of Knole would have remained within Vita's immediate family instead of moving to Lionel's younger brother Charlie and then to his son Eddy, Vita's cousin. Even better, if Vita herself had been born a son the house would have remained hers. However, for as long as Young Lionel remained alive, and even though she had moved away, Vita still considered herself to be the child of Knole.

Soon after their marriage the Nicolsons bought Long Barn,

an ancient house, with claims to have been the birthplace in 1422 of William Caxton, the inventor of the printing press. Long Barn's appeal for Vita was threefold. Not only did it boast its own literary-historical associations, but it was only a mile away from Knole and had the potential to make a lovely garden. For the next ten years, she visited her feuding parents almost every day. And as her role as go-between grew more demanding, her position as daughter of the house remained as strong as ever.

At the beginning of the war, Victoria was still not ready to accept that Lionel's affair with Olive Rubens had become a permanent arrangement. But when Lionel joined the West Kent Yeomanry, and went away to fight in the Dardanelles and Gallipoli things changed. With his first experience of professional leadership, Lionel at last found the self-confidence that Victoria's dominant personality had made impossible. And this new-found confidence emerged in the courage he demonstrated in his private life. The ambivalence with which he had been behaving towards his wife and his mistress at last reached a conclusion. One day in May 1919 Victoria caught her husband in an embrace with Olive beneath the tulip trees 'kissing like any soldier and his girl in the park . . . an occupation that was not much in accord with their both saying to me that their friendship was purely platonic'. She announced she had suffered enough. She was leaving.

Victoria's departure coincided with Vita's own romantic crisis. In 1919, when her two sons, Ben and Nigel, were aged five and two and Harold was a junior delegate attending the Paris Peace Conference at Versailles, Vita ran away to France with Violet Keppel. Violet was engaged to be married to Denys

Trefusis, a friend from childhood. But Violet intended the move to be permanent. The two women were madly, overwhelmingly, dangerously in love with each other. Meanwhile, the tension between Lionel and Victoria had been stretched to the point of rupture. Responding to desperate pleas from both her husband and her mother, Vita and Violet returned home briefly. Trying to comfort her parents during the weeks when her own marriage was also on the point of complete annihilation, her awareness of the responsibilities of daughterhood and occasionally her love for Harold and the boys were the only fleeting considerations that interrupted her and Violet's plans. 'I spent a miserable weekend going up and downstairs carrying messages between my parents', she wrote in May 1919 as her mother loaded up seven luggage vans with her possessions and left Knole forever.

During Vita and Violet's short stay at home Violet married Denys, a distinguished major in the Royal Horseguards who owned a pilot's licence. As soon as the two wives left the country again, swearing that this time they would never return, Denys and Harold hired a rudimentary aeroplane and with Harold shivering in the passenger seat the two husbands chased their wives across the Channel to Amiens where Harold, tipped off by his suspicious mother-in-law, challenged Violet's disingenuous oath to Vita that she and Denys had never been to bed together. Violet confessed the truth and Harold brought his betrayed and furious wife home by train.

Lionel and Olive in the meantime were relieved of Victoria's presence. She moved permanently to Brighton, but refused to divorce her husband and allow him to marry Olive, even though after Walter's death from tuberculosis in 1920 she was free to do so. But there was no such respite for Vita. After Victoria left Knole she imposed on her daughter a further twenty years of blackmail, alternating blame with neediness while Vita responded with pity, affection, financial dependency, exasperation and guilt. In January 1928 Young Lionel became ill with a flu that developed into an inflammation around the heart. His death came quickly. Victoria remained in Brighton, shaken and excluded. With rare but exemplary discretion, Olive moved out at once and did not reappear for the funeral. And for a few extraordinary days Vita had Knole to herself at last, the solitary chatelaine organising a funeral, a daughter making autonomous decisions that needed no ratification from anyone, a daughter at last in charge at Knole. This was the culmination of the bargain she had made with herself as a child. She would allow herself to love the place, in return for the chance to seize it as her own for a while, even though she knew she would eventually lose it forever. If the time of total possession was brief, it was worth having.

But within the week the huge mental strain that had been building up within Victoria over many years, stretching back even to the death of her mother, finally reached its climax and she fell apart. Isolated and offended that she had not been included in the final farewell to her husband, she let loose all her anguish in a wail of anger and despair. On a piece of blue paper torn from an exercise book that I found hidden among Vita's things, Victoria's huge and chaotic black writing covers both sides of the page. Referring now to Vita as 'Vipa', Victoria expelled all her misery, hurt and isolation, the letter to Vita a cry of deep hurt about being thoroughly neglected not only during the last three weeks of Lionel's illness but during the last three years. 'You are a selfish, callous, ungrateful child to the best mother anyone could have ever had.' Vita was at a loss about how to handle her mother's breakdown and at first tried to treat her with as much gentleness as she could. But in April Victoria stormed unannounced into the Sackville-Wests' lawyers' office in London, where she knew Vita was discussing Lionel's will. There, in front of the astonished assembled legal team, and using 'the most dreadful language', she accused her daughter of stealing all the family jewellery. Vita followed her mother into the street where Victoria had retreated to her parked Rolls-Royce, a victim shuddering with hurt one minute and a lunatic yelling abuse at her daughter through the open window the next. After being called a liar and a thief to the entertainment of every passer-by, Vita stood in front of the Rolls and cut up a precious and disputed pearl necklace with scissors as her mother watched, powerless and fuming, from her car window.

After the dreadful scene in the street Victoria refused to speak to Vita for nearly two years, communicating with her only through her grandsons. Although Vita maintained her end of the silence, she continued to feel guilty, aware that 'she must be feeling very lonely, somewhere in her strange heart'. Throughout her life there had always been times when a brief whiff of heliotrope, a click of the delicate fingers, could hypnotise Vita all over again and break her latest resolve not to trust her unpredictable mother. Their reconciliation during the Christmas of 1929 proved that nothing had changed between them. Victoria remarked that although Vita appeared 'very handsome' it was the 'regrettable moustache' that detracted from her beauty and that despite her 'beautifully waved' hair, she had become 'stout round the hips and looks exactly as if she was enceinte'. Victoria's critical habit was as vibrant as ever but Vita remained steady, instinctively forgiving even while Victoria's mental neuroses and paranoia deepened. Soon her mother's physical health began to deteriorate as diabetes and heart problems depleted her strength. She would sometimes answer the door in a nightgown fastened by a priceless emerald-and-diamond brooch from which, in case of emergency, she had hung a threepenny whistle from Woolworth's. Often Vita would find her mother still in bed, but barely visible, submerged beneath half-eaten jars of Fortnum & Mason's best pickled peaches, tins of truffles, cans of foie gras, soap from Coty, boxes of old stamps, bottles of cherry brandy, a fly whisk and piles of books written by Vita. Not once did Vita stop loving her. The day after Victoria's death on 30 January 1936 she wrote in her diary that she felt as if she had been 'hit over the head with a mallet'.

Orphanhood and physical displacement fractured the existence of an only child with a particular loneliness that persisted, unassuagable by anyone, not even a loving husband, nor any number of lovers. For a few years Vita's annual diary entry on 9 March, her own birthday, continued to record how much she missed her mother. In the late summer of 1936 when the Spanish Civil War began to tear Pepita's motherland apart, Vita began to write her book about her grandmother and mother. Eventually she recovered from the death of her parents but never from the loss of Knole. With her mother's death the final childhood link to the place she loved above all other had gone. She could not bear to return there, even though her uncle had given her a key to the garden gate. After the National Trust took on part-ownership of Knole, Vita wrote with emphatic conviction that 'it will never be the same – never, never the same – never, never, never'. Four years after her mother's death, the suicide of Vita's greatest friend, Virginia Woolf, only heightened her isolation. But Virginia had left Vita a precious legacy. In 1930 Vita had made her own personal claim on Knole with the publication of *The Edwardians*, her best-selling fictional memoir of her upbringing. But it was *Orlando*, Virginia Woolf's delicious and daring work of magical realism, inspired by Vita, that identified her with Knole in a way with which primogeniture could never interfere. The character of the title travels through several centuries, everything, including his own sex, changing as he crosses the boundaries of time. The constant of the story is the presence of the great house which has always been and – if fiction is to be believed in the way it should be – always will remain his family's home.

My father considered *Orlando* 'the longest and most charming love-letter in literature'. The romance of the novel was bound up in his own idolisation of Virginia, a sort of maiden aunt to him and his brother during their childhood, and a hero for the rest of his life. In 2002 Jeanette Winterson made a film about the writing of *Orlando*, in which Saffron Burrows who played Vita and Joely Richardson who took the part of Virginia brought their characters into disbelief-suspending reality. I spent some days at Knole with my father watching the filming, the mist rising above the silhouetted deer as dawn eventually broke on a sequence of magical November mornings. Nigel sat opposite Jeanette in the Great Hall where Victoria had once thrown a sumptuous dinner for the future Edward VII. I was allowed to crouch in a corner as my father spoke with his usual eloquence about the past life of that room, and of the Christmas parties he had attended there as a boy when all the estate staff came for a slap-up tea. The sense of time past and time present collided as I watched my father speaking at the age of eighty-five, the sparkle and amusement still dancing in his voice, as he remembered his childhood over which Vita and her mother had presided.

In the same year that *The Edwardians* was published, Vita, for whom place had always formed her fundamental sense of self, found somewhere that might compensate for, if not replace, the loss of Knole. Sissinghurst, a once grand Elizabethan manor house in the Weald of Kent was a ruin for sale, a place crying out for rescue. When Vita first saw the crumbling walls and the graceful Elizabethan tower at its heart one rainy day in March 1930, her response to this broken place was visceral. She fell, in my father's words, 'flat in love with it'. A muddle of separate buildings remained standing after the house spent seven years as a prison camp when England was at war with the French in the eighteenth century, and more recently had become the local poorhouse. The ruins of the once great house suited Vita and Harold well. After many months of clearing away centuries of rubble they made a home there. The arrangement was almost collegiate. Crossing outside courtyards from one part of the house to another, they slept in separate bedrooms in the South Cottage, above Harold's workroom; Vita had the exclusive use of the tower for her own writing; the dining room and kitchen were on the other side of the garden in the Priest's House, while the boys had bedrooms in the long low building that had once stabled Elizabethan horses. There were no spare bedrooms, although occasionally a very favourite friend or lover was given a room when Ben and Nigel were away. There were generous spaces in their marital togetherness, and for my grandparents that was the secret to contentment.

Sissinghurst became Vita's refuge. It mattered to her more than anyone or anything except Harold and Knole. It became hers. Neither law not man could take it from her. Harold did not own so much as a blade of the Sissinghurst grass. And it was at Sissinghurst that Vita could write and at Sissinghurst, in the earth on which it sits, where her creativity found its enduring memorial. Her distinguished reputation as a horticulturalist grew quickly, partly through her newspaper articles but especially through her garden. Its originality, intimacy and romance has made it one of the most famous, most visited, most copied and most loved gardens in the world. The particular poignancy of the place lies, for me, in its fragility, the permanence of her creation all the more precious for its inherent transitoriness. Sissinghurst felt to Vita like Knole's younger sibling and any suggestion that it might also one day be owned and managed by the National Trust prompted a rage of defence. In 1954, when Nigel floated the idea, Vita's response in her diary was unequivocal. '*Au grand jamais, jamais*. Never, Never, Never. Not that hard little plate at my door. Nigel can do what he likes when I am dead, but as long as I live no Nat. Trust or any other foreign body shall have my darling. Over my corpse or my ashes; not otherwise. It is bad enough to have lost my Knole but they shan't take s/hurst from me. That at least is my own.'

Isolation became essential to Vita's creativity. However, there was a time when too much of it tipped into loneliness. The more I read about how much time she spent alone, worrying about her creativity, uncertain whether she would ever write anything lasting or worthwhile, allowing herself to doubt herself, the more I understood her feelings. For different reasons, I had felt like that too. Both Harold and Vita were enthusiastic, lifelong sherry drinkers. But during the war, when Harold was away in London for long periods at a time and Sissinghurst lay beneath the flight path that German bombers took to make their raids on London, Vita found that alcohol helped her to pass the dark and frightening nights as well as alleviating the pain of creeping arthritis. On returning to find her 'muzzy', Harold would revert to his habit of avoiding discussion of uncomfortable personal truths face-to-face and resort to letters. In March 1941 when Virginia Woolf went missing, her suicide still only suspected, he came down by train at once from London to be with Vita as soon as he heard the news about her dearest friend. But during that whole evening neither of them mentioned Virginia's name once or the reason for Harold's sudden arrival. The following day he wrote Vita a loving letter about Virginia. Later he wrote again. 'I get anxious when I see you with a bad colour and not listening to anybody and speaking slowly and with difficulty. I always know that those moments mean staggers and it frightens me.' But then his courage to continue with what he knew to be the truth failed him. 'I think it is something to do with glands or the gland which makes one balance properly . . . I want to persuade you to see a doctor and know you will not agree.' His fear of confrontation enabled her to continue drinking. An alcoholic's greatest fear is being caught out. Lies are easily told if the recipient is willing to believe them. On a few occasions the gardeners found Vita passed out in the flower beds, returning her to the cottage by wheelbarrow. Their loyalty and discretion about these shameful incidents was admirable, the truth emerging only after her death.

If Knole had been her source of strength for the first thirty-six years of Vita's life, Sissinghurst and Harold were the props of her later years. Harold's early career as a diplomat was succeeded by a less successful period as a politician before he became a biographer, a broadcaster and a celebrated diarist. His intelligence, charm and vivacity ensured that he was present at some of the most socially and politically significant moments of the mid-twentieth century. He died in 1968 but his distinguished professional and literary reputation has endured. Only one of his achievements has been overlooked: Harold was never credited fully for his creative partnership with Vita in the making of the garden at Sissinghurst.

The early crisis in their marriage was never repeated. Harold's patience with and love for Vita during the most testing moments of her relationship with Violet Trefusis had tempered Vita's need for escape. While Harold had frequent, if short-lived, flings with beautiful young men, Vita indulged in passionate, sexually charged affairs with, at some estimates, a total of more than fifty women. She was predatory, her compulsive habit necessarily fed by constant change, her behaviour that of the addict for whom instant gratification is by nature transitory. Her sexual voracity included poets, journalists, butch women, feminine women, neighbours and even her own sister-in-law. She was ruthless about the feelings of those who risked other relationships for her, cavalier about those who fell deeply in love with her. Some of her lovers had been heterosexually content until trapped in Vita's lustful headlights, most famously Virginia Woolf, whose affair with Vita was the only time in her marriage that she was unfaithful to Leonard. Although some of the women, Virginia in particular, became and remained her greatest friends, as lovers even Virginia was exchangeable and disposable when Vita had tired of her in bed. In a letter written to Harold in November 1960 Vita blames him for not 'warning' her about homosexuality because 'it would have saved us a lot of trouble and misunderstanding'. She claims somewhat disingenuously, considering her premarital affair with Rosamund, that she knew nothing about homosexuality, male or female, before she became engulfed in the sexual typhoon, namely Violet, that nearly swept her out of her marriage forever. In the same letter she admitted that she loved him 'much more than I loved you on October 1st 1913', acknowledging with bemusement and pride the unlikely but enduring nature of their forty-year marriage. Almost twenty years earlier, during the war, she had written Harold a poem, a confirmation of her love. I cannot read it aloud without my voice cracking.

I must not tell how dear you are to me.
It is unknown, a secret from myself
Who should know best. I would not if I could
Expose the meaning of such mystery.

I loved you then, when love was Spring and May.
Eternity is here and now, I thought;
The pure and perfect moment briefly caught
As in your arms, but still a child, I lay.

Loved you when summer deepened into June
And those fair, wild, ideal dreams of youth
Were true yet dangerous and half unreal
As when Endymion kissed the mateless moon.

But now when autumn yellows all the leaves
And thirty seasons mellow our long love,
How rooted, how secure, how strong, how rich,
How full the barn that holds our garnered sheaves!

Harold was the hero of the pair. He was a snob, an anti-
Semite, a racist and a hedonist, but despite that he was also a
force for good. His greatest personal challenge was to stand up
to the selfishness of his wife because he loved her, and they
remained emotionally if not physically committed to one
another. The maverick nature of their marriage was accepted
by their closest friends and even became a source of gentle
amusement between husband and wife. During a joint lecture
tour in America in 1933 a journalist asked Harold if he and

Vita had ever collaborated on anything. 'Yes, we have two children' was Harold's honest reply. Marriage to Harold was probably the most significant act of Vita's life. He had offered her escape and reassurance during the often difficult path that single daughterhood imposed on her, while accepting and never being threatened by the power that Knole held over her.

Harold would have been a wonderful father of daughters. He filled the sensitive maternal role for his two sons, writing to eleven-year-old Nigel a marvellous letter about the trials of puberty. 'Spots come from picking – not just picking blackberries or strawberries but from picking spots. Also from not taking Eno's fruit salts when one is bunged up. I used to have spots something dreadful at your age – and now I have got a complexion of which any school girl would be proud.'

Motherhood baffled Vita. Perhaps she could not really understand the male sex, although I think it unlikely that daughters would have found her an easy mother either. She had little understanding of or interest in children. My father and his brother grew up admiring but fearful of her. They sensed that she felt obligation rather than love towards them. They considered themselves an interruption within the privacy of her day. They were never invited to visit her in her writing room and were wary of upsetting her. One Christmas my father unpeeled a banana in front of her, with the ringing of the church bells at Bethlehem on the wireless in the background. As he began slowly and noisily to eat the banana she lost her temper and shouted at him for his insensitivity, sending him from the room. Half a century later his retelling of the story to me could still evoke the ferocity of her reaction and the depth of my father's regret at angering her. In his auto-biographical attempt to make sense of his experience as a son he admits that Vita had 'posthumously become more central to my life than when she was alive because of the books that I and others have written about her'. Vita's sons chose to confess the anxieties of spotty adolescence not to Vita but to Harold. Neither of them had any experience of what it was like to be nurtured by or indeed to nurture a woman. For all Vita's creativity, and her own need for intense relationships, she had been unable to make her boys understand her own sex. They would have to look outside their own family boundaries to try and discover what womanhood, or at least femininity, meant.

# 6

# Philippa
## Loneliness

During my mother's lifetime I knew little and cared little about her past. While my father's family had long been concerned, well, to be more accurate, obsessed, with the business of recording and recounting everything that happened to them, no one wrote anything much down about the elaborately named Tennyson d'Eyncourts. There were no diaries and curiously few photographs of Philippa's family, and with an attitude that now seems unforgivably arrogant, we almost entirely overlooked her side of things. When her stories of wartime deprivation made their way to the surface we did not listen. Instead we yawned. We were intolerantly and demonstratively bored. I knew almost nothing about where she had lived as a child or gone to school. When I was much older I used to wonder a lot about her childhood. My ignorance saddened me. I found myself longing to discover that there had been some gaiety and real happiness in those early years before her marriage. All those years later I wanted that so much for her. But I was fearful of finding out the truth.

I regretted not having paid attention to Philippa's stories of her schooldays and to the moments when she tried to balance things among the mass of achievements notched up by Nigel's overdocumented antecedents. She would claim connections with famous people she had only met once, stressing how her ancestry was littered with distinguished politicians and writers. It is only recently that I have looked into her assertions and found that her claims had much truth in them. Her mother Pamela was a cousin a few times removed of William Gladstone, the prime minister, and her father Gervaise's family was only a cousinly generation or two away from Alfred, Lord Tennyson. The Tennyson ancestral home, Bayons Manor, was in Lincolnshire. An old copy of *Country Life* featuring the manor sat on my mother's glass-topped coffee table next to a valuable leather-bound first edition of Tennyson's *Idylls of the King* with Gustave Doré illustrations, bought by her at auction. Philippa's paternal grandfather was a naval architect who received a baronetcy in 1930 for his outstanding contribution to the wartime ship-building programme and for his work on the design of the military tank that rumbled onto the shattered battlefields in 1917, instrumental in defeating the enemy. There was even an Archbishop of Canterbury, a remote cousin on her father's side (extremely remote), who had preached the sermon at Nell Gwynne's funeral.

The wedding photograph of my maternal grandparents shows a couple well at ease in each other's company as they leave the precincts of the elegant St Margaret's, Westminster, after walking down an aisle chosen for the same purpose by Samuel Pepys and Winston Churchill. They are on their way to the reception at the Hyde Park Hotel. The wedding was grand enough to feature in *The Times*, the *Morning Post*, the *Lady*, the *Queen* and the *Illustrated London News*. Pam is pictured gap-toothed and beaming, carrying an armful of long-stemmed lily of the valley, her cream-coloured ankle-length satin gown clinging to her tiny frame while a long Honiton lace veil lined in shell-pink chiffon has been fastened to her hair in a 1920s flapper-style coronal. Gervaise who escorts her is slim, proud, tall, his shoes so shiny Pam could have eaten her wedding breakfast off them. Gervaise, who eventually succeeded to his father's baronetcy in 1951, was a financially cushioned man with a substantial country house in Hampshire, a rented shooting lodge in Perthshire, a ten-bedroom villa in the South of France and a suite at London's Dorchester Hotel. He conducted his professional life as a successful stockbroker with vigour, buying and selling securities with impressive acumen, and studying and maximising his own investments. He also found time to attend to the demands of his role as prime warden of the Worshipful Company of Fishmongers and president of the Shellfish Association of Great Britain. He was a flamboyant figure in the City, his devotion as a husband tending to outweigh his paternal responsibilities. The object of his devotion was an unlikely one. Disapproval and contempt were Pamela's default settings. Elegantly belted tweed suits were worn over cream and lemon silk pussy-bow-tied blouses. Her holiday-blue eyes fogged over with affected incomprehension when someone said something she did not approve of. She had become jagged and medicinal-scented after a severe attack of tuberculosis when she was in her forties, which had resulted in the removal of her entire left lung and also part of the right one by Sir Clement Price-Thomas, the King's own doctor, no less. In order to reach the lung a rib was lifted out, the pioneering operation leaving the patient with a weakness from which they were unlikely to recover and making my grandmother's already slender frame lopsided, a void at the heart of her. She was wholly unhuggable, and in her own way just as unmaternal as Vita.

My mother Philippa was unlucky. She arrived in the world at a bad time to be a daughter. She was brought up after the carnage that destroyed such a high percentage of male youth during the First World War and which had made boys matter so much more than girls. As a child she was shunted away from home to avoid the bombs of the Second World War, later her presence was obscured by the post-war gloom that preoccupied adults in the late 1940s. As a young woman the desire to escape from the dullness of home life made her ready to compromise in the 1950s. A decade on she had become tethered by marriage and motherhood and was too late to take advantage of the youthful emancipation of the 1960s.

She was born in London in December 1928, just as the generation that preceded her was abandoning their Edwardian sensibility. The Great War was a spectral presence, a shadowy part of the landscape of children's existence, haunting them with reminders of their good fortune at having dodged the tragedy of the century. An awareness of the vast deficit of young men prevailed. They had become the country's precious commodity. Boys played revenge-inspired team games called Us versus Jerry. Military-minded London park attendants retained their soldier moustaches that seemed to Paul Johnson, the writer and critic who was born a month before my mother, to have been 'hammered into their faces from inside'. Bowler-hatted men suffering from what was not yet recognised as post-traumatic stress, sold matches on street corners. Philippa's brother Giles watched Mr Butler, the keeper of the playing fields at Eton, tuck his empty left coat sleeve into his jacket pocket while keeping his spare arm on a shelf above the boys' washbasins in the cricket pavilion. His false limb terminated in a hand smartly clad in a brown leather glove. It was worn during matches and other formal occasions, the holding pin screwed into a metal plate in the stump as tightly as a hot-water bottle stopper so the arm didn't fall off during the match.

But if the male-dominated awareness had lingered for a decade after the end of the war, the political, social, sexual and cultural context of Britain began to shift from 1928 onwards. Philippa was born a few months after the death of Liberal Prime Minister Herbert Asquith, a politician who at his pre-Great War zenith had prevaricated over the protests of the suffragettes during the long hot summer of 1911, prompting women to carry out ever more drastic acts of violence and the government to punish them with imprisonment and the barbaric practice of force-feeding. In 1928, only one generation later, the voting age for women was lowered from thirty to twenty-one, Amelia Earhart became the first woman to make a solo transatlantic voyage in an aeroplane, and three works of literature that would have a lasting impact not only on what was read but on how people thought about sexuality were published to responses that varied from horror and censorship to qualified optimism. Radcliffe Hall's novel *The Well of Loneliness*, in which the prosecutors claimed the lesbian relationship was made explicit by the single phrase 'and that night, they were not divided', was removed from legal sale in England. Virginia Woolf's *Orlando* with its gender-ambiguous hero was applauded for its originality and imaginative breadth, and D. H. Lawrence's *Lady Chatterley's Lover* was banned in Britain and the United States for sexual obscenity but published in Florence in 1928 and in Paris the following year. Children like my mother settled happily for A. A. Milne's new book *The House at Pooh Corner*.

Adults knew they were living in limbo. The government's claim that the Great War had been the war to end all wars was gradually being eroded. The revolutionary leader Leon Trotsky had been arrested in Moscow under the instruction of the new Soviet leader Josef Stalin, and in 1928 was exiled to Kazakhstan. The Fascist threat in Italy and the Communist influence in Spain were intensifying as the economic health of a wounded but increasingly defensive Germany was on the rise. In October 1929, when my mother was ten months old more than thirty billion dollars were wiped from the New York Stock Exchange and the Great Depression got under way. Children grew to hate the overuse of the word 'crisis', popular with adults since the publication of Winston Churchill's book *The World Crisis* in 1923. 'Will our children bleed and gasp again in devastated lands?' he had asked. My mother's generation grew up under a national apprehension that the First World War would have a sequel just as my own generation were fear-fogged by the adults' anxiety that the Cold War would fulfil predictions of a third.

Like many families of the time, the Tennyson d'Eyncourts secretly valued their sons more than their daughter. Philippa was a middle child, neatly and inconspicuously shelved between her two brothers. The boys were sent away to expensive schools while my mother's education was reduced to the minimum, skimmed over, in the expectation that her blonde curls and sweetness of nature would eventually land her a husband, preferably with a title, who would keep her in the manner to which he would assume she had been accustomed. Despite the mood for women's emancipation, Philippa remained trapped by her parents' conservatism. With so little encouragement, she was as unlikely to pursue a career as the privileged members of Vita's generation had once been. Pam and Gervaise did not neglect their only daughter but for much of the time they ignored her: they were even more preoccupied with themselves than with their precious sons. A reaction to the deprivations of the First World War still hung over families like Philippa's, the post-war well-off. Many were determined to compensate for the long grim days when hedonistic excess had been discouraged by the King himself, the serving of alcohol at Buckingham Palace prohibited in order to encourage temperance among the affluent. Pam and Gervaise had swiftly become expert post-war cocktail mixers, their days filled with tennis parties, bridge games and travel to sunny places.

Philippa spent her early years near Hyde Park in a white-painted Georgian square around which uniformed nannies heaved enormous prams and discussed the indiscretions and infidelities of their employers. Her early life followed a path as conventional as that set down in the *Lady* magazine, which advised its readers in December 1930 that 'many a tomboy's hands (and incidentally her manners) have been improved by the possession of a manicure set'. Philippa was taught the rules, handed on in turn to me, that stressed how important it was to finish everything on your plate except the pattern, to wear Chilprufe vests next to the skin, to say 'vulgar' rather than 'common' and 'grown-up' not 'adult', to choose Cadbury's chocolates over Fry's, to pass round the cigarette box at parties, to eat peas with the fork humped, that 'bugger' was an acceptable swear word for women to use, that whistling was not for ladies, that the Church of England was aristocratic, that farting was funny, and never to address or even refer to a grown-up by his or her first name. The inspirational example of the King's second daughter, Princess Margaret Rose, some eighteen months younger than my mother, was dangled above Philippa like an ermine-lined balloon that might lift her to celestial rewards. Princess Margaret Rose was never late for meals and never forgot to wash her hands before tea. Reverence for the monarchy was stitched into her sensibility from birth, impregnated into the 'By Royal Appointment' terry-towelling nappies from Harrods.

But one morning in September 1939 during a week of softly lit, autumn-sunny days the swallows gathered on the telegraph wires, talkative, shiny, preparing for their imminent departure across the sea. That same week gas masks were placed next to tapestry kneelers on the floor of church pews, and my ten-year-old mother was released from her place beneath the flimsy domestic net and unwittingly embarked on a long pattern of flight that was to bookmark her life. The refuge from her parents' stuffy way of life was a small, private, girls-only boarding school called Lady Walsingham's in the heart of Norfolk. On the first day of the first term she found herself on the railway platform at London's Liverpool Street Station standing next to a pretty, dark-haired girl of her own age who looked sad but nice. Only a month earlier Sarah Freeman's mother had tripped on her own hairslides, carelessly and inexplicably left on a slippery wooden staircase, and tumbled to her death. Sarah's father had married his dead wife's best friend immediately after the accident, catapulting Sarah from motherlessness to stepdaughterhood within a week. Heading across the fens with the schoolgirls chattering and the steam train clattering, a friendship was formed between two neglected daughters. Half a century later a framed photograph of Sarah, my godmother, still sat on my mother's dressing table, shining with the conspiratorial smile of a schoolgirl.

My mother loved the time she spent in Norfolk. Everything good that she remembered about her early life was rooted in her schooldays; riding, bicycling, friendship, freedom. Lady Walsingham's school was based at Westmere House, a small manor in the centre of what had been a 34,000-acre estate and where the Walsingham family had been the local landowners since the arrival of William the Conqueror. In the late nineteenth century, the 6th Baron Walsingham, a member of the hedonistic Prince of Wales's set, ran his heirs into tremendous debt after investing and losing everything in the fledgling Argentine railway. The 8th Baron had enough money left to send his only son away to board at Wellington School but none for the private education of his three daughters. His wife Hyacinth was determined that Lavender, Margaret and Katherine should have a decent start in life with proper tuition, and started a small school in the mid-1930s at home where the daughters of her friends and friends of her friends would join her own three girls in the classroom. Lady Walsingham, born in 1890, had no formal educational training other than what her son called 'etiquette in the dining room and withdrawing room'. But her inexperience did not deter her from adopting an intimidatingly headmistressy manner. She claimed she was psychic, the reincarnation of an Egyptian princess with Anglican beliefs. But the maids knew better, aware that the mistress of the house and school kept herself informed of all the goings-on below stairs by standing silently in the tiny serving lobby between the kitchen and the dining room, eavesdropping on their chatter. But preserving the respect due to one in her position, the maids never failed to curtsy to Lady Walsingham nor the male servants to salute His Lordship, and none of them dreamt of taking a place in the front pew in the church which was always reserved for the family from the Big House.

Known to the pupils as Lady W, or when out of earshot as Dub, the school's figurehead was a handsome woman, and a keen knitter. Encasing her well-built figure in one of three woollen gowns of her own making, she would give her maid a second dress to wash while unravelling the third into a twirly pile before knitting it up all over again into a new pattern. Hyacinth's unusual taste in extravagant headgear challenged her otherwise unconditionally approving husband to query, 'You're not going out in that hat, are you, Cinter?' She could not abide the fashionable bobbed cut, wearing her own thigh-length hair, plaited daily over half an hour, into a Victorian chignon encircling the top of her head. In photographs it looks like a French loaf ready for the oven.

Lady W advertised her school in *The Times* personal columns on 1 August 1938. Riding side-saddle was her own favourite outdoor occupation and RIDING, capitalised in the newspaper promotion, became the central focus of the school. Sixteen ponies were shared among the thirty-two girls, a figure that rose to sixty with the school's popularity and as well-off city dwellers sent their children as far as they could from the advancing threat of war. The pony obsession is evident in a sepia-coloured photograph of riding-breeches-clad figures ice skating on the frozen pond. Lady Walsingham's became a happy, even idyllic place to spend a war.

During the summer the fields of the estate were dense with clover-rich grass, grazed by cows that provided each girl and teacher with half a pound of delicious butter a week. In a world where from 1940 onwards most of the country was rationed to a meagre two ounces, Lady W's girls were spoilt. The dairy shop in the basement of the house sold the excess milk, butter and cheese to villagers who came to fill up their trays and jugs and cream churns. In order to earn some extra cash from fields thick with rabbit warrens that prevented the soil from flourishing, Lord Walsingham grew asparagus in two long strips on the land in front of the house. He planned to supply the fancy London hotels but discovered the crop would take eight years to reach both the maturity and quality worthy of London diners. Instead, the Norfolk schoolgirls thrived on the sweet and delicate nursery stems, adding to the school's reputation as an indulgent establishment floating in melted butter and devoted to horsing around.

There was little formality between staff and students, with girls calling the teachers by their first names. In the summertime there was tennis (three grass courts) and swimming (one swimming pool and a muddy pond that froze over in the winter to form the skating rink), and all year round there was dancing, cooking and needlework and in winter, meals of thick and delicious rabbit stew. Lavender Walsingham maintained that the four things she learned during her school years – darning socks, cooking, how to have children and Morse code – served her well through the subsequent years. However, Lady Walsingham's school did not entirely neglect the academic curriculum and lessons in English literature, English language, scripture, French, maths and music were given in small classes of no more than eight girls. One reluctant student, who preferred horses to books, had been told by a fortune-teller in the holidays that she would pass her School Certificate with flying colours. On her return to school she gave up lessons, saddled her horse and waited for the prophecy to come true. She was the only girl in her year to fail every exam.

The wrong religion was the one acknowledged impediment to admission into Lady Walsingham's school. Although Lady Walsingham was not a fervent Anglican, she considered observance of the Church of England services to be an essential part of patriotism. Both Lady W and His Lordship had been very shocked when a niece of theirs was ensnared by a Roman Catholic convent and became a devout 'Mackerel Snapper', following the Catholic custom of eating fish on Fridays. As a consequence of this family upset, Lady Walsingham's advertisements stressed from the start that the school would accept 'Protestants only'. When the school's attendance levels were threatened by war and the extra financial pressure on parents, Lady Walsingham dropped her termly fee from fifty to thirty-five guineas. But her advertisements retained the religious caveat. And there was another undeclared prejudice. Lady Walsingham's was a school for posh girls. Only one exception was made, when a place was given at reduced rates to the daughter of the local vicar. The unfortunate girl was quickly identified by her fellow students as different, made acutely conscious of her charitable status and hated her isolated schooldays there. In the distant meadows and riding paddocks of Norfolk, snobbery and the class system were endemic. The girls remained their parents' daughters.

The little community was further segregated from the rest of the world by the remoteness of the landscape. The village shop was a mile away but a generous sweet ration was kept in a big cupboard at school. When the enemy bombs began to land on London and the fear of a German invasion gradually spread through the country, there was little sign of the conflict in that part of Norfolk. For three years the schoolgirls rode and swam and knitted and sewed and laughed and played games and ate asparagus and made alliances to last a lifetime. Parents rarely visited. The girls were no longer a disparate grouping but a community of unrelated sisters, bonded in friendship rather than blood.

The all-female environment was interrupted only when

Wellington School broke up earlier than Lady W's and the Walsingham son and heir, John de Grey came home for the holidays. From the ages of thirteen to eighteen he steeled himself to return to this daunting establishment. 'Like all males in their teens,' he explained to me recently at the age of ninety, 'I was naturally homosexual and found mixed-sex card games difficult and mixed swimming impossible.' John and the vicar's daughter were among the few at Westmere to feel out of sorts.

Love inevitably flourished among the desks. The lively romance between two of the staff members was followed as keenly as a popular magazine serial. Miss Gummersall, the matron known as Gummy, fell uninhibitedly for Miss Joy, the maths and geography mistress. A frisson ran around the school whenever the two were spotted holding hands, a running risqué joke that the expression on Gummy's face confirmed that she had recently been filled with joy. Romantic attachment between the girls also thrived. An excited queue would form before lights out as younger girls waited their turn to kiss Lavender, the very pretty and oldest Miss de Grey, goodnight. She was recognised as a 'mother figure', and according to her sister Katie, Philippa was invariably the first in the queue. Philippa gravitated towards any kind of proxy-maternal reassurance, even that offered by a fellow schoolgirl. A deprivation of attention at home had left her with a craving for a hug, some sort of intimacy, a physical connection with another person.

The years Philippa spent at Lady Walsingham's nourished her growing sense of individuality and of belonging. It provided an environment free from challenge, a jolly, girly, privileged place where schoolgirls were sometimes referred to by teachers as 'our daughters' and life seemed to hold such promise. She blossomed into the sort of pupil who was naughty enough, loyal enough, merry enough and pretty enough to be popular. She made people laugh and practised her gift for mimicry until she became an expert. More than seventy years after they had left the school, the youngest de Grey daughter still remembered how she and Philippa would make a midnight dash from their dormitory to the swimming pool for an illicit swim by the light of the moon. Racing back, wrapped in nothing but towels, on one occasion they were summoned to the headmistress the following morning, incriminated by their wet knickers which they had inadvertently dropped on the path. 'I liked her because, oh glory, she was fun,' Katie told me.

But even Lady Walsingham's protective walls could not keep out the war forever. The government had begun to look around for military practice sites, especially those with habitable buildings in which the army could rehearse tactics. One afternoon in June during the summer term of 1942, the villagers on the Walsingham estate, the farmers and their families were summoned to a meeting where Lieutenant General Anderson, the head of Eastern Command, announced that 18,000 acres, 150 houses, three schools, two pubs and thirty-four miles of roadway on the Walsingham estate had been identified for military occupation and every villager, man, woman, child, and those in residence at Lady Walsingham's school were to be evicted for the remainder of the war, however long that would be. Lord Walsingham acknowledged in front of the silent gathering that this was indeed a calamity. The villagers, many of them related to one another, were given a month in which to find themselves alternative places to live. On 19 July, the day the evacuation was completed, the RSPCA arrived to dispose of all the newly homeless pets, the reproach in the animals' eyes never forgotten by their owners. Although Lady Walsingham moved her school to other buildings on the estate, many of the girls, including Sarah, were taken away by parents who felt it was no longer safe. Philippa only stayed on for another year before her education ended at the age of fifteen and she left Lady W's for good.

Philippa's eventual return home made little difference to the lives of my grandparents. Sarah would come to stay and was taken aback by Gervaise and Pam's lack of interest in their daughter and her friend. Barely looking up from their game of canasta or bezique, unless it was to mix another super-strength martini, they would spend the evenings playing card games and shaking cocktails before edging their inebriated way to bed.

Gervaise was a presentation in pastel. From his slick grey hair – faintly yellowish from a regular infusion of tobacco smoke – downwards, he appeared bleached out. He wore baby-pink and lavender shirts with white collars and cuffs like a nurse, and his soft, damp-from-the-flannel complexion was so pale as to appear almost bloodless. He took a womanly care of his appearance. His skin was wiped clean of blemish by the Trumper's barbers in St James's while his fingernails were buffed, shaped and grime-innocent. He smelled nice. Even the snap of a new five-pound note being flicked years later from the wad he carried in his leather wallet and handed out with abundance to us grandchildren smelled as good as it sounded.

Dirt was to be avoided. Dirt smelled of poverty. Gervaise smelled rich.

As a small granddaughter I instinctively avoided physical contact with Pam, recoiling from the knobbly pearls at her neck that dug into me during the obligatory embrace on arrival at her house, while fascinated by the red lipstick stains that muralled her teeth. They lived in the New Forest in Hampshire in a mock-Tudor house. The silky fringes of her two identical Yorkshire terriers, Yorkshire and Bartie (her private, jokey shortening of Baronet), were combed to a gleam and tied neatly between the ears in pink and blue silk ribbons. Our favourite person in the house was the cook and our favourite room was the kitchen: both smelled deliciously of newly baked cake. Upstairs the uncomfortable, lemon-striped, horsehair sofas abutted sharp-angled side tables made from mottled walnut bearing china horses and silver ashtrays. Paintings of hunting scenes and fishing scenes and shooting scenes and all manner of other outdoor sporting scenes hung on the walls. On our visits there in the 1960s a pre-war lifestyle endured. At breakfast time, the electric hotplate on the sideboard was laden with fishcakes and chewy grilled kidneys, food we associated with lunch. The stables had remained untouched for years. Dozens of rosettes, many of the red first-prize variety, were attached to the beams with drawing pins, but I remember being more intrigued by the rows of ancient cans of tomato soup that had been rusting on the surrounding shelves since rationing began in 1940. One end of the garden terminated in a ha-ha, a terrifying hazard if you were on a bicycle, while the rest of the garden was surrounded by barbed-wire fences stopping the New

Forest ponies from wandering onto the lawn and eating the flowers. The vegetation beyond the fence was largely yellow gorse, full of prickles. It was a hostile environment without and within. My grandparents never questioned their position of superiority within the village, but behind their backs the villagers referred to them, in true E. F. Benson style with an affected double tap of forefinger to nose, as the Tennis-Courts.

Shortly after the outbreak of war, together with most country householders with rooms to spare, Pamela and Gervaise had been legally obliged to give a home to young evacuees from Britain's larger cities, especially London where the danger of attack was greatest. A million children had been evacuated by the end of 1939 and received no schooling for four months. The distress of the parents at the parting was mitigated by the knowledge that their children were going to stay in safer and healthier surroundings. But parents had no control over how much compassion would be shown to their children by the temporary guardians. Three little girls arrived at my grand-parents' diamond-paned, well-ordered, polished-mahogany, stiff-chintzy house, nervous, disorientated and miserable, saved from the threat of falling bombs but ripped out from the rootedness of their own houses. They carried few reminders of home with them other than a change of clothes and each other.

At the first supper, one of the little girls eyed the plate of greyish meat in front of her and asked if she could please have some of her father's favourite sauce. Except she did not put it like that. 'Daddy's favourite sauce' was what she said. I came to dread my mother's retelling of this story, and the accompanying affectation of a cockney accent to emphasise the almost foreign nature of these children. In an attempt to identify Daddy's favourite sauce, Pam encouraged Philippa, home from the very different society of Lady Walsingham's, to join the guessing game as together they went through every sauce they could think of. Tomato, Worcester, Tabasco and salad cream were swiftly dismissed in favour of béarnaise and hollandaise, each of these two options delivered in an exaggerated French accent. Goodness, Daddy must have a very unusual sauce as his favourite if it was none of these! The little girls had begun by shaking their heads at each suggestion, but when all recognisable possibilities had been exhausted they sat still in their chairs and began to sniff and then to weep. And then Pamela finally guessed what she had known all along. Daddie's Favourite Sauce was a spicy, sticky, messy, glutinous, brown liquid, sweetened with a hint of molasses. The brand became well known during the war for the Daddie's Girls, the brown-sauce factory workers whose flirtatious notes of encouragement attached to the consignments headed for the men at the front had resulted in marriage proposals featured in the popular press. But kitchens in nice houses in Hampshire villages were not acquainted with such nasty substances, even though the angelic curly-haired girl on the bottle's label looked exactly like the daughter of the house.

Pamela's cruelty towards these innocents was not yet complete. When she discovered the girls had washed their underwear and strung it up to dry between the chimney pots, defiling the dignity of her nice well-appointed house, she took a photograph and presented it to the child refugees' housing authorities as evidence that the children could not be trusted to behave properly and must be moved to another family. Years later, at the same age as those evacuees, listening to my mother telling this story and of her collusion with her mother, I wondered if she realised that it was not as funny as she had once thought. If this episode did not demonstrate to Philippa, even in hindsight, the extent of her skewed approach to children, it certainly did to me. The failure to understand, let alone love, children, together with the overriding snobbery that dictated Pam's conduct in most matters, was impossible to miss, and in part became my mother's own learned behaviour. Snobbery was the means by which Pam and in turn Philippa reassured themselves that they were significant individuals. Snobbery masked their own deficiencies. If they could not be happy within themselves, and who knows whether Pam and Gervaise, with all their martinis and indolence, were truly happy, then they could at least comfort themselves that they were superior to these frightened children.

Part of the reason why my mother had not supported the children against my grandmother's cruel taunts was because she did not know how to stand up to those taunts herself. Although Philippa was the daughter of the house and not a visiting refugee, she was not exempt from her mother's expressions of contempt nor from her regime of domestic discipline. She swept and cleaned and, in her own later interpretation, Cinderella-ed her way through those final two years of international conflict and well beyond the end of the war. Just as the Victorian daughter had been raised to help her mother with the running of the home, now in the 1940s and 50s the unmarried daughter in families who once had afforded servants became indispensible in maintaining pre-war standards. The difference between them and the housemaids who had preceded them was they were not paid. But the bitter resentment that my mother felt about the 'skivving' that she was required to do, a resentment that she often voiced to us, so much luckier, she reminded us, in our chore-free adolescence than she had been, is more easily explained by the knowledge that Philippa's parents were not poor, just mean.

Throughout the war Gervaise had spent time in the splendour of his suite at the Dorchester in Park Lane, a hotel owned and built by McAlpines, the family construction firm run partly by the father of an old school friend of his from Charterhouse. Gervaise had clearly not neglected his investments, so Philippa had the impression that she was being unnecessarily punished for a crime that she had not committed. She saw herself as a daughter without any marital prospects (she was still only seventeen!) and therefore as a burden who must be made to earn her board and lodging. There was one period of respite from the tedium of keeping house. Lavender, the eldest Walsingham daughter, had left school to enrol as a trainee in undercover surveillance as part of the Special Operations Executive. Just before the end of the war her sister Katie persuaded my mother to go with her to the same 'finishing school' as Lavender had attended. It was in London's Queen's Gate and run by Mrs Renee O'Marmy, known to her students as Mrs Really So Smarmy. Philippa and Katie were publicly hazy about exactly what they were learning in this strange establishment. They told friends they were studying 'Public Speaking'. My mother lasted one term and never spoke of this period in her life but something dreadful upset her there. Neither my brother nor I remember any talk of a dashing career in espionage before her marriage but whatever it was that Philippa got up to during those few unhappy months at Queen's Gate, she begged to be allowed to return home to Hampshire where she continued her job as unpaid housekeeper.

Eventually Gervaise turned his attention to his drifting daughter. He seems to have realised that, despite her youth, her attractiveness and her sense of humour that had flourished so freely at school, she was beginning to wither, alone in Hampshire with few friends and often only the New Forest ponies as companions. There seemed little chance that Philippa would ever find a husband among the card-playing Tories with whom he and Pam spent their time in the country. Through Gervaise's connections with the owners of the Dorchester, the hotel's Swiss chef, Eugene Kaufeler, was persuaded to take Philippa on as an apprentice in his kitchen. Of all the hobbies and passing interests of my mother's life, cookery was the one that endured. She became a wonderful cook, adapting the haute cuisine of Park Lane recipes to those she eventually served for us at home. My brother remembers 'enormous cartwheels of mushroom quiche, sole in creamy sauces, giant pieces of roast beef and roast potatoes which she fried to make crisp', the delicious food of our early childhood, while I, misty with nostalgia, still dream of the Elysian sticky toffee pudding and the roast chicken that melted into my homesick mind during the first weeks of each new boarding-school term. Eugene Kaufeler's kitchen served a clientele of movie stars, but while clouds of Grand Marnier soufflé wafted up the Dorchester stairs to the luxurious suites, the chef fell paternalistically for my mother. Their pupil–student relationship lasted far beyond her year-long apprenticeship and we children were the dubious long-term beneficiaries. Our own birthday cakes, ridiculously rich and elaborate with thick glacé icing and a filling of whipped cream embedded with out-of-season strawberries, would be delivered by special van on an annual basis to our boarding schools. Taking its place among the fish-paste sandwiches and ginger biscuits provided by the school for all birthdays Monsieur Kaufeler's embarrassing cake stood out like a fur coat at a nudists' colony.

As an apprentice chef Philippa stayed down in the Park Lane kitchens during the day, but in the evening she came out. After a five-year break during the war the debutante season resumed over the summer months of 1946. The season kicked off with Queen Charlotte's ball in the Great Room at the Grosvenor House Hotel where one hundred virginal beauties including my mother curtsied to a cardboard cake before twirling off in the hope of landing a marital contract with a suitably well-bred bachelor. The plan was to spend the next nine months negotiating the deal under the cover of flirting at a Lyons Corner House, at garden parties in Buckingham Palace, on the race course at Ascot, in the dining rooms of London's smartest residences, on the dance floors of nightclubs and at the weekends in Britain's grandest country houses. The trick was not to find yourself alone at any point with someone who was NSIT (not safe in taxis) or who insisted that he MTF (must touch flesh, or specifically the gap between the top of the stocking and the elastic of the knicker) or, as some were warned, allow yourself to be kissed by a boy in case that made you have a baby.

There are some joyful pictures of my mother at a picnic, loafing around, playing leapfrog, being silly, unselfconscious, happy. They are precious pictures, the only ones I have of her at this time in her life when she was so obviously free from any anxiety at all. Friends from those days remember her enviable femininity, her lovely figure and her gaiety during tennis games at Woods Corner and at evenings with the Montagues at Beaulieu Abbey. And she was in love. Patrick Plunket was the Catherine wheel, the fizzing pivot around whom all of London society, including the two royal princesses, spun. An Irish peer with crinkly, smiley eyes who was equerry first to George VI and later to Elizabeth II, he enchanted everyone he met, including his young boss. He lived in West Malling, on what Kentish people knew as 'the cherry blossom route', in a pretty pink house with a lovely garden and a conservatory overflowing with orchids and geraniums. My mother was one of many young women to be smitten by him, hoping they might become The One in Patrick's eyes. To the frustration of them all, he remained a friend to dozens if not hundreds of young women, but never relinquished his bachelor status.

As her time as a debutante and the traineeship at the hotel both came to an end my mother returned to the New Forest, with her Border terrier Romeo as chief companion, confined once again within the ivy-coated walls of her parents' house. She nearly ducked out of a New Year cocktail party at a neighbour's thatched cottage where she knew Bournemouth colonels and their tweed-suited wives would be out in force to meet the guest of honour, the hostess's lodger, the new Conservative MP for Bournemouth East. But Philippa went, partly because she had become the diligent secretary of the New Forest Young Conservatives Association, a role she took seriously, and partly because her parents, aware of the shortage of men after the war and of the stigma of spinsterhood, wanted her to accompany them, just in case.

Nigel Nicolson was twelve years older than Philippa but decades younger than the other guests. He was tall and dark, with a creditable war record in the Grenadier Guards. He was the son of well-known, if rather bohemian parents. As he mingled among his Tory supporters, among them a pleasing number of pretty young women, his eye fell on my mother and he was smitten. Or so he said to himself at the time. Early in the new year he took her to a white-tie dance, and, although entirely out of character and experience, kissed her in the car on the way home. Then he took her to lunch at the House of Commons and began writing her letters of 'mounting affection'. He was touched by her sweetness, her responsiveness.

Five weeks after the cocktail party, and having met no more than half a dozen times, Nigel proposed. He had never mentioned marriage to Philippa herself and the first she knew of it was when Nigel approached Gervaise in the sitting room, where he and Pam were taking their pre-dinner drinks. Nigel described the moment in his diary. As Philippa stood to one side, he cleared his throat and asked Gervaise if he might have Philippa's hand in marriage. It sounded like a business proposition from one man to another with the two women acting as witnesses to the negotiation. A gasp, some tears, acceptance and champagne all followed as my mother's parents congratulated

Nigel on his arrangement to 'take Philippa off our hands'. Soon afterwards Nigel took the train to London, leaving a bemused Philippa alone with her parents. The following morning Nigel woke up in the Piccadilly flat he shared with his father thinking, 'My God, what have I done?'

7

# Philippa
Trapped

Nigel maintained at the time that he had chosen Philippa as
his bride because she was 'unblemished, creamy, innocent' and
'the loveliest flower of the New Forest'. He felt, or at least
convinced himself to feel, that the motivation behind his
proposal was entirely honourable, even laudable: he had fallen
in love with her. But in an unpublished memoir written years
later he admitted that he had decided to propose mainly because
the acquisition of a wife would do him a lot of good in his
constituency. Philippa's version almost concurred. Although at
first she truly believed he had fallen in love with her and she
with him, she was under no illusions as to the practical advantages a marriage would produce for Nigel. She discovered
through her Young Conservative friends that a few weeks before
their meeting, Nigel's constituency agent had given Nigel some
personal advice. The Conservative Member for Bournemouth

East was in his late thirties, unmarried, and people were beginning to talk. He had to consider his majority. The agent could help. Suddenly Nigel became very gay, attending numerous cocktail parties at which a series of pretty girls were dangled as potential wife material. Philippa was the prettiest. She would enhance his professional reputation.

In 1953, however, he pretended quite successfully to himself as well to his constituents, Philippa's parents and Philippa herself to have met the woman of his dreams. 'I fantasised my own romance,' he wrote thirty years later, 'and acted the role I had created.' And, love apart, he felt he was doing Philippa a favour. 'I was rescuing her from a stultifying life of cooking, riding, mowing the lawn and would show her the delights of literature and politics and London and literature.' And that is exactly what she thought he was doing too. At least that is what she thought at first. Nigel wrote her wonderful love letters, all put neatly away in date order in the 'Philippa from Nigel' file that we found after his death. But later Nigel would confess that he knew 'I was not as head over heels as I pretended in the letters'. He was simulating in-loveness. In his unpublished memoir, he cites the fact that his fiancée was 'barely educated' as his earliest fear for the long-term success of their marriage. Within weeks Nigel was bored by her. He thought, dangerously and arrogantly, that although she was 'unformed intellectually' he would be able to 'mould' her, to erase the Tennyson d'Eyncourt-ness from her.

Philippa's replies, which are all the more touching for the evident genuineness of the emotion, are interleaved with his in the file. For the twin escape routes that marriage offered, escape from the dreary demands of home and escape from the ever-present fear of spinsterhood fostered by her mother, Philippa also wanted the marriage to work. But she did not know what to expect nor did she have any experience with which to compare her feelings, having never had a boyfriend before. The weeks leading up to the wedding were difficult ones for her. Nigel took her to meet his parents. Her two letters of thanks, one each to Vita and Harold, written after her first visit to Sissinghurst are full of gratitude for their 'gentleness and under-standing' and 'acceptance of me as Nigel's wife to be'. The response from the Nicolson side was less straightforward. In an ambivalent letter to his other son, Ben, that I found among Nigel's papers, Harold described his future daughter-in-law as a racehorse owner might assess a new filly. 'Very pretty in a rather chocolate box way. Pink and white complexion, a ready smile with flawless teeth, saffron-coloured eyes, fair hair, good figure, about five foot ten inches . . . obviously straight and reliable and competent and decent. Not clever I should think in the intellectual sense . . . enormously presentable and Niggs will be proud of her.' But the Nicolson parents had not conducted themselves in a manner to make their son proud. Before Vita's first meeting with Philippa she was so worried that she might make her future daughter-in-law nervous that she gave Harold the 'impression that she had been drinking heavily', an observation he passed on to Nigel, not by way of criticism of Vita, but more as an explanation of her 'muzziness'. And during an encounter between the prospective in-laws, Harold's archaic suggestion to Gervaise that the father of the bride should provide a substantial dowry went down predictably badly. Philippa herself, however, was won over when Harold urged the reserved girl to call him by his first name. 'I think you will find it comes very naturally,' he assured her, 'after fifty years of practice.' But on 8 April 1953 Nigel wrote separately and ominously to his mother. He had been engaged to Philippa for a month. 'I can already see her shaking off the rather dull conventions of her family and becoming a Sissinghurst person. She is an unopened flower, a strong bud. It will be fascinating to see her develop.' She had become an experiment for Nigel not only to shape to his own ideal but to reflect well on himself. At the age of thirty-six Nigel was still looking for his parents' approval. And they gave it, but with reservations, joining in the Nicolson family conspiracy that Philippa would have to be taught how to be a satisfactory Nicolson wife. 'Can she open a bazaar well?' Harold asked Nigel. 'She'll have to learn,' Nigel told him. And in a shocking letter to Vita shortly before the wedding, Harold wrote, 'I do not think she is an interesting or intellectual girl, but Niggs would not have wanted that – what he wants is an adoring slave.'

Beyond the need for parental solidarity, there was another and potentially more dangerous indicator of Nigel's immaturity. He was frightened of Philippa, or at least of her femininity, a quality of which he had been almost entirely unaware as he grew up, resulting in a naivety compounded by sexual igno-rance. He was unable to recognise that his own terror of humiliation would lead to resentment of the very person whom he wished to impress.

Nigel had been a virgin until the age of thirty-one. He had

once removed the socks of a girl he adored but with such evident nerves that she told him to return for the rest of her clothes after he had mastered the art of seduction. Desperately in love with this girl, he sought expert help. Over a drink in London in the Guards' Club, my father's business partner, George Weidenfeld, a man of the world, gave Nigel blow-by-blow instructions. George was an Austrian émigré who had escaped the German annexation of his country and arrived in Britain in 1938 and, fluent in several languages, he at once landed a job with the BBC wireless. Through his work there he had met Harold Nicolson, who, impressed with the young man's brilliant intellect and entrepreneurship, had identified a potential work colleague for his younger son. An uncertain and unconfident Nigel, demobbed from the army, had intended to retire to the countryside and become a woodman. Instead Harold made the introductions and in 1948 George and Nigel founded a publishing firm together, an ampersand joining their two surnames. The commercially unpromising title of their first published book was *A New Deal for Coal*. But George and Nigel were convinced that its clever young author had prospects. His name was Harold Wilson. The future leader of the Labour Party, and Britain's future twice-over prime minister, was the first of an increasingly eminent list of writers who soon signed up with the new firm.

George was not only clever, he was also irresistibly charming and unfailingly practical. He was experienced in the Art of Understanding Women. He knew just the person to lift Nigel out of his restricting inexperience and made arrangements. A few days later Nigel went round to the flat of a young actress called Olga, whose role as handmaiden to Vivien Leigh in a film of *Caesar and Cleopatra* had been considered most accomplished by the critics. Olga gave Nigel the essential knowledge he needed, although he wrote in his memoir that 'in no sense was this affair with Olga a sexual liberation'. By the time he was engaged to Philippa he was *still* inexperienced, diffident and rather horrified by the whole sexual rigmarole. He thought of sex as 'nasty, something one was obliged to do only occasionally, almost like going to the loo'. When a friend of George's 'pressed her leg against mine' at one of George's parties, 'I hastily withdrew it'. During the few months of his engagement, he comforted himself that Philippa's lack of expectation would see them through when the time came. My mother was heading towards an emotional and physical trap of which she was quite unaware. The thought of her innocence terrifies me.

Unlike his fiancée, Nigel had not warmed to *his* new parents-in-law considering them 'a menace in duplicate'. The distrust was mutual. Each thought the other vulgar, 'vulgar' being the fiercest charge Pam could make against another human being. Long afterwards Philippa confided to friends that Pam had asked her several times whether she was sure she should go through with the wedding. Her mother was caught between the attraction of her daughter marrying into a famous, aristocratic (if not rich) family and her distaste for these unconventional individuals who did not change for dinner, wrote books and got up to all manner of deviant things behind their bedroom doors. Neither mother nor daughter's anxieties were softened when six weeks before the wedding, as Philippa was assembling her trousseau of slim-waisted summer frocks, Nigel presented his bride-to-be with a small brown book. *The Civilisation of the Renaissance in Italy* by Jacob Burckhardt, a distinguished Swiss historian, had been published in 1860, and was described on the jacket as 'the standard work on life and manners in the Renaissance between Dante and Michelangelo'. A section at the back carried black-and-white reproductions of paintings of popes, doges and Carpaccio's depiction of the English ambassadorial party arriving at the Venetian court painted between 1495–1500. Nigel had inscribed the flyleaf of the densely printed pages: '*To Philippa from Nigel. A pre-honeymoon present June 10th 1953.*'

Homework was expected of her. We found the book on a shelf in Nigel's bedroom after he died. Certain passages had been highlighted by him in the margin in pencil but many of the flimsy pages were still suspiciously new-looking, suggesting that apart from the places containing Nigel's annotations, the book had probably never been opened again.

Nigel favoured the beautiful Christchurch Priory on the coastal flats in the heart of his Hampshire constituency as the church in which to be married, but Pam insisted that her only daughter should follow her own footsteps up the aisle of St Margaret's, Westminster, one of London's grand society churches. Photographers from the press were waiting to record the first sight of the new Mrs Nicolson, who emerged from the church on the arm of her husband in a gown of oyster satin looking young, happy and cautiously confident. Following close behind were the respective mothers, Vita in a black straw hat, pearl necklace and sensible flat shoes, Pam in strappy toeless sandals and an incongruous dark enveloping coat despite the July weather. Both looked miserable. The fathers were all merry buttonholes and cheerful optimism. A reception for six hundred people was held at the Fishmongers' Hall, courtesy of Gervaise's elevated position there. The guests were largely members of the constituency and Hampshire locals. Harold and Vita knew no one and stood in the shadows, Vita feeling especially out of place and, as Nigel wrote in his diary, looking 'as timorous as a doe caught by the hunt'.

On the first night of the honeymoon at Sissinghurst, the excuse of tiredness postponed for the nervous couple what on the second night was described by my father as 'an ordeal'. He rated his own 'performance' as 'adequate', hardly the trumpet blast and clashing of cymbals a virginal bride in love might expect, even wish for. Philippa had married a man who although twelve years older had almost as little sexual experience as herself. Nigel's hopes that, without previous comparisons, Philippa would not notice his inadequacy and humiliation may have been realistic at first, but practice did not dispel his unease nor her disappointment. While his sexual inhibition and reticence and even distaste remained causes of lifelong secret shame for him, they became an increasing source of frustration and distress to Philippa. In an interview about his parents' love life given to America's NBC network in the 1970s at just about the moment his own marriage was ending, Nigel declared that 'the most important lesson of all is that the sex element of a marriage, anybody's marriage taken over a lifetime, is about 10 per cent'. Poor Philippa.

For the remainder of the honeymoon, their first holiday together, the newly-weds had planned to drive through the northern towns of Italy, but after a few days in Venice they reached Verona, that most romantic of cities, where their car hit a tractor full on. Their injuries were minor but the car was a write-off so they came back early to Shirley House, their first home together, a small white farmhouse in Nigel's Hampshire constituency. That autumn the local doctor confirmed that Philippa was to have a baby. With almost audible relief, Nigel observed in his diary that Philippa was 'engrossed in something at last'. Impending motherhood brought contentment and focus to her life and even some temporary softening of the relationship between Nigel and Pamela. On the night of 9 June 1954, Pam stayed at Shirley House playing dominoes with Nigel downstairs as the drama unfolded upstairs in Philippa's bedroom. Ten decorously punctual months after the wedding a daughter was born. They called the baby Juliet, the name chosen in part as a neat reflection of Philippa's love for her Border terrier Romeo. All seemed well enough until a few months later when a frail-looking Philippa was diagnosed with tuberculosis, the disease that had weakened her mother. But much had changed since Pam's day, and the dramatic surgery that had been necessary to treat Philippa's mother a decade before had been replaced by a new drug-based treatment that became a familiar element of our family life. Despite medical progress, the convalescent period for TB remained severe. After two weeks of observation at St George's Hospital at Hyde Park Corner, my mother was allowed home. But she did not return to Shirley House. Instead, she moved in to her parents' home a few miles away, an adult daughter in isolation in her childhood bedroom, forbidden to touch her own infant daughter, or even to be in the same room as her, for fear of handing on the infection. There was to be complete bed rest for four months with as little movement as possible.

Deprived of her own home and of her independence and separated from her new baby, she was quite unable to bloom in any way, least of all in the way that my father had predicted or at least hoped she would. A misty black-and-white photograph taken from the bedroom door shows her slight figure far in the distance, propped against the pillows, wearing a woollen bedjacket edged with a collar of swansdown, the photographer, perhaps it was my father, allowed no nearer than the door. Her bed tray straddles her blanket-covered knees, its supports made of open wicker baskets into which an unfinished tapestry has been tucked. A few months later a picture of me looking apprehensive sitting on her knee reveals her thinness as she holds me with some caution. Maybe the picture was taken to record our reunion? She had just returned home to Shirley House.

Gradually Philippa began to feel better and to put on a little weight, but most nights Nigel remained in the separate bedroom into which he had moved during her illness. As she continued her long convalescence she went on regular beneficial visits to the healing sunshine at her parents' villa in the South of France. At Villa Arabe Philippa was able to recuperate from her illness and join her parents' friends who came to snooze on sunloungers on the large terrace far from the cold English climate.

My father stayed at home. Busy with his parliamentary career, Nigel became involved with many of the social reforms of the 1950s. In 1955 public compassion was running high for Ruth Ellis, a glamorous, peroxide-blonde, twenty-eight-year-old nightclub hostess who had shot her boyfriend. Her defence counsel maintained that the boyfriend had driven Ruth to the point of insanity. While Ellis acknowledged that she had pulled the trigger, she was adamant about what had happened that day. 'It was quite clear to me that I was not the person who shot him. When I saw myself with the revolver I knew I was another person.' Her '*crime passionnel*', it was argued, should not carry the death sentence. But Ruth was hanged in Holloway Prison on 13 July and the abolition of hanging became the fierce focus of public and parliamentary debate. The American novelist Raymond Chandler, who was living in Britain, wrote to the *Evening Standard* about 'the medieval savagery of the law', voicing the opinion of many, including several parliamentarians, my father among them.

On 4 September 1957 the Wolfenden Report was published, recommending reform of the law that made sex between men illegal. Homosexuals were regarded by many as deviants and the witch-hunt in America for gay men and women known as the Lavender Scare became every bit as virulent in 1950s Britain. The Home Secretary, David Maxwell-Fyfe, had pledged there would be 'a new drive against male vice' and to 'rid England of this plague' that resulted in the imprisonment of a thousand men a week. A neighbour and friend of Philippa's from before her marriage, Lord Montagu of Beaulieu, had been convicted and jailed for a homosexual affair in 1954, and Nigel, at heart a liberal and, in this case especially, his parents' son, was fully supportive of the legal changes, antagonising many members of his party and more seriously his profoundly shockable and conservative Conservative constituents. His disillusionment with the way the Conservative government led by Anthony Eden was handling the volatile situation in Suez became the most serious cause of his moral separation from the Government. When he abstained in the crucial vote of confidence in Britain's invasion of Egypt, he alienated himself from his constituency irrevocably.

Two years after Philippa had been given the all-clear from tuberculosis, a son, Adam, was born, her gratitude for his safe delivery reflected in her invitation to the family doctor, 'Doccor' Howard, to be a godparent. Breastfeeding was forbidden for fear the agitation would exacerbate the currently dormant TB otherwise, for a while, our growing family seemed happy enough. But despite the arrival of Adam and the apparent domestic contentment of life at Shirley House, Philippa was drifting away from Nigel, squeezed out from his attention by the demands and anxieties of his work, and not interested enough in that work to make herself a sympathetic companion with whom he could share those worries. 'I wish I was like Romeo,' Nigel wrote as early as 1957 when he realised he was losing her. 'Romeo just has to look at you with loving eyes.'

When my left-leaning father, reactionary Bournemouth's unlikely MP, was forced to resign his seat over his disagreement with the government over the Suez crisis, there was no longer any need to live near his old constituency. My parents closed the gates to Shirley House on 12 January 1961 and my father saw my mother's eyes fill with tears. They were moving to London, away from the rootedness of home. And in London everything began to go wrong. London left Philippa disorientated. She was thirty-two years old, a mother of two, a two-hour car journey away from her parents, and her upbringing, domestic circumstances and age disqualifying her from taking part in the revolution that was going on in the clubs and pubs and restaurants and houses and flats and attics and cellars of Swinging Chelsea. Nonetheless, she tried to join in as best she could. Her skirts became a little shorter, and she smoked Benson & Hedges cigarettes that came in a gold box and which she lit with a little flourish and a click of a Dunhill lighter, blowing out the smoke while she spoke, very glamorous, very Julie Christie. She listened to Chubby Checker and Herb Alpert on the record player in the sitting room of our small terraced house. She zipped through the Chelsea streets in a lavender-coloured Triumph Herald, a 'racy coupé' as described by the manufacturers, a sexy Italian-inspired number that had only been on the market for a year and could turn on a sixpence just like a London taxi.

From the outset of their marriage Nigel had kept a dressing room of his own at Shirley House with a single bed in it. He had moved out of Philippa's room when she became ill and had never gone back. His 'distaste for the ultimate act', he wrote in his confessional memoir, had become so entrenched that it was no longer due to 'squeamishness but to the fear of revealing my inadequate potency'. In London he maintained his own tiny bedroom next to Philippa's large airy double-windowed room, one half of her silky bedspread forever intact in its perfect unruffled smoothness. Each morning my father pushed his bed into a vertical position as he had once done as an Eton schoolboy, where it was held against the wall with clips to give him more space to move around.

In 1962, two years after Penguin's successful case to publish *Lady Chatterley's Lover*, and after narrowly winning a censorship battle themselves with the Director of Public Prosecution, Weidenfeld & Nicolson brought out Nabokov's novel *Lolita*. If Nigel was preoccupied with censorship and sexual boundaries at work, the interest also spilled into his private life, but not the part he shared with Philippa. Tucked into the springs of the upended mattress of his monastic single bed was a pile of magazines with pictures on the covers of young women wearing bathing suits that were too small and too tight for them, their hair in high ponytails, smiling in a very friendly way indeed at the camera. A copy of the uncensored, sexually explicit Penguin edition of *Rabbit, Run*, John Updike's first *Rabbit* novel, had been squeezed between his classics books on the top shelf of his bedroom. Every day he went to work at his publishing office. Like Philippa, he travelled. But his expeditions were infrequent and conducted for work rather than play. He was at home a lot, and despite Philippa's loneliness, his presence, his all-consuming career, his critical intellect and his failure to make love to her swamped, stifled and depressed her. He recorded in his memoir that, in her frustration, she would often become angry with him, and once she bit his thumb. Yet his awareness of his contributing part in an obviously disintegrating marriage appears in the diary to be non-existent. My mother seemed unable to find her way through the claustrophobia of her situation. With marriage she had escaped the imprisonment of daughterhood only to find herself once more trapped, the pain of loneliness forcing her into isolation and apparently preventing her from recognising that rewards might have been found in motherhood. A month after we moved to London she returned to her familiar if unsatisfying sanctuary, leaving her children to settle into new schools as she flew off alone to the South of France.

Pam and Gervaise had recently made friends with Dorothy and Daniel Silberberg, an American couple who lived near the Villa Arabe. Dan Silberberg was a successful self-made businessman from the Bronx, the exact source of his wealth Gatsby-mysterious. As an antidote to the precision of the business world, he supported up-and-coming artists with whom he became friends. Philippa used to emphasise Dan's commercial brilliance by telling the story of how he had made his contacts as a shoeshine boy in New York's financial district, charming his way to a career as he buffed up Brooks Brothers' loafers worn by Wall Street whizz-kids. Dan was the same age as Gervaise and they had either met over the barter of the trading floor or maybe simply as like-minded neighbours in the South of France. On one of Philippa's frequent visits, Dan took a shine to Gervaise's young, restless, unfulfilled and vulnerable daughter and soon his own house at the newly fashionable fishing village of St Tropez, a few miles along the coast from the d'Eyncourts' Villa Arabe at Cannes, became her latest refuge.

In 1962 St Tropez was the most seductive place on earth. With its Gauguin-pink bougainvillea, lavender-scented air and cicadas chattering in the fig trees, this ancient and tiny fishing port had been attracting the rich, famous and glamorous ever since the film *And God Created Woman*, set in the town, hit the cinema screens in 1956. Its previously unknown star, Brigitte Bardot, the twenty-two-year-old wife of the director, Roger Vadim, played a sexually energised eighteen-year-old called Juliette. Bardot had bought a house on the edge of the town, positioned at right angles across the bay from the twin terraces of Dan's own splendid house. Everyone knew when Bardot was in residence, buzzing around the tiny streets on her moped, blonde hair streaming out behind her, a bottle of wine and a stick of bread in the basket in front. Her well-known predilection for removing the top half of her bikini while sunbathing on the rocks outside her house was trumped by her habit of dancing shoeless, a never forgotten thrill for those lucky enough to find themselves touching toes with her on a nightclub floor. Everything about Bardot smouldered, even her alliterative initials.

Dan was sun-leathered, square-faced, flat-faced, his darting lizard eyes predatory, alert, constantly assessing everything they lit on. His long-fingered hands were covered in liver spots. He spoke rarely and slowly, as if the effort of articulation exhausted him, and when he did say something the volume was turned down so low that one had to lean in to hear him. He smelled of dust. He wore espadrilles with the backs down, the flap-flap of the sole on the red-tiled floors giving warning of his imminent arrival. During the day he would take his house party out on his boat, the *Darcey*, rarely travelling more than a short distance from the shore before anchoring in the clear warm Mediterranean water. A member of the crew would swim alongside the older English guests holding an umbrella up high in order to protect the sensitive English skin from an undesirable suntan. After the swim, lunch was served beneath a canopy on board while guests lounged and smoked on white cushions drinking rosé and surveying the party scene on boats moored nearby. Sometimes Dorothy went out on the *Darcey* with the party, her particular skill for dressing the tomato salad praised with gusto by the guests. Sometimes she stayed behind, apparently unconcerned about her husband's mesmeric power over younger women. With quiet dignity she closed herself away in the darkened mosquito-screened dining room at the house, to be massaged by professional healing hands.

A glamorous mixture of artists and businessmen, British aristocrats and beautiful girls assembled for the evening fun. There was a pub-like bar off the sitting room with a full range of exotic alcoholic drinks lined up on the shelves. Dressed in baggy lilac trousers and an oversized linen shirt, his eyes barely visible behind his thick-lensed tortoiseshell glasses, Dan would stand behind the counter mixing the pre-dinner cocktails. He would trickle a thin stream of scarlet *framboise* liqueur or deep purple cassis into cold white wine, easing out the cork as if pulling a ripened carrot from moist earth. Or he would squeeze lemon juice into a silver shaker, capped by a sieve to catch the pips, and add a splash of Bombay gin and a measure of Cinzano. Then he would give the concoction a good shake before pouring it into glasses with rims that had been dipped in sugar. He was an accomplished sugar daddy.

My mother was enchanted by this sunshine world, so distant from her dull, domestic life in damp and rainy England. St Tropez became her favourite place to go, the scent of wild mimosa that grew so prolifically her favourite smell. She could not stay away. Any reproach by Nigel at Philippa's absence was implicit. Perhaps he did not dare acknowledge that she was able to find greater contentment somewhere else, thus showing up his own inability to make her happy. Her mother, on the other hand, was not pleased, becoming increasingly disapproving back in the New Forest, writing to my father about her growing consternation that Philippa was spending so much time abroad with 'aging Jews'. She began to suspect that her daughter was not only flirtatious, but lustful. It did not occur to her that Philippa was justified in longing to be desired, to be valued for herself, rather than considered inadequate for not matching the intellectual standards demanded by her husband. To Nigel's continuing frustration and reproach, she never listened to classical music and rarely read what he considered a 'proper' book. From the earliest days of their courtship, Nigel had made it cruelly clear in his letters to his parents that she was incapable of discussing philosophy, literature, architecture or politics. But his plans to 'educate her' had not worked out satisfactorily, and as illness, motherhood and then loneliness intervened, Nigel made his irritation with her all the more evident. So when Dan Silberg, rather than judging her for her superficiality and frivolity, praised her for her pretty face, her lovely figure and her gaiety, she began to glow. Praise and an unprecedented awareness of her own attractiveness gave her a power that she had never enjoyed before and it proved addictive.

## 8

# Juliet
## Confusion

My mother began her nine-day recovery from my birth at home in her pink quilted bed, surrounded by flowers and messages of congratulations. My father, entering with characteristic hyperbole into the drama, recorded that on the first day of my life I was given a spoonful of water that I accepted 'with the maturity of a marchioness sipping Cointreau'. I was not only a first child but a first grandchild. The Sackville flag was raised at the top of the tower at Sissinghurst in honour of my arrival, Harold wrote to Philippa to say the news had made him feel 'thirty years younger', and that night Vita wrote in her diary: 'May God please be kind to Juliet all her life. And if she ever inherits Sissinghurst may she love it and care for it. Amen.'

But when my mother fell ill with tuberculosis when I was eight months old, her incarceration at first in hospital and later in isolation in her bedroom at her parents' house took her from me. Although 'Mumma' was my first word and the name by which I continued to address her all my life, the drugs that helped her get well ensured that 'Strep-to-my-cin' was my first sentence. Her long and tiring illness established not only a relationship that was undercut by her absence, but put the emphasis of parental presence on my father. Despite his total lack of experience with children, he rose at once to the challenge. He was supported by a series of nurses in starched and belted *Carry On* uniforms. When I was just a few weeks old, the first of these surrogate mothers came with us to spend the weekend with Vita and Harold at Sissinghurst, the long since forgotten site of a prisoner-of-war camp for French soldiers. After the nurse had put me to bed, she went for a walk in the garden and spotted a column of men beside the moat, talking in an incomprehensible language and wearing a strange version of military dress. On reporting the intruders to my father, she was immediately replaced by another nurse. My father did not go in for ghosts. They terrified him.

I did not seek out ghosts but I spent a lot of time hiding away with the fairies. They lived in a clearing in the little wood beside the stream at the bottom of our garden in Hampshire and from an early age I sat for hours alone in conversation with this diminutive, alternative family in elemental secrecy, the damp earth underneath me, the strip of dancing water in front, the sunlight catching particles of dust in the air around me. When it was too dark or cold or rainy to see them, I knew they were sheltering inside the hollowed-out trunk of the oak. Once I misstepped in an attempt to join them and fell into the stream, my gumboots filling with water. Back at the house I was rebuked, stripped and plunged into a warm bath where the autumn leaves sticking to my knees detached themselves and floated off towards the taps. After that I was forbidden to go down to the stream alone, and instead took refuge in the garden in the tiny caravan, an old painted baker's cart that my grandfather Harold had given me for my fourth birthday.

When Adam was born, in order to share the new responsibilities, to allow my mother time to recover and to concentrate on the new baby, my father became voluntarily immersed in the care of his elder child. In his diary he wrote a detailed account of the morning routine established by a three-year-old daughter and her forty-year-old father, who at that time was sharing her room along the corridor:

At 6.00 am Juliet batters me into wakefulness. I shout at her to go back to her cot and keep quiet. For the next hour there is a constant pattering to and fro to fetch various dolls and books. She carries on a conversation with her rag doll Fiona in hoarse whispers. I'm not asleep at all but I pretend to be. At 7.30 I tell her to dress. With mounting modesty she goes next door and puts on, usually back to front, her knickers and vest. She reappears at my bedside for inspection. With great care we then choose the frock or trousers to go over the vest. Hair is combed by me still from my bed. Shoes are buckled. And then after a cat-lick washing of hands and face she bounces off to P's room . . . It is a very happy life.

The physical weakness of his wife allowed Nigel a chance to participate in the earliest days of his daughter's toilette in ways he would not otherwise have welcomed. The experience softened him. He loved being a father. We also had nannies and rabbits – Flopsy, Mopsy, Cottontail, Peter and several dozen of their immediate descendants – a marmalade-coloured cat, Chunky, a budgerigar, Budgie, my male counterpart, the Border terrier Romeo, and each other. When my brother Adam was old enough he joined me in the baker's cart. He called me Duster because he couldn't say Juliet. We were allies, dressed in clothes cut from the same cloth, blue, red or yellow Viyella dresses with collars for me, short trousers for him.

In 1960, when I was five, Jenny, the daughter of Doccor Howard, asked me to be her bridesmaid. In a short sequence of movie footage from the wedding, my mother, immaculate in her black broad-brimmed hat and a sleek black-and-white linen costume, stands at the church porch waiting for the arrival of the bride. I am standing beside her in a white, ankle-length dress made of stiff organza, a pale blue velvet ribbon at the waist, and holding a small wicker basket filled with lily of the valley. One whiff of the sweet scent of those delicate bell-like flowers, the same flowers that had been given to Vita on her return home from the Sackville-West inheritance trial, takes me back to childhood in an instant. The memory mutates into the unusual sensation of the fabric of a new dress, a bridesmaid's dress, brushing against bare calves, scratchy and thrilling at the same time. In the film Philippa bends down to speak to me, her hands encased in pristine white elbow-length gloves clasped tightly behind her back, well out of the way of sticky fingers.

Later in the footage and after the service I am skipping about in Doccor H's summery cottage garden. I look up to my father, and as I stretch up my hand, his answering hand reaches down to enclose mine. Hands mattered. Holding a parental hand was like being called 'darling'; rare but special.

At times Philippa had seemed happy enough. In my favourite photograph of those days, my mother is in the middle of the picture, wearing a creamy mid-calf dress. She is holding the hands of her two children – on her right is a six-year-old blonde girl in a striped summer frock, a cardigan and a hair-band made of blue ribbon, while on her left her three-year-old son stares up at the hulk of an enormous white ship that is docking in front of them. We are in the London Docks, waiting for our new Finnish au pair Brita (the latest in a long line) to disembark from her ship, the *Baltika*. I had privately longed for the ship to sink before it arrived because it was a day when we had our mother all to ourselves and I did not want it to end, especially because she was holding our hands.

Much of the time my mother felt quite unreal to me, never tethered, floating off, always busy, remote, disconnecting from me in mind and body. And yet for a while it was her remote-ness, her elusiveness that made her so seductive, the night-time rustle of satin close to my ear as she bent down to kiss me goodnight before going out to a dinner, a passing mist of rose-tinted scent that lingered even after she had closed the door and gone downstairs. Years later at boarding school when I was a teenager, I would still mouth her name over and over again, wanting her to come to me, to be near, to stay with me. Perhaps she did not realise how much I wanted her to show me that she loved me. Perhaps her own mother had never shown her how.

I did not want to leave Hampshire for London. I loved Shirley House and all the animals, and I did not want to leave Alison, my best friend from school, who had yellow hair like me. Our new house in Chelsea was just off the unsmart end of the King's Road. Council houses and blocks of flats had replaced the Victorian slums and stood among the Georgian terraces. Although it all felt very modern and taxi drivers knew the area as the World's End, we missed the country. The garden at the back of the house smelled musty, and was filled in all seasons with dead sycamore leaves, the flaky surface of each leaf swollen at one end to house a tiny nut, like the aniseed that is left behind at the end of a sucked gobstopper. Adam and I would dig up the stale urban earth around the sycamore leaves with a spoon and fork, excavating a tunnel that would lead us down to Australia, or at least back to the Hampshire fields. But it was also exciting to be living in a city where the ice-cream van stopped right outside our front door and played the Popeye tune to announce its arrival. Every afternoon the rag-and-bone man clattered down the middle of the street, shouting for any old iron, his horse oblivious to any car traffic as if the pair of them were still working in the eighteenth century, while the oddly illicit, acrid smell of hops fermenting at the local brewery swirled in the air.

Each morning four of us would leave the house in Limerston Street. In the beginning Adam walked to his kindergarten with Brita while my father bussed me to my school in South Kensington before getting on the Tube for the onward journey to his Oxford Street publishing office. Within a year it was considered safe enough for us go to school by ourselves and at the age of seven and four we began to lead lives that were frequently unsupervised. I would catch the double-decker bus directly outside our door, getting to know the conductors who kept an eye on unaccompanied schoolchildren. At the same time my little brother, wearing his red-and-green uniform, his cap covering his blond hair, was put on the number 19 or 22 to Sloane Square, from where he had to walk by himself along the remaining stretch to the school door. We undertook the journeys in reverse each afternoon, and sometimes after school we were allowed to go round the corner to the local toy shop that sold Dinky Toy sports cars for boys and Sindy dolls for girls. Occasionally, the owner produced a gem from under the counter, a battery-operated telescope that ranged round the night skies with an especially powerful beam, or a miniature spade-and-fork kit that would have taken us to Australia far faster than a spoon and fork. Once he showed us his own model of a 1911 San Francisco fire engine that set both our hearts racing. Further along the road, the baker's home-made doughnuts claimed our weekly pocket money. The sugar stuck to the upper lip, and the blood-red jam squirted out of a hole in the dough, no matter how carefully we tried to staunch it with the paper bag. The baker's assistant (or was she his wife? his sister? his daughter?) had a huge goitre on her neck. We stared. Her slightest movement between the trays of currant buns, jam tarts and pastry horns filled with artificial cream caused the huge growth to wobble from side to side like a balloon filled with water. The streets around us were packed with various kinds of uniforms, small children in school uniforms accompanied by nannies in nanny uniforms, old Chelsea Pensioners in uniform red coats with gold buttons, and lots of pretty girls with uniform fringes that were so long you could hardly see their eyes and skirts so short you could see their knickers.

On the left-hand side of the King's Road, beyond Old Church Street where the painter Augustus John had kept his studio in 1910, was the fire station from which scarlet engines burst like flames with alarming regularity, and nearby was the Manresa Road library, where I was a newly enrolled junior member and their latest happy inhaler of the smell of old books. Along the next stretch of road after the Town Hall the anarchic clothes shops began to arrive. I stared through the windows of Granny Takes A Trip and Mr Freedom, and ventured into Stop the Shop with its revolving platform that you had to leap off if you wanted to look at any of the clothes on the racks. The sales assistants, dressed with more flamboyance than any of their customers, looked disdainfully at anyone who interrupted their conversation, enquiring whether they might actually make a purchase. Punctuating the great fashion parade, at the top of the King's Road was the solid presence of Peter Jones looming up on behalf of an older generation, as if to say 'enough's enough'. This glass-walled department store was a bastion of courtesy and efficiency for locals, grand old ladies with their newly shampooed poodles and even royalty. Ever since the building had been completed in 1936 it had presented a symbol of reassurance in a fast-changing world.

A year after we moved to London I developed osteomyelitis in my left leg, a serious infection of the bone marrow that can lead to amputation if not treated with urgency. I was taken immediately to Great Ormond Street Hospital, and after the operation, undertaken by a delightfully flirtatious surgeon named Mr Lloyd-Roberts, my mother brought me a pale gauzy bedjacket edged in pink swansdown. I had seen one like it before, in a photograph of her in bed when she had TB. The bedjacket was one sign, but the seriousness of my illness was confirmed by an expression on my mother's face that I did not recognise. I had never seen her so frightened. I was in the hospital for six weeks and she came to see me every day. Once, her visit coincided with a flurry in the ward, a tightening of nurses' belts, a smoothing-down of starched skirts. Prince Charles was recovering from appendicitis in the adjoining room and his mother had arrived to see her son, bringing her own mother with her. For Philippa, the royalist, the sight of her newly convalescent seven-year-old daughter in close proximity to a current and future monarch was nearly overwhelming. I made friends with William who was in the bed next to me. While his mother had been pregnant she had been given Thalidomide, a tranquilliser prescribed as an antidote to morning sickness. The drug had not been properly trialled. The resulting deformities detected in around 10,000 newborn babies worldwide and many more who died in the womb made Thalidomide the worst disaster ever to hit Britain's medical profession. William had been born with arms and legs that were not fully formed and which would never grow. My temporary incapacity was nothing in comparison to his life sentence.

On the day I left hospital my mother cooked my favourite supper and as I ate the hamburger, chips and frozen peas, followed by ice cream rolled in sponge for pudding, I had never been happier to be home. But a couple of weeks later she left for a holiday in the Bahamas with her new friends from St Tropez and·I continued my convalescence in Hampshire at the ever-dependable home of Doccer Howard and his wife and near my maternal grandparents. The neighbours I liked best apart from Doccer and Mrs H were the always smiley Simmondses who had a swimming pool shaped like a nurse's kidney bowl that we were allowed to use whenever we liked. Mr Simmonds had a red sports car without a roof that I admired and a twirly moustache that I was not so keen on because his hello kiss felt like an encounter with a scratchy toothbrush. Mrs Simmonds smelled good, had a pronounced but attractive gap between her two front teeth and left pretty lipstick imprints on the stubs of her numerous discarded cigarette butts.

My father made little objection to Philippa's frequent visits abroad, and to her close friendship with the Silberbergs. Only when he was confronted with maternal rather than uxorious absence did any discomfort show. But although he always involved himself in our day-to-day welfare, his attempts to bath us on the latest au pair's evening off were not always welcomed. In March 1962, he wrote to Philippa describing a bathtime with Adam, and the challenge that his four-year-old son presented to his own naked-phobic father:

> Verity is rather nice. She looks like sin itself, with a long hank of black hair hanging over one shoulder and a pint-sized face, very wicked, but she is considerate and sweet and Adam adores her.

'I want Verity to bath me.'

'Well she can't. She's going out for the evening.'

'Who will bath me then?'

'I will.'

'But I don't want to be seen by you.' I insisted and there was a lot of hiding behind towels and loud complaints that the water was too hot, then too cold and I had chosen the wrong coloured bath mat and the pyjama jacket goes on *first*, Dadda, didn't you know that?

I would watch my mother's departure, waving stiffly from the steps of our house as she got into a taxi, calling out to her at the final moment as she slammed the door, asking if she really had to go. Or I would see her leave from my position at the sitting-room window, kneeling up on the cushion of a sofa covered in yellow satin material that shone in two stripes, like the line of hackles on a dog in which the hair faces in the opposite direction, putting my face into the not quite clean net curtains that smelled bitter and were rough to touch, crackling a little when the nylon rubbed against itself. As the taxi drew away I would swallow down the ache in my throat, and go upstairs with our new and permanent nanny Shirley to watch *Coronation Street* on the tiny television in the cupboard next to the Baby Belling where Shirley made us comforting toast. Shirley had been born twenty-eight years earlier in Sissinghurst village and Horace, her father, had been indispensible to Vita and Harold when they first arrived at the house. He was an expert builder and bricklayer who mended the crumbling Elizabethan walls and built others up which Vita trained her roses and clematis. Shirley came to work for us when she was in her twenties and remained with us for fifteen years.

In some ways the marriage of our parents was still clearly a viable relationship despite the growing separateness of their lives. Shirley had arrived shortly before the birth of my sister Rebecca, a gap of almost nine years separating us two daughters. She was a constant, discreet, no-nonsense presence, showing unfaltering love to us children and without whom my childhood would have been infinitely poorer. Although a good part of her time was inevitably concentrated on Rebecca, she gave our entire family more than maternal reassurance. While my father grew to rely on her wisdom and practical support whenever my mother was away, Shirley also provided my mother with the companionship and human presence that diluted Philippa's increasing hostility towards Nigel. She would often try to persuade Shirley to delay her day off until after lunch so that she would not be left alone with her husband, fearful of their antagonistic intimacy.

I was not enjoying school and my report said I did not take part in sports or indeed in the classroom. I felt 'unsatisfactory', a word weighted with doom and used by both my parents with unhesitating frequency. Characters in books felt like better friends than the real-life girls I met in London. I found sustenance in literature, especially in Narnia's Lucy, Wonderland's Alice, and particularly any motherless or fatherless little girl who had a secret. They all became my imaginary companions. I longed to meet Mary Lennox and Colin, the sickly son of the house, whose father lived abroad and barely ever came to see him or the secret garden growing behind the locked door. These children's secrets were my secrets too. The wardrobe with a concealed panel at the back that led into Aslan's snowy kingdom was as real to me as any piece of furniture at home. I envied the unexpected friendships and the implicit criticism and eventual approval of unsatisfactory children; spoilt Mary Lennox admired the boy Dickon who charmed the animals and showed her a different way of behaving; the indulged Little Princess Sarah Crewe could not have survived the tragedy of her father's death without the love of Becky, the girl who cleaned the rooms in horrible Miss Minchin's school. And there were reassuring surrogate parents, mothers like Mrs Sowerby who cooked and listened and instinctively knew when a skipping rope was all that was needed to make a lonely child feel happy.

Then school life improved. We were suddenly in the news. A girl in the sixth form called Twinkle who wore pink lipstick in morning prayers went on television with her top-of-the-hit-parade pop record about a boy called Terry who crashed his motorbike and died, giving even the youngest pupil a sense of drama by association. Twinkle's glamour increased when a mystifying rumour went round the school (forever unsubstantiated but still thrilling) that she was going to have a baby *without a husband*. And there were other excitements. A famous pop group called the Yardbirds rented rehearsal rooms in a shed next to our lacrosse pitch and busloads of screaming girls would arrive to catch a glimpse of them.

And then a new teacher arrived. Her name was Mrs Fitzgerald, she taught us English, history and scripture, and she lived on a boat on the Thames. She was distracted by life, running into the classroom at a tilt, unbalanced by a huge pile of exercise books covered in red-biro corrections, her face full of movement and anxiety, freckled and breathless with strands of hair the colour of ripe crab apples escaping from a untidy bun. Swinging her legs as she sat on the teacher's table facing the class she would time-travel us schoolgirls away from 1960s London and into the world of Dickens's French Revolutionary knitting women, the *tricoteuses* of his *Tale of Two Cities*. The domesticity of their occupation and the unnerving placidity of their demeanour contrasted with the blood-curdling executions taking place in front of them, as they sat 'knitting, knitting, counting dropping heads'. Nothing unnerved Madame Defarge, the chief knitter, as her needles expertly and covertly encrypted the names of those to be killed within her stitches. We shared Mrs Fitzgerald's horror and admiration and never forgot the scene. Later on, children became the inspiration for several of Penelope Fitzgerald's books, but it had long been children whom she inspired. Once she spoke about how she longed to see a blue poppy. I picked one for her in the garden at Sissinghurst and brought it to school. When the absence of the poppy was discovered I found myself in terrible trouble. But I had not known it was the rarest flower in the garden. I only knew that I wanted Mrs Fitzgerald to have it.

Nor was I aware that while the *tricoteuses* were using their knitting to lethal effect in our classroom text, Mrs Fitzgerald was knitting at home for her family's survival. Struggling to pay her bills, she would unravel her daughters' sweaters and reassemble them with a little more wool to make them last longer. How could any of us have known that when she was not introducing a roomful of girls to her love of books, she was managing an alcoholic husband, trying to keep her daughters in food and clothing, darkening that grey-red hair with a tea bag for economy, and eating chalk for nourishment? How was I to know that the battered, leaky Thames barge on which Mrs Fitzgerald lived was sinking into the river at the World's End just a few yards from my own home? And how was I to know that all the time the theatrical showiness of Chelsea was settling itself in her mind, waiting to re-emerge years later in her wonderful novel *Offshore* where 'the King's Road fluttered, like a gypsy encampment, with hastily-dyed finery while stage folk emerged from their beds at a given hour, to patrol the long pavements between Sloane Square and the Town Hall'. All I knew was that Mrs Fitzgerald's lessons were better than any of the other lessons and made going to school fun for the first time.

At home, my mother's life in London was unravelling too. My father recorded, not altogether uncritically, in a letter to his parents that she had become 'soignée'. She had her nails painted scarlet and sat beneath an upturned metal flowerpot that wooshed warm air onto her fashionably straightened curls once a week. But she was seldom at home to greet us when we got back from school. Even when she was not in France she never seemed to be around when she was needed and wanted. One day my brother pulled out some nylon stuffing from the cushion of his kindergarten chair and shoved it up his nose 'when I wasn't looking', he explained later with charming guile-lessness. He was having severe difficulty in breathing and his teacher was worried. My mother rushed to the school after a telephone call to say Adam needed urgent medical attention. By the time she arrived the stuffing had already been hoiked out with a pair of tweezers by a doctor. Her newly painted blood-red nails did not escape the matron's silent glare of disapproval, nor did the rarity of her appearance at school.

Once when I returned to find the house empty as usual, the inevitability of her not being there and the unfairness of not having a mother like the other girls, one who would help me off with my coat and ask me about my day, suddenly swamped me. I stood on the top step and weighed up the options. None were very appealing. An old friend of my father's who wrote screenplays for television lived opposite, but he never spoke to us children. Two doors down was an MP who never spoke to us either. Mrs Lamont next door looked kindly but she had a horrid snappy dog and lived behind a dark privet hedge. So I ran away to my own friend Ellen who lived a few streets away in a house with a mother who was always there to help her off with her coat and ask her about her school day. An hour later Ellen's doorbell rang. A policeman was standing on the step and told me my mother was on the warpath. There was a dreadful row when I got home and I thought how unfair it was because it was not my fault that I'd been left all alone.

We had never visited our grandparents' house in France but in August 1963 my mother took us with her to St Tropez. It was the first time we had been abroad. Adam and I were anxious misfits in a sophisticated playground, an exotic land of ice creams, crêpes, warmth and being undressed. We would escape the rosé-infused grown-ups on their sun loungers to examine Brigitte Bardot through binoculars, trying to control our sniggers as the local goddess lay on a rock across the bay from the villa wearing only the bottom half of a blue gingham bikini. She was the first naked, well, semi-naked adult we had ever seen.

When we came home I wanted desperately to see the undressed motherliness of my mother. I had never seen her without clothes. The grown-ups' bathroom was directly underneath our own, the door always locked whenever one of my parents was inside. With a nail file taken from my mother's dressing table, I managed to cut a flap in the blue linoleum floor beneath our basin. Prising up a loose wooden board, I had a clear view of the bath fifteen feet below me. I put the linoleum flap back in place and waited until the evening when I heard the bath running. Lying on my stomach and carefully lifting the lino, there was the grown-up bath with my mother sitting in it, her knees drawn halfway up to her chin. But I had forgotten how her curls frizzed up with heat in a way she did not like. Covering her head and, from my bird's-eye perspective, concealing her entire body, was her large forget-me-not-speckled bath cap. One short but audible indrawn breath of disappointment gave my game away. She was furious. How had I *dared* to do such a thing? I was put at once in 'disgrace', a word loaded with consequences including the threat that I would be carried away to the 'Kiddymart'. We were very familiar with this establishment although we had never actually been there. Not yet. The Kiddymart was a special supermarket where parents took their unsatisfactory children and swapped them for better versions, the type who would not spy on their naked mothers. I was given a reprieve from barter this time but made to understand that adult nudity was both private and in some way shameful.

When our mother was away again the following summer and Shirley took Rebecca to stay with her parents in Sissinghurst village, Adam and I were sent to our cousins on the Norfolk coast. A family friend of theirs, a painter, was also staying, using the garage at the back of the house as a studio. He was very solicitous of me and called me darling and invited me to come and see him in the garage. I was now ten years old, a sucker for being darlinged, a fan of pop music and liked the song playing on the garage radio, 'Doo Wah Diddy Diddy' by Manfred Mann. The family friend said I was beautiful and then he asked me to take off my knickers. I fled. I wrote to my mother and told her what had happened and asked her to come back to England and take me home, posting the letter in the red postbox at the end of the twitten in the village. I had assumed it never reached her because she never came to get me. Except the other day I found it, opened and tucked away in a file containing my childhood drawings.

Sometimes Nigel took us on excitingly rigorous holidays, travelling in a rented Dormobile to Scotland or Ireland, or taking the ferry from Harwich to Norway to shiver and twiddle down the fjords. Nigel's solo parenting attempts on these trips were sometimes clumsy and inhibited. 'I hope you aren't consti?' he would mutter, using an expression that had died out with the war but feeling he should somehow enquire whether our digestion systems were still functioning on a diet of reindeer meat and Polo mints. One year we went to Amsterdam and could not understand why women were sitting in the shop windows. 'They're waiting for their lunch' was all he could come up with. But in contrast to the uneasy sophistication of St Tropez and the *Darcey* they were wonderful adventures and we were never happier than when huddled and freezing in our macs on the floor of a waterlogged rowing boat in the Hebrides, belting out 'Over the Sea to Skye'.

Sometimes when my mother was away we stayed in London under the care not only of my father and Shirley but also of Mrs Tremson, our cleaning lady. Mrs T was of indeterminate age, but to my eyes her careworn face made her ancient. She ran her sudsy empire from the linoleum-floored kitchen in the basement, mopping it twice a week with a soapy sponge attached to one end of a long pole, working it up to a skating-rink shine. We spent a great deal of time down there with her, having tea at the trendy breakfast counter covered in dark green Formica, on uncomfortable stools with seats that whirled round and round. Occasionally there would be Twiglets and crisps, the modern food a treat in contrast to our usual Spam sandwiches and slices of luncheon meat and corned beef, the attendant layer of yellow fat clinging to the sides of each slice. Pausing to squeeze the dirty water from the sponge into her bucket, she would push back her long, yellowish-grey hair, and lean her chin on the pole. With ash dropping from a roll-your-own balanced on a whiskery lower lip, she would caution in her nicotine-lined voice: 'Another war is right round that corner, mark my words.' Beaten about by gloom and despair, she feared all over again for her East End birthplace where in the 1940s so many buildings had tumbled in flames.

'I thought the Germans had gone away now, Mrs Tremson.'

'Well, that might be. And good riddance to them. But it's those Russians that are coming now. Taking over from where the Germans left off. Coming over to finish the job.' Whistling involuntarily as she sucked in her breath through a gap in her teeth, she fashioned another cigarette from her tobacco tin, the stub of the last one neatly stowed away in her flowery apron pocket, muttering about the new threat that would be the death of us all. Gesturing with the ragged end of her mop, she hinted that an explosive was probably hovering nearby, perhaps even hidden behind the Hoover in the broom cupboard. I dreaded the day when we would all have to shelter from destruction in the coal-hole under the street with nothing to eat except Mrs Tremson's wine gums. She was big on wine gums and kept a stash of them in her pocket, from which they would emerge slightly grubby with flecks of Kleenex and ash. I would go to bed terrified about the advancing Russians. Like Mrs Tremson, I was convinced they were coming to get us just as the Germans had come to get our mother when she was a child.

During the two decades that followed the end of the Second World War, the threat of a third remained disturbingly real. In the early 1960s, memories of the misplaced optimism that had grown up after the First World War had not been forgotten by those of Mrs Tremson's age. Not long after our move to London I found several wads of food-ration book stubs, bound in elastic bands, shoved into the back of a chest outside my mother's bedroom. In the new post-war generation of children, a rudimentary political awareness began at an early age, especially those growing up in cities, and above all in London where buildings and confidence had not long ago been violated. With a ubiquitous struggle to make ends meet and a class and gender divide still defiantly entrenched, one did not have to look very far for evidence of inequality and deprivation. Without the means to articulate my growing sense of the unfairness of my own good fortune, Mrs Tremson's worries troubled me. It never occurred to me to ask why she worked so long into the evening, or whether she faced a long journey home 'on that bleedin' bus'. She protected her privacy with monosyllabic vehemence. All she would admit to in answer to my mother's enquiries about her persistent yawning was 'needs must'. Hard work and pride guided her through her life, and when daylight hours ran out, she responded by fitting in the last of her cleaning jobs well into the night. Anxious to help, I would steal a handful of threepences from my mother's purse and balance them in a wobbly hexagonal tower on the Formica counter but the pile would remain untouched. Although she was always known as Mrs T, no one knew if she had a husband or any children. If they did exist there was little doubt who was the chief bread-winner in her household. But now I wonder if her mop-shaking anger had originated when those dammed bombs had fallen in Bethnal Green twenty years earlier and deprived her of a family. Her commitment to us was unconditional. She never made any demands of me, never asked for homework to be finished, teeth to be cleaned or hair to be brushed, and she tolerated my presence in her shiny kitchen without comment. Her reliability and constancy provided reassurance in that emotionally broken house.

*

A sequence of deaths both public and private marked the first half of the 1960s and resulted in big changes in all our family's lives.

During Vita's lifetime we had been frequent visitors to Sissinghurst. Vita wrote and has been written about as a novelist, a poet, a biographer, a feminist, a lover, a lesbian, a home-wrecker, a wife, a mother, a gardener, a friend. But she was also four times over a grandmother. The contrast between Vita and my mother was evident even to a small girl. On our weekend visits I would join Philippa, all femininity in her belted summer dresses, bouncing curls and sweet scent, as we followed Vita, striding ahead of us through the garden. Snapping her secateurs open and closed with one hand as if unlocking and cocking a gun, in the other she held an old tortoiseshell cigarette holder, her words drifting towards us through a spiral of smoke as she drew the cigarette to her lips. Long-limbed in breeches and knee-length lace-up boots, a creamy pearl necklace hung in the indent of her neck above a silk shirt, her earrings dangled low, the jewellery her only concessions to the conventions of her sex. Sitting next to her at lunch, I was close enough to inhale the tobacco impregnation of her flattened hair. She was terrifying and thrilling, as tall as my father, her voice aristocratic, deep, silky, seductive, disturbing. She sounded like a male version of the lady on *Listen with Mother*, elongating the vowels as in 'cleassic' and adding an h to endings as in 'summah'.

On paper she approved of the idea of me, her granddaughter, the feminine line restored. And yet she was uncertain how to show much warmth to a reserved child. We would sit at oppo-site ends of a garden bench warily examining one another, but twice we had an encounter that came closer to intimacy. During the hop-picking season she took me down the lane that runs behind the moat and out into the ancient Wealden fields. I had to trot beside her to keep up; no encouraging hand was lowered that day to meet mine. But as we left the lane and walked between the rows of bitter-smelling hops, plump in their muted green summeriness, stopping to examine their leaf-layered heads, looking like miniature artichokes, there was a companionship in her authority that might have developed into something more if she had lived longer. I felt pleased to have conquered the fear of being alone with her. In the spring of 1962, she was diagnosed with bowel cancer. Nigel took Adam and me to Sissinghurst to say goodbye. We had learned to dance the twist and had been practising on the brick terrace in the garden in London. Vita sat in a deckchair on the lawn, her knees covered by a favourite rug made from cream and pale brown llama skin, the rumble of her deep tobaccoey laugh and the expression of delight softening a face exhausted by illness. She died a few weeks later on 2 June at Sissinghurst on a glorious early-summer's day. That evening our father came as usual to read us a bedtime story but instead lay down briefly beside me and closed his eyes. When he drew the curtains and went downstairs, leaving me in darkness, I could feel the wetness of his tears on my pillow.

Vita left Sissinghurst to my father in her will and we moved in at once. Adam and I were given the old apple storerooms in the Priest's House, across the stairwell from our mother. Nigel slept separately in the front wing of the house, just as he had done as a boy. But Vita's legacy proved to be a financial headache for my father, especially with the punitive inheritance taxes of 1962. He had no capital of his own and Vita had spent the bulk of hers on making the garden. Much of the money Nigel earned as a publisher and writer was absorbed by the huge fees of the private schools to which he sent his children. The only immediately obvious way to raise the money owed to the Inland Revenue was to sell Sissinghurst itself. But Nigel had another plan. Over the next few years he devoted himself to negotiations with the National Trust who eventually accepted the house and garden for the nation in lieu of the tax. Despite his mother's '*jamais, jamais*' echoing in his mind, he signed the agreement. He had negotiated well. The family was to be allowed to live in the house and garden rent-free in perpetuity. He had saved Vita and Harold's beautiful creation for posterity.

That same sad summer that Vita died was made still sadder when Romeo, my mother's Border terrier who had accompanied her into her marriage, became ill. In the middle of our school holidays, when Philippa was yet again away at the French seaside, the dog died of old age. 'There will be nobody to comfort Mumma in France,' I said to Nigel, horrified to think of her being so unhappy and so far away. My father wrote to tell her of our distress but she did not come home. On 31 July he spent their ninth wedding anniversary alone with us. Still she did not come home. Then her grandmother died. Nigel went to the funeral on behalf of his absent wife. A week later a blue, flimsy airmail-paper letter arrived for my father. Phillippa wondered whether he would mind if she stayed on for yet another week. She was having such a lovely time. Nigel wrote back describing the reception her letter had received. 'Juliet came and sat on my tummy on Thursday morning and flung down your letter. I read it in bed. It caused universal upset that you were not coming home till the 16th.' Maternal abandonment was chillingly familiar for Nigel. His mother had left her husband and temporarily eloped with Violet Trefusis when he and his brother were young children. Now Nigel's own wife was behaving in exactly the same way.

There were further upsets to stumble through before my parents could attempt to find stability in their new life away from London. Six months after Vita's death, on 29 December 1962, Pamela, my remaining grandmother, also died. She was fifty-eight and had been unable to fight off a virulent attack of pneumonia with her remaining half lung. Years later my father suggested to me that her constitution had been further weakened by too many martinis. Unlike the shock I felt at my father's tearful response to Vita's death, I have little recollection of my mother's reaction to the loss of her own mother. We were sent to stay with our cousins in Norfolk while Philippa went straight from the funeral to the Bahamas to find comfort in the warmth of the Caribbean sunshine, liberated from maternal disapproval at last. Gervaise was still alive but he soon found a new wife, Vinnie, a jolly, rich Texan widow with winged diamanté glasses, with whom he moved to happy tax exile in Bermuda. We rarely saw him again.

In October 1962, during the two weeks after the Cuban Missile Crisis had erupted, a war between the United States and the Soviet Union, who had joined forces with the Cuban leader Fidel Castro, had appeared inevitable. There was, however, a mitigating factor in this new international threat. Hope for a resolution lay in the charismatic new American president. Jack Kennedy was a man whose male potency and movie-star aura had travelled across the Atlantic, reaching out through television screens across the country. Youth, good looks and an even younger, equally glamorous wife made this president seem invincible to my idol-struck mother, who never tired of remarking how by the strangest of coincidences the president and his wife were identical ages to herself and my father. Hers and many other people's fears about the USSR growing territorial ambitions were dispelled when the joint diplomatic skills of Kennedy and Nikita Khrushchev ensured the crisis was averted. A year later, late on the evening of Friday 22 November 1963, we crept down the stairs in the Priest's House at Sissinghurst in our pyjamas and slippers. A thick tapestry curtain lined with green hessian obscured the dining room's view of the staircase and ensured that anyone sitting on the stairs could not be seen. Parting the curtain one inch, we watched pictures of chaos on the small black-and-white set below us, a scene of madness, cars travelling at speed and police sirens yelling. People with serious faces were holding one hand across their chests and a woman in a hat like an upturned milk pan was being helped into an aeroplane. But our attention was soon diverted from the frantic pictures on the screen onto Harold, Philippa and Nigel, who made no effort to restrain their grief, their adult watertight invincibility suddenly revealed as porous.

And there was yet more disturbance to come. One January morning in 1965, just over two years after we had become grandmotherless, and a little more than a year after the assassination of Kennedy, we returned from our Saturday riding lesson to find our mother slumped in sorrow. For my mother, as for so many of her generation, Churchill's death felt like the death of a parent.

She took us to his lying-in-state at Westminster Hall, having arranged to jump the queue with a special pass provided by her soldier brother. We were smuggled in through a side door and made sure we put on dramatically sad faces when we were confronted by the coffin lying on top of the catafalque. But the emotion we felt was the thrill of being part of an important occasion rather than any sadness for a large old man forever smoking a cigar whom we had never actually met. Two days later we came back from our lesson and sat with our mother in our jodhpurs and riding boots watching Churchill's funeral on the television. After the heavy coffin was carried slowly and precariously down the steps of St Paul's Cathedral by eight young guardsmen, it was placed on a boat for its journey down the river, past the Houses of Parliament. As the huge cranes along the Thames dipped their heads in respect my mother held our hands and wept. The *Observer* journalist who wrote afterwards that 'This was an act of mourning for the imperial past. This marked the final act in Britain's greatness', spoke for my mother, my father, and all those hundreds of thousands of people for whom the olden days were now over forever. With first her mother's and then Churchill's death the adult world that had formed such a large part of the structure of Philippa's life was disintegrating.

Not long afterwards, a photographer from the local county magazine came to the house to take pictures of the newly renovated part of Sissinghurst. He wanted some family shots.

My mother had just heard that Rip, Romeo's successor, had been run over by a car at the top of our lane. She had been told that although he had survived he might be brain-damaged. I remember watching her as she sat for the photographs, looking beautiful, wrapped in a green woollen cloak edged in black, gazing into the far unfocused distance, her eyes washed with tears. That day I loved her very much.

Although Adam and I were still at school in London where we continued to live during the week, the family began spending every weekend at Sissinghurst immediately after Vita died. Soon a new piece of luggage appeared in the boot of our mother's car but we were forbidden to unload the squat black leather case, 'Mumma's face case', with her initials in gold lettering stamped next to the brass lock. Officially it held her shampoo and pots of face cream but we sometimes got a glimpse of the unfamiliar medical jumble crammed inside before she hastily snapped the lid shut. Once or twice when she was out I would creep into her bathroom and examine the contents. There were large white tubs containing Rip's new epilepsy pills and mysterious silver bookmarks indented with three neat rows of tiny white tablets, the individual days of the week printed above each row. I was a teenager before I recognised their purpose and an adult before I worked out why my mother needed contraceptives. Brown opaque bottles of varying sizes with screw-top lids had been tossed into the bottom of the case, leaning tipsily against each other. The bottles contained hundreds of small yellow capsules. That summer on the radio stations Mick Jagger was celebrating the wonders of Valium, mother's little helper, singing of how it helped alleviate a sense of loneliness, lifted you out of being present in a dull and confined life, and dissipated the sense of what a drag it is getting old.

After a while we left London altogether to live at Sissinghurst full-time and my mother's position as mistress of that lovely place seemed briefly to give her confidence. Just as Victoria had found when entrusted with the running of Knole, the beauty of Sissinghurst provided an almost human ability to nurture. Philippa took a new interest in things. She began to take extra care with her clothes; using the small legacy from her mother she bought five jaunty kilts of every colour which she wore with matching cashmere polo necks. And she began to cook again, making us delicious lunches of roast chicken and crunchy new potatoes, joints of beef with creamy, home-made horse-radish sauce. But she was lonely, with even fewer friends in the country than she had in London.

If the grown-ups were preoccupied with their adult anxieties, Sissinghurst was the best thing that had ever happened to me. The key to a small opening built within the huge swing doors that fill the central entrance arch and shield the garden from the world at night is not like any others on my chain. It is smooth and unmarked, giving away no clue as to what it opens, a secret garden key. Letting myself in feels not so much like an arrival as a completion, a slowing of the rhythm of my heartbeat as I lock the door behind me, a coming home. The absence of both my parents and my grandparents has made no difference to my feelings, except perhaps to strengthen my sense of incred-ible luck at being part of the place where I have always felt both a daughter and granddaughter, a cherisher and cherished, protector and protected. This is the place, in all its tumbling, flowery romance, that matters to me more than any other, my certainty whenever I am uncertain. At times in my life, before motherhood, I have loved it more than anything or anyone else. I understand without any difficulty what it meant to Vita. They are my feelings too. When I was living abroad or whenever I was away from home and unhappy, I would walk the rooms of both house and garden in my mind. In my mind I would seek out the reassurance and peacefulness of the tower, and the encircling garden. I would summon that image of great beauty, concentrating on the moment when, in Yeats's words 'midnight's all a glimmer'. At times of anxiety I would dream that the house had crumbled away, or caught on fire and burnt down or that there had been an apocalyptic flood, the tower floating out to sea, balanced on its side like a slimmed-down Noah's ark.

The loveliest, luckiest time to be there is after the garden has closed to the public, when the chatter stops and the National Trust institutional hoo-ha that buzzes around the place ceases. When I am alone there, late on a summer evening, I can sense Vita's presence in some places, in the shed where her gardening tools are kept, in the sunken garden on the lower courtyard, on the far side of the moat, in her own bedroom. Sometimes a little puff of dust escapes from a bowl of dried rose leaves and lavender grains, the relics of Lady Betty Germaine's recipe abandoned long ago on a windowsill and momentarily caught in a shaft of light filtered through the diamond-pane windows. Once when I was living in Vita and Harold's South Cottage by myself the switch fused on a new television set I had installed in Vita's bedroom for company. The man who has been mending televisions at Sissinghurst for decades explained that ghosts do not like excessive electric currents in their bedrooms and tend to make their displeasure felt. The television worked perfectly from then onwards. Vita had made her point.

When we moved to Sissinghurst, her writing room on the first floor of the Elizabethan tower remained undisturbed, just as she had left it. There is something thrillingly daring for a child about looking through a grown-up's possessions, knowing their owner will no longer walk in and challenge you. After Vita died Adam and I climbed the tower steps up there for the first time. We would sit at her desk and rifle through the drawers, marvelling at a passport that would never be used again, at the engagement book with forever blank pages for the second half of the year of her death, coveting a pair of scissors with handles wound round with red raffia and a pen made of bamboo. The words on a page of blue writing paper, hidden at the back of the desk drawer puzzled me so I kept the page. *'Darling, I left a pearl earring on your side of the bed yesterday. Keep it safely for me? your Mary.'* Sheets of brand-new stamps were tucked within the folds of the leather blotting pad. A corner cupboard, painted green by Vita in 1930, the year she bought Sissinghurst, hung on the wall to the right of the desk. Inside was a bottle of emerald nail polish that seemed exotic, even indecent, for a grandmother, and a pot of Gloy, a liquid glue with a red rubber slitted top, that was slipped with speed into an acquisitive child's pocket. On the top shelf of the cupboard lay a small box containing the sole of a delicate dancing slipper that had been fashioned into a shape so flat and slim that it looked like a cooking spatula, but one too fragile ever to be used to stir a stew. Childlike writing covered the underside. *This represents the sole of the shoes worn by my mother. My father told me he had this paper-knife done from one of her shoes in 1871. (Left to me by Papa) Victoria Sackville 1908*. Vita's mother had identified Pepita's shoe a few days after the death of her own father.

As well as the idiosyncratic seductiveness of her exuberant garden, where the roses sometimes trailed so low over the paths one had to duck to avoid becoming ensnared, the interior of the house was redolent of Vita, crammed with her treasures and her clutter. The Sackville coat of arms was stamped on the silver sconces in the dining room, Georgian silver wig stands for overheated judges were displayed on the big desk, tapestries that had once hung on Knole walls now hung in Sissinghurst bedrooms, a much-loved pottery jug shaped as a chicken clucked water into glasses on the dining-room table. Many years after Vita's death and heavily influenced by my father, I began to pay attention to her writing, her trailblazing, her unconventionality, her conventionality, and I grew proud of my association with the alarming old woman with a chewed tortoiseshell cigarette holder in her mouth. She had been an intimidating grandmother who had demonstrated little empathy towards children but also an exotic grandmother whose stories of Old Lionel's coach journeys to London accompanied by outriders armed with silver pistols passed their way from Nigel to me. As I grew older my impression of her changed. I was eighteen and in my first term at university when *Portrait of a Marriage*, the book that made her posthumously famous as a ruthless rule-breaker, was published, and I applauded my father for his long-deliberated decision to make public her shocking story of same-sex infidelity. The timing suited my own bid for emancipation.

Some of her old treasures are now mine. A green leather case with the word 'Vita' scrawled at a diagonal in gold script across one corner lives beneath my bed. The case is lined in cream satin and a series of indentations create little silky beds in which jade-handled instruments nestle neatly. There is a small pair of scissors, a hairbrush, a nail file, a nail buff, a comb and two glass pots with smooth green lids. Inside one pot is some sinister-looking cream, yellowish and crusted. The other jar is empty but the contents, brackish powdered rouge that accentu-ated cheekbones a hundred years ago, have spilled all over the case, damp staining the satin inlay pink. The expense of the case is obvious, this talisman of affluence belonging to an earlier age, but although Vita kept it safely among her precious things, or at least never threw it away, she had obviously never cared for it in the way a more fastidiously girly woman might. The purpose of the case seems to have sat at an uncomfortable angle to its owner, while the owner, at her own estimation, proceeded at an odd angle to life. After Vita died Harold gave me the three-foot-high wooden angel, painted in dull gold, that had been in her bedroom ever since they had rescued it from a deconsecrated church in Venice half a century earlier. Nigel put it on a plinth in the eaves above my bed from where he said it would always bless me.

After she died Harold continued to live in the cottage he had once shared with Vita. Without her he was almost inconsol-able, incapable of shaking off his grief. His existence without her became what his biographer James Lees-Milne called 'a slow and steady diminuendo'. When I was alone with him he would chant a little rhyme to me: 'He for a little tried to live without her, liked it not and died.' One day when we came across the garden to see him, he was up his red wooden collapsible ladder in his writing room in the cottage. He was searching for a book on the top shelf. Realising Adam and I were looking up at him, he momentarily lost his balance. 'No one will ever call me Hadji again,' he said very slowly as he came down the ladder, holding open a book with an inscription that Vita had written on the flyleaf. 'Hajji' was originally a respectful term used to mean a Muslim who had completed the pilgrimage to Mecca. Throughout their marriage, in private and in Vita's letters to Harold, she had called him Hadji (her spelling), what she understood to be the diminutive Arab word for old man, and the sight of the word in her handwriting and the great absence of her had suddenly overwhelmed him. 'We will,' I said. And we always did.

In old age Hadji suffered from the combined effects of several small strokes, the most recent of which reduced his mental agility. Most days Adam and I would collect him from the cottage and bring him across the lawn to lunch in our part of the house. He would sit at the head of the table. As my father attempted cheerful conversation, my grandfather and my mother would barely respond, lost in their own sad isolation. Occasionally Hadji would cry out, 'Oh Viti, Viti, Viti,' while my mother remained silent, never touching the delicious lunches she had cooked for us. Instead, a plastic tub of cottage cheese mixed with tinned pineapple and a carton of yogurt sat on her own plate, the control she imposed on her figure, apparently giving her some sense of influence over an existence in which she otherwise felt powerless.

However, away from the tension of the dining room, Harold still felt to me like a marvellous grandfather, a blueprint for grandfatherhood. Before Vita's death, when I was six years old and Adam just three, he had helped us plant a sapling oak on the bank of the moat opposite the huge trees that had been there for hundreds of years. The planting was a marker of our belonging there. The sapling took root and thrived, and now the tree is enormous, a source both of pride and of slight shock that we have both lived for so long. Harold loved us children from the beginning and was made demonstrably happy by us coming to live permanently at Sissinghurst.

'Can I join you in the paddling pool?' he would ask without waiting for an answer as he stepped straight into the water wearing his shoes and socks. 'May I offer you a light?' he would suggest, footman-solicitous as we placed a sugar cigarette on our lips while he flicked a match to the red-painted end.

There were dares known as courage tests. 'I dare you to jump off the top of the tower steps with your eyes shut.' Or, 'I dare you to climb to the top of the wall on the lower courtyard.' The long drop from the top of the tower steps to the lawn below required our small legs to be courageous, but the Bagatelle urns that Victoria had given Vita from her Wallace Collection legacy, and now planted with sweet-smelling viburnum, acted as hand steadiers. The wall was a greater challenge. A fragile crumbly Elizabethan affair, it was sturdy enough to support a fully bloomed Madame Alfred Carrière rose but hardly robust enough for the combined weight of two boisterous grandchildren. My mother would appear and shout, 'Oh, Harold, I have asked you NOT to endanger the lives of my children.' 'What about my wall?' he would reply as he gestured for us to climb higher, his moustache rising up his face and expanding with his smile. He invited physical affection. I would run the length of the long yew walk at top speed as he waited for me at the other end, a white figure in his cream linen trousers and bashed-up panama, holding out his arms wide as I hurled myself into his embrace. When it was time for him to get on with his writing or when he simply needed to be on his own, he guaranteed sixpence to whoever could hide in a cupboard for longest.

We spent a lot of time with Hadji in his cottage. He kept a bisected mug on his desk, a present from his secretary that said 'I only asked for half a cup of tea' in gold letters, which we thought very funny, and he kept his paper clips and rubber bands in two little blue-lidded pots marked Odds and Ends. We used to watch him shave in the mornings, using dark orangey-transparent Pears soap to work up the lather, joining in with his loud shouts of pain when he pretended to cut himself. As he became increasingly frail, he was looked after by a sequence of single male companions, all of them known as 'My Man', who cooked and cleaned for him and took care of his well-being. Michael Kirk was in his early twenties with twinkly blue eyes and curly dark hair and he was our favourite Man, a sort of dashing elder brother and nanny rolled into one. Michael adopted a newborn lamb called Jacob who had been abandoned by its mother and brought him into Hadji's cottage. Sucking a real-life baby's bottle with a power and urgency far beyond the capability of an infant, Jacob's hooves made a little sliding tap dance, cha-cha-ing on the slippery brick floor of Vita's flower room. We loved Jacob the lamb until he grew into Jacob the sheep when he became smelly and annoying with his headbutts and we left him in Michael's far more patient care.

The garden was our playground. The miniature maze formed of box hedge outside the Priest's House was the exact height for a child's hand to brush along the feathery surface as we ran through the narrow paths of the White Garden. Most of the time we bicycled everywhere, along the grass paths, sometimes past Vita's brightly coloured caged budgerigars, although their frantic flapping and cries for freedom meant that was a route I avoided. Occasionally Michael took us swimming in the sea at Camber Sands at nearby Rye, but most afternoons we escaped across the stile by the thyme lawn, leaving the garden and its showy publicness behind us, running down the poplar avenue that crossed the open field, past our oak-seated swing, through the clattery collapsing bottom gate and taking the path into the wood. We would climb into the small wooden boat and row out onto the lake almost unpassable in some places for the thickness of the duckweed, disturbing the paddling moorhen that vanished in a spray of water among the reeds. Trailing our fingers over the side in the green slime, tadpoles slithered from our grasp, the sun catching the momentary translucent shimmer of the dragonflies as they tipped their wings on the water's surface and made iridescent circles around us. Vita described that radiant place as one of the few that could 'repair the cracked heart, the jangled temper or the uneasy soul'. Years earlier she had pushed her own boat down the slope onto the lake, a skiff ordered on a whim from the Army & Navy soon after she came to live at Sissinghurst, as she too watched the dragonflies 'darting off on their blue and brown nuptial flight, so lean and so oddly joined and jointed'.

On summer weekends we went 'boat racing' with our father, dropping our own carefully selected stick into the stream and watching as it was carried along with the current before urging it in increasingly noisy and desperate terms to out-float the competition. Only when our wooden boat encountered a stone or the waterlogged root of a tree were we allowed to give it a helping prod along past the obstruction with a 'hoiker' cut by our father from the bendy hazelwood that grew there in profusion. There was inherent cheating and our father, the chief cheater, invariably won the race. The boat-race route took us past the small fenced cemetery devoted to the graves of Vita's dogs, with Byron's lines to his own Newfoundland terrier Boatswain quoted on their tombstones: 'Denied in heaven the soul he held on earth' – an epitaph which we found incomprehensible but nonetheless desperately sad.

In winter, we would put one foot on the ice at the edge of the lake to test the strength before inching as near to the centre as we dared. One year my father lost his balance and fell backwards on top of me, crushing my head onto the ice beneath him. As I returned to consciousness, still lying on the frozen surface, the worry on his face was replaced first by an expression of relief at my survival followed quickly by another of even worse anxiety. 'Never, never tell your mother what I have just done, promise me?' I promised. Years later he would describe the moment as one of the most frightening of his life, my near icy death made worse by the prospect of admitting responsibility for it. He hated me reminding him of it. Even as a tease.

Towards the fields on the other side of the house, the Victorian red-brick farm buildings huddled together, the sweet, sickly ammonia smell clinging to the cowsheds and mixing with the earthiness of the surrounding fields. Behind the sheds was a huge tap that ejected dead frogs, drowned in the rusty discharge. At teatime, milking time, Daisy and Marigold and all their florally named companions swayed back down the lane, returning from a day's munching in a hip-butting mass. Following the familiar twice-daily procedure, we watched the wellington-booted farmer martial his herd into the milking shed, the pink fleshiness of the cows' udders swinging above the grey clanking milk pails. In late summer the hop pickers arrived for their holidays from London's East End, sleeping in the huts and tents around the hop fields above the cowsheds. The men would pick from the vines while the paisley-scarved women sat on long trestle benches in the oast house, exchanging gossip while sorting good hops from bad with darting fingers, the palms of their hands smoothing the hard green buds that jostled and jumped past them on the conveyor belt. Further down the hill were the chicken sheds and off to the side the low building that housed the pigs where a dozen newborn piglets lay under a warming light in a neat row along the underside of their deep-breathing wiry-haired mother; pigs under a maternal blanket. Once we left the always-closed door open on purpose and the old sow lumbered into the yard, her tired eyes opening and closing, confused by her liberation, her piglets vociferously frantic, running circles around her. We were in disgrace for days.

In the orchard we had a den in the clammy, fetid air-raid shelter. Adam and his friend Simon dug for potatoes abandoned there during the Second World War and I commandeered the only shelf, on which I stored a comb and a banana and basked in the sense of keeping house. I like to think we rarely conformed to gender stereotype but for some reason the dug-out inspired those roles. On rainy days we hung about in the old brewhouse, lurking at the bottom of the haunted staircase, swinging off the carved post on which a sixteenth-century Sissinghurst laird was said to have chopped off the hand of a pretty young servant reluctant to follow her master upstairs to the bedroom. Sometimes I took my book and went alone to the attic floor, where no one ever came and from where I could eavesdrop on the voices below me or could listen out for the weekly travelling baker who kept a basket of sweets and chocolate for sale in the back of his bread van. Vita's chauffeur, Jack Copper, stayed on with us for a few years after her death to do all sorts of odd jobs as well as making home-made cider in the garage. After a hefty tasting session, he would weave up the lane at the wheel of the old black Zephyr as we bounced in the back seat on our way to buy starfish-pink fruit chews, four for a penny in the village sweetshop. Shirley had moved with us to Sissinghurst from London, remaining our invaluable nanny. Sometimes she took us to see her mother, Aunt Pun, who lived in the village. Aunt Pun, with her long grey plait coiled and pinned round the back of her head like my mother's old headmistress, and wearing a periwinkle-patterned overdress and polished stout brown lace-up shoes, made the best teas I have ever eaten. A bowl of just picked tomatoes, still warm from her sunny garden, and another containing lettuce, pulled from the earth moments before, sat next to a plate of of ham, thickly sliced, a newly baked loaf and a pat of creamy butter. A jug of marigolds sat at the centre of the white cloth, and after we had dipped the tomatoes in salt to illogically enhance their sweetness, a tray of floury currant scones would appear with a dish of home-made raspberry jam. The feast always ended with a generous slice of Victoria sponge that barely made contact with the tongue before melting away. Occasionally I was invited to make up Aunt Pun's bingo foursome in the village hall where she was inevitably in charge of the tea and scones. I sat with her friends, inhaling the sweet scent of violet cologne, while young and old marked their cards. Eighty-eight, two fat ladies, always got a chortle and a couple of accomplished wolf whistles invariably accompanied Legs Eleven. Aunt Pun, authoritative, no-nonsense, all-providing, consistent, smiley, was my idea of a mother.

My own mother was becoming more and more unhappy, her moods switching between semi-hysterial laughter on the telephone with her friends, when she would snort through her nose, to anger and to silence. Her existence at Sissinghurst had been made more uncomfortable by her reluctant agreement to condense four of Vita's gardening books for publication into one volume. She had always shown a real interest in the garden which Nigel appreciated and valued, and he thought this suggestion would give her 'an occupation' and therefore make her happier. But by imposing on Philippa the old family pattern of writing about the life and work of an earlier generation, he only emphasised her lack of self-confidence. Fourteen years after the pledge to his parents that he would make Philippa 'a Sissinghurst person', rather than allowing her to establish her own identity, he was still trying. He was a man for whom presentation and show, rather than emotional honesty, often held priority. And when those required standards fell below his expectations he judged harshly.

Nigel's idea for the anthology held no appeal for Philippa. In the summer of 1967 when he was abroad researching a book, she wrote him a letter, exasperated by her sense of her own inadequacy for the task and angry with him for making her feel that way. 'I'm very panicky about the garden anthology,' she wrote in scratchy green ink. 'I'm certain I don't have the knowledge, competence or concentrated dedication to complete this minor project on time . . . I'm frightened it will be terribly amateur . . . I try to remind myself how well praised were my prècis [sic] and paraphrases at school. But if my name is attached to this anthology I'll feel my stomach switch-backing at my lack of push for nepotism.' The letter continues chillingly. 'You don't think I'm now happy to die having given Juliet, Adam and Rebecca life but I am.'

This is a tough letter to read, her waning confidence barely concealed beneath her defiance. By giving birth, she suggests, she has achieved all she ever will. And yet she goes on to end the letter with a real understanding of the beauty of Sissinghurst as if to demonstrate what she might be capable of. It is impossible not to be moved by her lyrical description of the garden that evening. She tells Nigel how 'the light of the sun lowered in purple stripes across the sky, the tower threw its long shadows sideways over the orchard. It was marvellous, the light. The bricks were gentle pink, the balsam poplars puffed their pungent smell across the orchard . . . Sybille [a head gardener] marched briskly down the flagstones to lower the flag and I watched as the dogs growled and tumbled in that pink dusk.' But the lack of confidence, the fear of failure and the seeking of approval where there was none were familiar. Every one of the women who preceded me in our family had felt like this at times. Pepita had felt judged and shamed in Arcachon, Victoria had felt marginalised and cast off by Lionel, Vita had not met her own rigorous standards, and now Philippa was trapped by Nigel's harsh treatment of her and by her own lack of self-belief.

Nature's wildness unnerved her. Despite her upbringing in the country and her enduring love of horses, the natural world seemed determined to catch her out when she least expected it. Once, when dusk was falling, she put her hand on a sleeping bat on the banister. The startled animal made straight for her curly hair. Another time a wasp flew into her ear and was floated out on a wave of olive oil, poured by the doctor into the insect's hiding place. One day we put a dead rat on her car seat just for the fun of hearing her swear. But there was also a human wildness in the air at home. I recognised the undisguised contempt on my mother's face as she watched my father from her end of the dining-room table. The silent glare was preferable to the stream of precious French dinner plates that had on one occasion flown in Frisbee-anger between my parents down the length of the kitchen table and from which we had fled upstairs to Shirley's soothing presence. During their rows I would concentrate on the plastic yogurt container that sat next to a silver twin-tubbed mustard pot, an A and an F imprinted on the inside lids, an Edwardian joke denoting Anglais and Français. Had Vita sat looking at the same glinting pot as her own parents' relationship unravelled during dinner? I did not want to catch anyone's eye. If I looked down perhaps things would be better when I looked up again.

# 9

# Juliet
## Escape

During the summer of 1969, the Rolling Stones lamented how a lack of sexual satisfaction leads to a deeper sense of isolation. And, as if she had by now given up on Sissinghurst, Nigel, marriage, the beauty of the pink dusk and on us children, Philippa went off on one of her regular visits to stay in St Tropez. And there she fell in love, not only with a man but with another kind of life. The new existence was offered to her by a fellow Silberberg guest and an old schoolfriend of her father. Robin McAlpine was a widower, a much older man, the wealthy chairman of a family firm of world-renowned civil engineers, who had built Wembley Stadium, the M1 motorway and the Dorchester Hotel where Gervaise had lived during the war. He flattered Philippa, he fancied her and he promised to look after her. The tug of the older man, a father figure, protector and provider attracted her. Just as Nigel had offered her an escape from a stultifying life with her parents in the New Forest, McAlpine represented an alternative to a critical, unloving husband. Robin's escape route included unparalleled riches and even the possibility of a title – he had been knighted in 1969 in the same honours list as Nigel's business partner George Weidenfeld. In return for financial affluence, she would bring him gaiety, sexiness, companionship and rejuvenation. She had made her first patriarchal bargain with Nigel. Now she was about to make her second.

On 1 May 1968 Hadji died at Sissinghurst of a heart attack while undressing for bed. He was eighty-one. The coffin was placed in the Sissinghurst library, known to us as the Big Room, and Nigel sat beside it for the entire night before the funeral, weeping, he told me years later, more than he had ever wept in his life. A joint memorial service for Harold and Vita was held in Christopher Wren's beautiful church, St James's, Piccadilly, and we children were given a day off school to attend. The light-flooded building with its huge windows and pews in the high gallery above the nave had been filled with flowers sent up from Sissinghurst. The art historian Kenneth Clark gave the address to a packed congregation and afterwards Gervaise gave a lunch at the Ritz accompanied by champagne for the whole family. I found the outing thrillingly sad. But I was not aware of the secret pledge that my mother had made with my father. She had given Nigel her word that she would not upset Harold by revealing their mutual unhappiness. As long as Harold was alive she would stay. The pledge had now expired.

My childhood now became dominated by secrets. There were secrets kept from me, secrets I suspected and there were also some secrets that I knew but kept to myself. I spent a lot of time listening at doors, silently picking up the telephone receiver and holding my breath to make my presence inaudible. It was supposed to be a secret that my parents were not getting on, but we had been long aware that although they slept beneath the same roof they lived separate lives. One day when Nigel was abroad on business, Philippa and we children were collected by a small plane in a nearby field and flown over the county boundary to lunch in a smart white house in Hampshire. Robin McAlpine greeted us from an upstairs gallery that ringed a large potted-palm-filled, centrally heated hallway. It was the first time we had met him and we were not sure of his precise relationship to our mother. He was wearing a black sling due to a recent fall and we watched him walk cautiously down the stairs, steadying himself on the banister with his good arm. As he reached the bottom to greet us, his sling acted as a shield that prevented him from shaking our hands. Despite his considerable size he seemed frail and old. In the dining room, silver swans with movable silver wings that opened to reveal a bed of salt had been positioned at intervals along the table. The first course was already waiting at each place. I was still feeling sick from the bumpy plane ride as I stared at the plate in front of me. The white of an egg was just visible through a murky blanket of aspic, one lettuce leaf and a tiny flower of parsley alleviating the gloom of the brown jellied blob. I hated eggs. As I cut into the mud-coloured sphere, the yolk ran free, staining the plate yellow and swamping the lettuce garnish, the only part of the bilious presentation I had been bracing myself to eat.

For the next few months, Philippa would shut herself in her bedroom at home, and although I could not make out her words, if I put my ear to a crack in the beam in the corridor, I could hear her whispering, a new sort of glutinous half-voice that made me shudder. She would remain locked away for more than an hour, a red light on the other telephone extensions in the house showing that she was still talking. I used to put one finger over the light to cover it up but the beam shone through, turning my finger into scarlet X-ray flesh. I wondered what my father thought and if he had noticed the way the red light stayed lit for so long, or if he listened in through the space between the beams and heard that cloying voice. I wanted her to stop gush-whispering into the receiver, to stop talking, to hang up. I knew who was on the other end and I did not like it.

That Christmas holidays she took us to London to see *Gone with the Wind* in the huge cinema in Leicester Square. The film, at four hours long, ended too late to catch the last train home. We were to stay the night in the London house belonging to Robin McAlpine. He had become a very special friend. He was a very kind person. His house in Mayfair was thick-carpeted and very hot. A glass bottle of water labelled like wine sat on the bedside table next to a glass engraved with garlands of flowers and a flowery cotton pouch containing paper hand-kerchiefs. In the bathroom the towels on the chrome rail were unexpectedly warm. In the morning the live-in cook brought a tray laid with a plate of paper-thin slices of brown bread, porcelain cups so fine one feared taking an accidental bite out of them and a miniature pot full of weak, scented tea that

My favourite photograph: holding hands with my mother,
the London docks, 1960

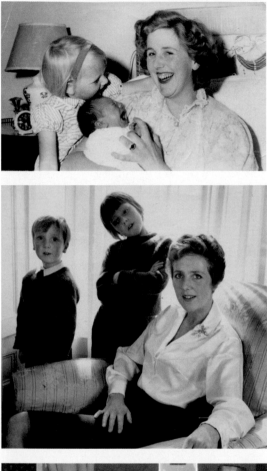

Philippa, me and
my day-old brother
Adam, 1957

A posed portrait
of motherhood,
London, 1962

Philippa on the
brink of departure,
London, 1968

Nigel's favourite
photograph of me,
hole-punched for
his diary, 1959

Nigel at work in
the gazebo at
Sissinghurst, 1972

Me and Nigel in
the Lime Walk at
Sissinghurst, 2003

Three generations of
daughters: Philippa, Vita
and me, Sissinghurst, 1959

Feeding the ducks with Hadji
at Sissinghurst, 1959

Adam and me with Hadji,
a week after Vita's death,
June 1962

Above: Me and James at Oxford, 1973

Below: Clemmie and Flora, Brick House, upstate New York, 1991

Top left: Clemmie, Nigel and
Flora during a long Sissinghurst
summer, 1989

Top right: Flora's first visit to
Sissinghurst, 1985

Left and below: A house
full of daughters, 1999

Top: Clemmie
with her daughter
Imogen Flora, 2013

Right: Me and Charlie,
Greece, 2015

Below: Me and Imo, 2015

Top left: The streets where Pepita learned to dance: me in Malaga, 2014

Top right: The gates of the Villa Pepa: all that remains of Pepita's house at Arcachon, 2014

Left: Imo playing in the sand, Arcachon, 2014

went grey when you put the milk in. On the way home on the train my mother said quietly to me that it would be best to tell our father, but only if he asked, that we had stayed the night at her brother's London club. My father was waiting for us in the kitchen. Had we had fun? Was the film good? Where had we stayed? I hesitated. I looked at my mother. She looked back at me steadily. She was counting on her daughter. Resistance thumped just under my ears. In silence I went upstairs to the bathroom at the top of the house and put the little piece of wood attached to a leather thong into the latch, locking myself inside. I sat on the linoleum floor and then got into the empty bath and stretched out full-length. For the next hour I remained there silent, my socked feet resting on the taps as my father and mother took turns trying to persuade me to come out. They pleaded, reasoned, bribed, wheedled, exasperated and raged, but the power had shifted from mother to daughter. I not only knew the honest answer about where we had stayed the night but also a more insidious truth: that my mother wanted me to lie for her. Victoria had imposed the go-between role on Vita when her marriage to Lionel was falling apart. But this was worse. My mother had asked me to join in on her betrayal and that day in the bathroom was a point of departure. Philippa had not taken into account the strength of my developing alienation from her. Her long aban-donment of me over many years was mirrored that day by mine of her.

I was not sure why I had been suddenly packed off to school on the Kent coast, a two-hour drive away. I didn't want to go.

My brother was sent at the same time and he was only eight years old. He didn't want to go either, but somehow the banishment from home of little boys whose small knees shone red with cold in their new uniform short trousers was presented as a wholly acceptable practice for a certain kind of family. My father had been sent away. My mother's brothers had been sent away. There was no reason to break the tradition. But I do not know how my parents justified their decision to put a sobbing daughter into such expensive exile. Perhaps it eased their guilt at arguing in front of us. My mother cooked roast chicken, my favourite food, for the last supper. I could not eat a mouthful. At the school the headmistress herself made a favourable impression on my father when she wept in admiration at the strength of my resistance to her establishment. I was homesick but not really for my own home. Hiding my face in a damp pillow, I would invent a place where there were no rows, an ever-present mother who always made my favourite suppers, and plenty of expeditions with a father who promised me I would never have to go back to boarding school. Dancing was the best lesson, as we were allowed to change out of the brown uniform and wear our home clothes and feel normal. I knew that my father missed me because he wrote to me every day for the first week, three times a week for the next three weeks, and after that once a week whenever we were apart for the next forty years.

I was entirely innocent of the facts of life, although my father's sixteen-year-old god-daughter, dressed in jeans and a black bra, had once let me watch her wash her hair while she listened to music on her own gramophone, in her own room. This glimpse into the unimaginable, sophisticated and seductive power of adult women alerted me to a deliciously mysterious life ahead. On the first night at boarding school two older girls in my dormitory told me about the imminence of the apocalyptic blood that no woman, whether a mother or a teenager, is able to avoid. It was a curse they said. I was eleven and had never heard of such a dreadful thing but I was terrified that it would soon strike me down. As I queued up with the other girls in the communal bathroom, with its row of rusty baths, early adolescence so uncompromisingly exposed, I tried to work out whether those in the tubs in front of me had yet been cursed. I wanted to keep my end up but a bluff at authoritative knowledge backfired when I compiled a list of rude words to read out after lights out and accidentally left the list in my gym knickers when they went to the laundry.

'What is this? Please read it aloud,' Matron demanded, holding out the piece of crumpled paper to me as I faced her across her office desk.

'Bra, bottom, fart, willy,' I began.

'Continue please.'

'Bosom, bust, knickers,' I went on.

'I'm afraid I will have to write to your parents,' Matron concluded as I slunk from her room. Although the inventory was never mentioned by either parent it might have prompted a conversation with my mother on my twelfth birthday.

'What I am going to tell you, this thing about what a man does to a woman to get a baby, sounds disgusting,' she said, crossing her legs as she lit a Benson & Hedges and exhaled the smoke with force. 'And it is.'

I never much enjoyed boarding school, the experience of

returning after the holidays always traumatic. In the spring of 1969, almost a year after Hadji had died, there was a sense of finality at Sissinghurst and yet I was feeling more miserable than ever at the prospect of another ten weeks away from home. My mother drove me back to school for the first day of the spring term with my trunk in the boot of the car. Sitting outside the school gate in her green Rover with the cream leather seats whose smell made me feel sick, the ignition turned off and the warm air from the car heater extinguished, she told me that she and Nigel were getting divorced. She would be leaving forever, she explained. We were used to the 'leaving' but not the 'forever'. Her words held the physical sting of a slap. In the late 1960s divorce was not a common state of parental affairs, at least not in my school, and it stigmatised me as one of several distinctive odd girls out, linked as a figure of whispered curiosity to the girl who was adopted, the foreign princess who shaved her lower arms, and the inconsolable one whose father had died. A day or two later a copy of the *Daily Express* had been placed on the low table in the house study. Several girls were sitting in front of the fire reading and chatting to each other and paying no attention to me as I picked up the paper and turned the pages. Part of the William Hickey gossip column had been neatly removed with scissors, the headline perhaps accidentally left intact. 'CHATELAINE OF SISSINGHURST PREFERS GARDEN IN HAMPSHIRE'. I looked up. Every eye was on me. They said they had cut the passage out to save my feelings but I knew they had been waiting to see my reaction. Yet I was not the chief casualty of the breakdown of the marriage. Philippa's decision punctuated a defining point both in the structure of our family life and in my mother's loss of identity. Until that moment she had been a daughter, then a wife, then a mother. For the next part of her life, she hovered between those two last roles, never quite sure which of them she wished to occupy, stumbling and falling with increasing damage not only to herself and but also to her relationship with us.

When we returned from a holiday in Ireland, Nigel left us at Philippa's new home, a large rented flat in a Victorian block just off Kensington High Street, before driving back to Sissinghurst alone. At one end of her large sitting room was a colour television, the first I had ever seen, while at the other end red-painted chairs with string seats were ranged around a trendy white-painted table. There were strawberries for supper in April, bought from the laboratory-clean supermarket down the road. In this seductive, sharp-edged, brightly lit city environment, tapestries and hessian and Sissinghurst fustiness had been replaced with the whiff of new gloss paint and beige carpets. Suddenly London had become a treat, no longer just the place for an occasional holiday visit to the cinema and the smart dentist who discussed his loathing of Harold Wilson's government with our mother while drilling ever more venomously into her children's mouths. Now, we ate ice creams in Kensington Gardens, went to the cinema and learned to eat with chopsticks in Chinatown. We went shopping in Kensington Market and I bought long silky Indian scarves and a silver necklace with little bells that jangled as I moved. We inhaled incense, sophistication and freedom. My mother and a couple of friends threw a teenage party in our flat for their four daughters. Carolyn and Bella Warrender were super-glamorous and I was amazed to find myself suddenly part of a cool gang. The third daughter, Rachel Pritchard, with her long blonde hair, was mischievous, irresistible. She became my lifelong best friend. There was a discotheque in the sitting room and I wore a mustard velvet trouser suit with a black wet-look shirt underneath. The next day one of the most popular boys at the party called by with a pair of silver hooped earrings as a thank-you present. I felt giddy glimpsing life's potential.

Throughout that year I was aware for the first time of being the envy of my contemporaries. For one lovely, spoiling, possibly guilt-induced interlude I had a mother who shone with demonstrative love. Maybe she was acting the part but I think not. Her own happiness came from the liberation from years of insecurity and unhappiness and allowed her to turn her attention to her children in ways she had been unable to before. She made us laugh with her mimicry of the man reading the news on the new colour television. I glimpsed the schoolgirl who had been singled out for her friendship and sense of fun in Norfolk, the young woman who had played leapfrog in London when she fell in love with Patrick Plunket, even the shy but eager bride-to-be whose sweetness and vivacity had struck my father among all the other guests at a party nearly twenty years earlier. Maybe, after her schooldays, this was the time when she was most free, happiest. When she was out, her rosy scent continued to drift on the air. At last the criticism and the obligations had gone and she had money and rooms of her own, the communal entrance to the flat giving her a liberating anonymity. Despite my new membership of the group of school oddities, I began to feel pleased that my parents had separated.

For that one year I felt I had cracked the knack of balancing life, seeing each parent whenever I wished. It was as if I had learned to run a bath to the perfect temperature with not one extra drop of hot or cold required, until one day the water ran tepid. Philippa's independence had been illusory. Robin McAlpine had paid for the flat in the old-fashioned way, his mistress housed, no questions asked, in a service apartment. But the arrangement could not last indefinitely.

Back at school I stood in the fusty little cupboard beneath the main staircase where there was a pay telephone that accepted incoming calls; the receiver, black Bakelite, was sweaty on my ear from the girl who had used it before. My mother was asking me to come to her wedding to a man I barely knew though knew I did not like. She was turning me against my will into a stepdaughter, an awkward link in the conventional family chain. I refused the invitation. She wept. I hung up. I was losing her all over again.

Was it unkind not to be more tolerant of her choice of a husband, need for a husband? Was I behaving selfishly by protecting my new-found contentment at receiving her attention without competing with other adults? Her friends questioned her decision, begged her not to go through with the marriage. She shared her doubts with them and cried the night before in the arms of one of them, but the next day her anxieties had apparently dissipated, her resolve hardened. There was a legal ceremony at Caxton Hall, the same registry office where in 1952 Elizabeth Taylor had married husband number two, Michael Wilding, and where in 1965 Ringo Starr had married

Maureen Cox. Philippa's legal formalities were followed by a church service at St George's, Hanover Square, during which a scratchy recording of the vows was made, the only audible words being Philippa's confirmation that she would remain married 'for richer'. The flowers at the wedding lunch at the Dorchester were regal purple, her favourite colour. None of her children were there for any of it. She returned all Nigel's love letters, handing him back what had become redundant and meaningless documents.

Philippa's second husband delivered the promised material comforts that took her beyond her wildest dreams. The reward for marriage included houses and live-in staff, holidays to exotic places, designer clothes to wear to the private box at Epsom racecourse, enough champagne to fill every en suite bath in the Dorchester Hotel and a private London taxi with its own peak-capped chauffeur. She once came to my school open day in a helicopter, her means of transport matched only by the mother of one other pupil, Princess Anne. There was an attempt on both sides to keep our relationship buoyant. But there was also a reluctance. I wanted to do the right thing and show that, despite not going to the wedding, I was pleased for her, but I wasn't. She seemed anxious to keep me involved in her new life and yet I annoyed her. A friend of hers meant well when he took me aside and said how it could not be easy for me, being neither one thing nor another. Although I had embarked on the bumpy trip through the no-man's-land of adolescent instability, tilting at times towards childhood and at others cautiously in the other direction, I did not want my limbo state pointed out. My mother's irritation with her teenage daughter, pustular with hormones, or what Philippa termed 'bolshiness', was compounded for her by having to contend with a stepchild and a stepparent who had found themselves connected in a way that neither had chosen.

Weekends at Robin's Hampshire house were a trial. The single thin chime of the clock in the hall would coincide precisely with the arrival of the Spanish butler bringing a tray of sherry glasses and a plate of mackerel pâté smoothed into perfect cones on top of Ritz crackers. Returning ten minutes later he would announce with a token bow that lunch was ready, repeating the ritual in the evening for dinner, when even though there were rarely any outside guests, women of all ages were required to change into long dresses before entering the dining room.

Dining rooms have run through my family as uncomfortable environments in which to be trapped. In Albolote, Catalina read aloud her absent daughter's letters to her embarrassed guests. At Knole, Victoria had tried to talk through difficult silences in the Poets' Parlour, and at the same table Vita had attempted to calm her arguing parents. In the dining room at Sissinghurst, I had watched the painful decline of my grandfather's health and my own parents' unmistakable incompatibility. In Hampshire, my stepfather sat at one end of the highly polished table in the centre of the overheated dining room, Philippa at the other waiting for the butler to bring in the grouse. Conversation centred on the weather and the state of the turf for the next race meeting at Epsom. Both my stepfather and Philippa were mad about racing. All forms of culture, especially books, were considered dangerous, subversive and narrowing of the mind. There was to be no mention of politicians except Winston Churchill, and any hint of interest in the Left Wing was like suggesting Chairman Mao should be invited for a game of croquet. Adam remembers an explosion at his mention of the Red Star parcel force. There was to be no Commy talk in that house. Desperate to find a topic and to interrupt the silence which felt like an expression of disapproval at our presence in Robin's house, I would stare at my plate considering and rejecting everything that came into my head. All possibilities were derailed as I watched my stepfather tap Tabasco onto the new season's oysters. He was a large man, not as tall as Seery but almost as bulky. But he had none of Seery's sweetness. He felt soft and dangerous. He reminded us of Goldfinger. Filling the wall behind Philippa was a half-length 1950s portrait of Robin's first wife who had died some years earlier. Looking like Grace Kelly in a pale pink, sleeveless, diaphanous evening gown, her beautiful, formidable, cold, painted eyes stared down at the back of my mother's neck.

Even as my parents' marriage was disintegrating, and especially after Philippa's failed attempt to get me to lie for her, my relationship with Nigel had deepened further. Just as in those few flickery black-and-white moments of film when, as a five-year-old bridesmaid, I had reached for my father's hand, I continued to reach for him after my mother left. After my parents' divorce I spent as much time with Nigel as I could, gradually assuming a new responsibility. A (wifeless and indeed parentless) man often finds himself in need of a wife, but when a wife is not available, a daughter, even a teenage daughter, has to do. Almost a hundred years earlier, and only a few years older than I was in the late sixties, my great-grandmother had arrived in America to act as her father's hostess at the embassy in Washington. Following her pattern, I stepped into a vacancy created by a mother's absence. And like Victoria, the arrangement proved equally beneficial to father and daughter.

My second boarding school was only a few miles from Sissinghurst and after Saturday-morning lessons I would look out of the small window on the upper staircase and down onto the school driveway where Nigel's orange Vanden Plas would be neatly parked waiting to take me home. Unaware of the extent to which he had been deprived of female affection, not only by his wife but also his mother, I wonder now if a nascent maternal instinct, a role reversal at such a young age, was already in place in me. During Nigel's early days of singlehood, when he required a woman to assume responsibilities suited to someone far older, I think he saw an opportunity to 'mould' me in the same way he had tried to mould my mother all those years ago. He made clear his determination that I should not be submerged into incurious conventionality by the ultra-conservative, unacademic boarding school that Philippa had insisted on. He would test me, push me, and often criticise and despair of me whenever he saw a reflection of my mother in my behaviour. I was shy, unconfident and prone to giving up. 'Little Miss Can't' was a favourite retort whenever I failed a challenge. I was frequently reminded of what was touted as 'the family motto'. 'If at first you don't succeed, try, try, try again,' he would chant, whenever I raised an obstacle to what he was suggesting. Much later he admitted that he had first heard the phrase from *The Children of the New Forest* by Frederick Marryat, a book that had been given to him by one of his constituents in Hampshire when I was born. He wanted to toughen me up. He was not satisfied with a weakling daughter and his confidence in my potential ebbed and flowed. A chance remark could finish me off, especially a comparison with one of my school friends who were universally assessed as prettier, funnier and cleverer than me. Perhaps Nigel was unaware of his daughter's acute sensitivity. I recently read that the *Sun* newspaper editor David Yelland sometimes regretted publishing an unkind story, feeling 'like a boy who kills a songbird with an airgun and only afterwards realises the power of his weapon'.

What I wanted more than anything was Nigel's approval. His endorsement counted. His conventionality, indeed hypocrisy, given his insistence that he was the most liberal-minded and emancipated of men was demonstrated in the demands he imposed on his pliable teenage daughter, expecting her to serve as his wife's replacement cook and hostess for summer lunch parties. Having sent him a shopping list by post from school earlier in the week, I would change out of my uniform into jeans and knock up cauliflower cheese, macaroni cheese, cheese on toast, cheese and biscuits, and an oddly infallibly delicious chocolate mousse while, accompanied by his own sibilant whistle, he picked purple clematis to float in the two silver bowls on the dining-room table. But at the time I was not in the least resentful, did not feel exploited, enjoying the part I played in his life, enjoying being needed, enjoying acting the grown-up, enjoying the praise, enjoying being with him, grateful for the sense of importance I felt when I accompanied him anywhere. And I loved him, happy to make my own patriarchal bargain.

'Unseen hands will clear up,' my father would promise guests at the end of lunch, implying the presence of several willing staff in the kitchen as we took his visitors round the garden before waving them goodbye and returning together to the twin sinks. The washing-up became a favourite place for difficult conversations, all inhibiting eyeball-to-eyeball confrontation removed as we stood side by side staring down into the soap-filled chrome tubs, me washing, him rinsing. He continued to take his parental duties as seriously as he always had, not sure if he could rely on his ex-wife to carry them out properly, and perhaps mindful of his mother's inability to communicate with her children. Given his queasiness over all matters sexual, he handled a hormonal and dislocated daughter with laudable skill. 'Do you know the facts of life?' he asked one day, clearing his throat and turning on the cold tap more forcefully. 'Yes, of course,' I lied. 'That's good. Then we don't need to talk about any difficult details. I have just one thing to say on the subject. Love affairs must reflect the pattern of your professional life. You must have three good stabs at your career and the same number at love. Change your professional as well as your romantic direction three times. The jobs and the men [he assumed it would be men] should all be rather different, none should become permanent or even necessarily husbands, but each of the three in both categories should be serious commitments and grand, all-consuming passions. The only thing I ask is that you neither fall for nor become a dentist. Mouths are horrible orifices into which to peer.' (He had a recurring aversion for orifices of all varieties.) He was a romantic. Like his grandfather Lionel, but at odds with my mother, he did not want dukes for me, although on Valentine's Day an unsigned postcard of a Bavarian castle would arrive with '*This is where your prince is waiting for you*' written on the reverse in his neat handwriting.

I was learning little at a boarding school where every girl was sent on a celebratory school picnic when the head girl won a scholarship place at university. Each morning we made our beds with sharp hospital corners that were inspected by Matron for precision. Our physical deportment was refined by walking up and down the classroom with books piled on top of our heads. We had embroidery, cooking and knitting lessons. White-collared velvet dresses in dark colours designed with the house-keeper of an Edwardian vicarage in mind were worn on Sundays, with a panel that flipped up at the back so the nap of the velvet did not get crushed by the schoolgirl bottom. We learned that the correct direction in which to shave a leg was from ankle to knee, to do the Scottish reels and the waltz. We had euphemisms when we had our period (a word that itself was deemed vulgar) like 'The Curse' or 'I am off games'. 'Charlie's dead' was code for 'your petticoat is showing', and everyone including Princess Anne had a photograph of their mother on their dressing table next to the pink Mum Rollette sold by the ton at the village shop. We were all confirmed by the local bishop, the Archbishop of Canterbury, not because we were believers but because the preparatory lessons were taken by a shy visiting nun who we interrogated in voices of touching sincerity about what the Bible meant by 'knowing' a man. After lights out, conversational topics progressed from breasts to buggery and soon I was far out of my depth. There was talk about 'positions' and although I could not work out how the five basic ballet points, with the variations of a foot in front or behind, could enhance or decrease sexual pleasure, I kept quiet. We were all astonishingly naive. At the beginning of one term, word went round that during the holidays a very beautiful sixth-former called Isabella had 'Gone All The Way' with her boyfriend. A little bunch of us would assemble on the side of the Lime Avenue waiting for a glimpse of Isabella to pass by, astonished to discover that she could still ride a bicycle.

There were attempts to prepare the student body for adult society. Sixth-formers were required on a rotating basis to eat a week's worth of lunches at the headmistress's table and practise the art of conversation. For seven days we were forbidden to mention the weather or sport while the stewed cabbage was handed round in an exaggeratedly polite manner, as if we were seated at a Lord Mayor's banquet. Filling conversational spaces once again became a thing to dread, just as it was in my step-father's house, and we would try anything rather than be reduced to the ultimate crime of discussing the nature of the food on our plate. I was useless at needlework, cheated during the practical for my cooking O level, hated sleeping in a dormitory, made few friends, and the only part of school life that I really enjoyed were the English lessons and the marvellously bosomy Mrs Innes Crump who rippled with emotion whenever she called upon herself to recite 'Ode to a Nightingale'. Poetry and fiction remained my escape route, my psychic refuge.

When Philippa suggested she might be able to persuade Nigel to let me do my A levels at a crammer in London, I jumped at the chance. She had found a college with a knack of getting non-academic girls through their exams with impressive speed.

London and blue jeans felt a lot more exciting than velvet dresses and the village shop. I would have a room and my own bathroom in one of Robin's two houses in Mayfair. Nigel agreed to the move, my academic success mattering to him more than my nearby availability as loving, compliant daughter and hostess.

Westminster Tutors was based in a series of Victorian rooms in Artillery Row, just down the road from Westminster Abbey, presided over by its formidable founder Miss Freeston and her rabid terrier Topsy. I discovered to my surprise and pleasure that my old teacher Mrs Fitzgerald was on the staff, the wisps of red hair that still escaped from her bun now highlighted with grey streaks as she ran into the fuggy little teaching rooms balancing a pile of books and a paper cup of soup. Perching the lunchtime mulligatawny on the bench next to the hazardous gas fire, her infectious love of literature, now transferred from Dickens's knitters to Tess and her illegitimate child, remained undimmed. I began to feel adult, emancipated. I started to smoke, secretly at first, practising by lying full-length on the floor of the bathroom before adjusting to the dizzying nausea as I stood up. I rehearsed my inhale–exhale technique during long Tube rides. I discovered T. S. Eliot. I had never read anything like it. At home I thought about Prufrock and listened to Don Maclean singing 'Everybody loves me Baby' and wondered if anyone would ever love me.

Philippa's ambitions for me did not include the intoxication of reading poetry and smoking on the Underground on my way to Artillery Row, but more the landing of a rich, preferably titled proposal of marriage, including a chauffeur and a country seat.

In preparation for a life of Bentleys and baronetcy, she wished me to come out as a debutante. On the day I left my boarding school, she somehow pulled a string and arranged for both of us to have our photographs taken by Cecil Beaton. I had been given a special candyfloss blow-dry by my mother's hairdresser and felt and looked like a shop-window mannequin as the dapper, bow-tied Beaton stood me in front of his camera. Forbidding all mention of 'cheese', a word guaranteed, he said, to produce a most unattractive elongation of the lips, he required me instead to repeat 'lesbian' very slowly after him, which produced a much more natural smile in the finished portrait.

Debutantes were still under the patronage of mothers who met each other at lunch parties before the beginning of the Social Season, ostensibly to organise the dates for their daughters' dances, to discuss the potential of that year's selection of 'Debs' Delights', but covertly to weigh up the competition in terms of wealth and looks. Philippa cultivated several new friendships with smart mothers, but considered herself slightly ahead of the game with the Beaton photographs under her belt and, through the connections of Patrick Plunket, an invitation to a party at Kensington Palace hosted by Princess Margaret. One of the other guests was at Westminster Tutors with me and her handsome brother Harry asked me to dance, as Lord Snowdon spun the discs in the large palace drawing room. Princess Margaret cruised among us, her eyes like mobile telescopes zeroing in on any misdemeanour, her own cigarette firmly in its holder while tearing a strip off my dashing dance partner who had dared to drop his stub on to the floor and grind it into the polished surface with his shoe.

The season kicked off as usual with Queen Charlotte's Ball at the Grosvenor House Hotel in Park Lane, an occasion that originated in 1780 as George III's celebration of his wife's birthday, attended by the Queen's virginal ladies-in-waiting, wearing white to demonstrate their virtue. The hundred or so snowy-gowned, sporadically virginal debs of 1972 had been coached by Madame Vacani, ballet teacher to royalty, on how to make a long, slow simultaneous curtsy to the battered old symbolic cardboard birthday cake, the same one that was familiar to my mother. It was brought into the Grosvenor House ballroom on a trolley draped in a faintly grubby white petticoat and pulled by the six prettiest debs. I was not chosen as one of those involved in the cake transportation. The Debutante Dress Show was the next social engagement, held in the bubble-gum-pink ballroom of the Berkeley Hotel. I was not chosen as a model.

For tutorials I wore denim pinafore dresses and jeans from the Etam shop nearest to Artillery Row, or a favourite pair of yellow bell-bottoms from Top Shop that were covered in Beatrix Potter figures. After afternoons at home immersed in writing A-level essays, I spent the evening at the deb dances choked in imitation pearls and rotating the six lacy, flouncy, flowery long dresses that Philippa had chosen for me. I was a disappointment to her, my physical appearance not up to scratch, the huge, intrusive Sackville nose that had troubled Victoria in Vita's wedding photographs re-emerging to ruin yet another daughter's profile. My front teeth were too large. They looked like tombstones. If I could have seen myself from behind I would have stopped wearing trousers. The habit for criticism that Victoria had directed against her daughter's appearance was inherited by Nigel and adopted by Philippa. She tried to improve the situation. In order to give me the best start in life, she announced that either she could throw me a big party at a grand London hotel with all the eligible young men she could muster, or, in order to make myself more desirable, she could pay for me to have a discreet Harley Street nose reduction followed by a small dinner at which to show the new nose off. I chose the party.

Secretly I began to feel that life was working out well. I had fallen in love. And I was prepared to take the next step towards liberation. What girl can feel that she has truly gained her independence before she has discovered sex? I went to the family GP to ask for the Pill. From behind his mahogany desk and looking at me over the half-moon of his bifocals, he regretted that as I was still too young to vote he would have to inform my mother of my request. Somehow I persuaded him to keep the transaction between us, as my emancipatory birthday was only a few months away. Not long after my visit to the doctor, we went for a day trip to the races in France with my stepfather, travelling in his private plane. While our bags were checked on a random search at the airport, my contraceptives, cunningly packaged as a powder compact in order to preserve discretion, were placed on the customs desk for examination next to a Tampax. I grabbed both objects, feeling as embarrassed by the tampon as I was incriminated by the contraceptives. I had not moved quickly enough to prevent my short-sighted stepfather from enquiring whether I had started smoking cigars. I swiftly though truthfully replied that I had. But Philippa had sharper eyesight. She knew I was slipping beyond her control.

She cheered up when she heard I was going to a ball at Blenheim (nose intact) before she realised my attendance would be contingent on being the unpaid assistant to London's most in demand travelling disc jockey. I would be eating in the downstairs kitchen with the resident chef rather than upstairs in the ducal ballroom, and lugging electric cables past the family portraits instead of waltzing beneath them in the arms of the heir. But she was even more taken aback to discover that the DJ had become my first proper boyfriend. I had met him at the discotheque company's promotional party at the beginning of the deb season. He was wearing a pair of Mr Freedom cream velvet dungarees covered in black stars over a scarlet T-shirt. He was irresistible. His parents were unknown to Philippa. He did not have a title, a stately home or a job in the City. With the looks of a young Byron, the dark romantic eyes of Heathcliff, the glamour of Charles II, the enigmatic charm of Jay Gatsby and an ambitious and clever mind, James Macmillan-Scott was the coolest man in London. When he was not DJing, he was a part-time house painter and moonlighting in an upmarket grocer in Knightsbridge. He was so handsome that people used to make excuses to go and stare at him, pressing their faces against the shop window. I could not understand what he was doing with me and my big nose. He wore ruffly lace shirts, a creamy silk scarf with a fringe and a long leather thong round his neck from which he hung a jangling bunch of keys. He shared a pair of red setter twins called Elvis and Jethro with his flatmate Ian, a photographer. He drove a Fiat Cinquecento in which he raced round Hyde Park Corner on two wheels and I was mad about him.

In the summer of 1972 I passed my English literature A level with a good grade, and to both my parents' and my own surprise Westminster Tutors recommended that I sit the Oxbridge entrance exam that autumn. If I was offered a place, I would join the university the following year. We all knew that my chances were slim. The competition was intense, especially for a place to read English. My mother did all she could to discourage such ill-advised folly. Maybe she truly believed that I would be hurt by the probable rejection. More likely I think she was jealous, and also a little fearful, emphasising to me that the route to adult success did not lie in a musty library rather than admitting her dread that academic opportunity might widen further the gulf between us.

She wrote to Nigel suggesting an alternative plan. 'Juliet is not exactly university material,' she said, and wondered if a nice establishment in Switzerland or France or maybe a course in the history of art in Florence might fit my non-academic inclinations better. In some ways she was a generational casualty of the incremental progress of female emancipation, a woman confused, no longer able to apply the rules and restrictions of her own upbringing to her daughter. Resentful, perhaps, that she had been offered so little encouragement by her own parents to follow any sort of intellectual or professional career, she did all she could to put a stop to mine. I knew that if she had her way I would be on track to follow her into an educational vacuum, the prospect of finishing schools threatening to finish me off. But I was lucky. My father had more confidence in me.

With his encouragement I returned to Westminster Tutors, filled in the forms and continued to balance my academic, social and love lives. At the end of that final term I sat the Oxbridge exam, and in early December I heard that I had passed the written round and had been invited by St Hugh's College, Oxford, to come up for an interview.

The night before the interview I had been to an ankle-twisting dance on a skating rink and limped onto the train to Oxford from Paddington still wearing my ice-skimming, red tartan pinafore dress. One hundred and twenty-four interviewees were competing for twelve places. Two weeks later and three days before Christmas, I arrived home blown dry and buffed up from my mother's hairdresser on the day of my own debutante party, for which a special chocolate pudding, 'Bombe Surprise pour Juliette', had been created by the head pastry chef at the Dorchester Hotel. A telegram addressed to me was sitting on the coconut doormat.

> Vacancy offered you Michaelmas Term 1973 Please Reply
> by Return. English Literature faculty St Hugh's College,
> Oxford.

I put the telegram in my pocket and went to the party.

I did not mention the St Hugh's telegram to anyone. I knew what my mother would want me to do. But my father's opinion would be difficult to argue against. James had been offered a job running the discotheque at the Tehran Hilton. He had asked me to go with him and I had agreed. I wanted to be with him all the time. Three days after the party I telephoned my father from my stepfather's house in Hampshire (where the first edition of Tennyson's *Idylls of the King* with Gustave D'Oré illustrations sat between the latest editions of *Country Life* and the *Field* on a table in a room where the walls were lined with the spines of cut-off books, a library in illusion in an otherwise book-free house.) 'Happy Christmas,' I said, asking about his own lunch with the neighbours, wanting the details, all the trimmings. 'Oh, and by the way, I got into Oxford,' I said 'But I'm not going.'

I heard the smash as my father dropped the remaining unbroken coffee cup from a favourite pair given to my parents as a wedding present. I explained that I would be turning down the place to read English at Oxford in favour of working at the Tehran nightclub with the man I loved. My father said he would write to me, and the following day a costly hand-delivered letter arrived, cleverly outlining the advantages and then the disadvantages of both options. In conclusion he pointed out that as fascinating as the interior of a Persian nightclub might sound, it would probably not differ much from the interior of any similar establishments in Berkeley Square. Whereas Oxford . . . the legacy would be lifelong, he said. The sight of the word on a jar of marmalade had never failed to thrill my grandfather. My father continued to dream about punting and of a Brideshead world. James could visit. I would make new friends. I would be living in one of the most beautiful cities on earth. I would never regret it. And he was right. For me, those three years at Oxford, concluding with finals week spent in my hero T. S. Eliot's rooms at Merton College, have backlit the rest of my life in a way that the dark basement of the Tehran Hilton never could have done, even for a moment.

My mother had little choice other than to accept my decision, and although I do not remember any expression of her pride, or even approval, I do remember my stepfather's sceptical comments about 'joining a bunch of hairy lefties'. Philippa had one last attempt up her sleeve to hold onto me, to 'finish' me. She put the Channel between me and James and sent me on a smart cooking course in Paris where I lodged with an impoverished count and countess who let out rooms to nice British girls. I spent weekdays heaving with nausea as I failed to skin a rabbit or dice a pair of lamb's kidneys, evenings in Maxim's wine cellar learning to taste the difference between a Lafitte and a Latour, and weekends attempting to arrange flowers in a vase suitable for a ducal ballroom. Every third Friday, unknown to my mother, I would take the coach from outside the central bus station at Les Invalides to Calais, a ferry to Dover and a coach to Victoria where James would meet me. I would return to Paris on the Sunday.

In October Nigel drove me to St Hugh's College in St Margaret's Road in north Oxford. As a surprise, he had brought with him in the boot of the Vanden Plas two framed prints of his own favourite paintings, Gainsborough's *Mr and Mrs Andrews* and Turner's *Fighting Temeraire*. Together we hung them above my bed as the autumn sun glinted on the leaves that fell from the sycamore trees outside my window.

Oxford was not very Brideshead at first sight. The long brightly lit corridors were school-reminiscent. Watery footprints darkened the cork floor that linked the shared bathroom down the corridor to the rooms. No male visitors were allowed in the college after 10 p.m. Dinner was little better than the meal that Virginia Woolf had described at Girton almost half a century earlier when the pattern on the bowl beneath the watery soup was clearly visible. Glasses did not 'flush' yellow and red as she had observed them do at men's colleges. But despite the water we drank and the institutional smell of the college corridors, I was at Oxford. I had a room of my own and a reader's pass to the Bodleian, after declaring to the librarian that I would not 'bring into the library or kindle therein any fire or flame'. James was my most constant visitor followed by my delighted father. Not only was his daughter at Oxford, the first woman of the family to follow in the Nicolson male tradition, but Nigel was able to indulge himself in a three-year-long nostalgia for his youth. He took me to tea in the Randolph Hotel round the corner from his old lodgings in Beaumont Street and opened an account in my name at Blackwell's where he set up a generous termly credit for new books. I went to lectures given by Dame Helen Gardner, who was rumoured to have been in love with T. S. Eliot, and by Richard Ellman on James Joyce. Ann Wordsworth gave her tutorials in a shed off the Crick Road. We sat on stools. Rings from the bottom of leaky bottles stained the carpet, a half-empty bottle of Burgundy was propped against a bookcase, the wine as dark as Mrs Wordsworth's red velvet jacket. We rolled our own. Sometimes we could not see her face through the gloom. We talked of Gerard Manley Hopkins and Keats and everything else that mattered, the soft encompassing darkness causing us to blink hard when we emerged into the harsh light of day.

*

I had made a new friend who had not been scrutinised for approval by either parent. Belinda Harley was my tutorial partner. With her shiny, fashionable, Purdy haircut, she was Oxford's Zuleika of the 1970s, a stand-out undergraduate in a college with a strong rowing community and a dining room that served chewy stews, strength-building spinach and quite a lot of beer. Belinda had vodka in her room and pâté. I had sherry. I floated about wearing frocks. Belinda strode down the High wearing black trousers and a skintight denim jacket with little beneath. The jacket had a zip sewn on a bias from shoulder to hip and she would move the zip up and down depending on her mood. I had never met anyone like her. We were inseparable. Belinda knew Francis Warner, the poet and English don at St Peter's College. Francis knew Samuel Beckett and Richard Burton and Francis helped us launch a literary society, encouraging us to invite our writing heroes to come and speak. They came. My father kicked us off with 'How much should a biographer tell?' and then the playwright Peter Nichols came, followed by the aristocratic biographer and historian Lord David Cecil, the American theatre director Charles Marowitz, and the artist and son of Bloomsbury, Quentin Bell. The exquisite Irish novelist Edna O'Brien came and insisted the audience sit at her feet instead of in rows of chairs as she read aloud to us from her latest novel in the sexiest voice on earth. When the controversial critic F. R. Leavis agreed to be prised from Cambridge for the first time in thirty years, every member of the university's English faculty joined the undergraduates to hear him, and even though we had moved the meeting into the biggest theatre we could find, it was standing room only as he began to speak. No one in the room could understand a word of what he said, but, delighting in the knowledge that they had actually been there, no one cared a jot.

One day Francis invited Belinda and me to a tutorial at St Peter's. Richard Burton, 'the world's Greatest Living Actor' as I wrote later to my father, was waiting for us in Francis's room wearing an academic gown. Burton's love affair with Oxford had begun during the war when he was briefly an undergraduate at Exeter College. Since then he had returned to the university as often as possible, had acted with the university's dramatic society, OUDS, and had long wanted to establish with Francis an Oxford theatre devoted to putting on Shakespeare's plays. Sitting beside him in an afghan coat, all hippy and ethnic, her thick black hair parted in the middle, was Elizabeth Taylor, whom Burton had just married for the second time. Her deep violet eyes danced with the audacity that comes after consuming most of a half-bottle of Jack Daniel's. I registered the convenience of the slim flat sides of the bottle that slid neatly into a pocket. The awestruck male undergraduates sat on the floor. Belinda and I, as token girls, shifted self-consciously in the two spare chairs. As soon as Burton began the tutorial with Henry V's magnificent entreaty to battle, 'Once more unto the breach, dear friends', his wife interrupted.

'Oh, for fuck's sake, Richard, you can't do the King properly with a fucking WELSH accent. Henry V was fucking ENGLISH for fuck's sake, hand it over. I'll have to do it.'

Reaching for the book with one hand, she took another glug with the other. But Burton would not hand the book over and there was a tussle and she walked out while he continued, apparently oblivious to her absence, that arousing, skin-tingling voice caressing us for the rest of the evening. My mother was thrilled by the story, which she considered almost as good as Princess Margaret paying me a personal visit. Burton was less star-struck by the experience. That night he wrote up an account of his day at Oxford in his diary.

> 21 November 1975, Oxford. Cheap. Everything very shabby. Clothes (my suit?) cars etc. Students unattractive. Beer warm. Depressing. Glad to get to bed.

I was still officially living in my stepfather's London house during the holidays, escaping across the park at night to James's flat and returning early in the morning, letting myself in stealthily so that my absence should not be discovered. When I left Oxford, although James and I were in love and wanted to move into a place of our own, we did not have the guts to 'live in sin'. Nigel intervened. One night at Sissinghurst after much whisky James and I were turning over with Nigel the options about how I might afford to escape from living at my mother and stepfather's when Nigel passed me a note in red biro. He had written: 'Juliet and James get married.' He was a man who liked neat endings, a parent following in the tradition of free dancing lessons negotiated by Catalina in exchange for her daughter's hand, and the subtle housing contract his grandmother Victoria had made with Young Lionel that ensured her continuing occupation of Knole. Just as his great-grandfather Old Lionel had been satisfied with his daughter Victoria's multi-purposed engagement to Young Lionel, Nigel was pleased about his own proposal to entrust my welfare to a good man whom he knew I loved, solving a financial and accommodation problem and achieving a legal outcome all at the same time. But there was an element of selfishness about his matchmaking. By making himself instigator of the arrangement, he was keeping me under his wing. He was not prepared to entirely relinquish his daughter, confidante and hostess, and for a long time I thought that was a loving, even exemplary way to behave. If the arrangement suited Nigel, it also offered me everything I wanted at the time. In accepting the move designed by my father, I would have a husband I loved, an escape route from my mother and I would make my father happy. Unlike the spirit of independence that motivated Pepita and Vita to loosen their parental ties after marriage, I was not only content but keen to maintain a post-nuptial closeness with my father. As he climbed the stairs to bed I could hear his semi-silent whistle. I handed the note to James and we both burst into tears. The wedding took place the following year.

My father organised everything and gave me away, or at least gave half of me away, at the altar. My mother showed her disapproval, disturbed not only by the lack of title but also by the life of poverty that she was convinced lay ahead of us. She showed little interest in the wedding plans beyond commissioning and paying for the dress that was designed and made by her own smart haute couturiers. At the fittings I became a child again, unassertive, miserable at her joylessness over my approaching marriage. Unlike Victoria at Vita's wedding, Philippa did at least appear, without Robin, at mine, arriving by helicopter, remaining downstairs as I put on my wedding dress upstairs in her old bedroom, alone with her hairdresser. Five minutes before we left for the church, I appeared at the top of the stairs in my expensive, diaphanous, bridal gown. My father was waiting at the bottom. His face fell. The fashionable 1970s absence of a defined waist was not to his conventional taste. 'You aren't going to wear that, are you?' he asked as I descended the stairs and tried to feel bridally beautiful.

With marriage I felt I had arrived at the point of irreversible and invincible grown-upness, the exhilaration of exclusive intimacy in which no one, especially not a parent, could interfere. I would never be treated as a child again. James loved Sissinghurst and my father loved us being there for the weekends. The ballast of becoming a couple even led to an unexpected but welcome easing of my tense relationship with my mother. We had little money but saved for a down payment on a small terraced house in Battersea, managing the mortgage between us. I was working in publishing and James left the discotheque and started an interior decorating company with a friend. He made our house lovely. We invited our friends for tea in our red sitting room, cooked shepherd's pie in the yellow kitchen, ate off a table made out of an old door in the green dining room, bathed in an old Victorian bath in the blue felt-lined bathroom and slept in a creamy bedroom. Our life was as straightforward as the colours that surrounded us and we were happy.

I understood why in her memoir Vita said the first four and a half years of marriage to Harold made her feel 'rescued from everything that was vicious and violent'. My husband and I were embarking on our marriage in a spirit of contented equality.

For me, the excitement wasn't owning the toaster, or the novelty of entertaining in my own home, but more the concentration of affection I received from my husband and the bonus of realising that the partnership of marriage can be like no other relationship. I loved working out problems together, discussing obstacles as well as opportunities. I discovered the fun of planning weekends, holidays, birthdays, Christmases, all of life together; the heady feeling of infinite possibility. I felt as if I had returned to the sanctuary of the baker's cart which had been my refuge as a child, complete with a door James and I could close against a difficult world.

## 10

# Juliet
### Guilt

My mother's second marriage was not working out. She had become frightened of her new husband. He was a busy man with little time for her. She was home alone, bored. The hot air balloon of luxury that might have lifted her up to a carefree heaven had instead lost its appeal and she was drifting slowly earthwards, in houses that were sweltering in temperature and freezing in atmosphere. Her existence became devoid of laughter or even much conversation. And she had begun to drink.

Sarah, her best friend from the old schooldays in Norfolk, would telephone and realise immediately that Philippa was drunk. 'Oh, Pippa,' she would say sadly. 'Don't Pippa me' came the go-away reply. So friends stopped visiting, uncomfortable at the deterioration of a woman who had once been so pretty and so gay. Like Pepita's more than familiar relationships with the local stationmaster Monsieur Béon and the builder Monsieur

Desombre, my mother befriended people who she paid to ask no questions and who would not challenge her. The manicurist and dressmaker would gather for lunch at the house where the air was scented with huge vases of expensive, out-of-season mimosa. Champagne and smoked-salmon sandwiches were served by the butler while the dressmaker convinced her client that she would look lovely in lilac, in navy, in stripes, in spots, in linen, in velvet, while imitating my mother's drunken grimaces behind her back. When the beautiful clothes eventually arrived months later, just in time for the five-day Ascot Race Meeting, protected by sleek grey dust covers imprinted with the 'By Royal Appointment' logo, they hung in her cupboard unworn as she had become unwilling and unable to leave the house.

But in the face of undeniable evidence she denied there was a problem. And we, her children, also became distrustful, avoiding her on the telephone and in person as we all got on with our own lives. We would visit reluctantly, briefly determined to confront her, to save her, but realising as soon as we saw her that there was nothing we could do. She would attribute our hesitant suggestions that we could smell vodka on her breath to the Swiss herbal sweets that she claimed had been relieving her sore throat. In the library, where she sometimes sat all day watching interminable horse racing on television, there was a cupboard containing boxes of expensive mint chocolates, board games and, on the top shelf, one upended, unwashed glass tumbler. Even though the bottle of vodka had been more imaginatively hidden, the purpose of the solitary glass, tucked high above the snakes and ladders box, was impossible to disguise. The indignity of my mother's appearance, old before her time, youth-drained, sometimes injured at ankle or knee from a fall, was shocking. She became bloated and reddened, angry and amnesiac, unloving and unreachable. We would leave her slumped on the sofa, disheartened all over again. She would absent-mindedly fondle the underbellies of her husband's basenjis, sinister dogs deprived of a bark who squirmed with Trappist pleasure under her touch. I would quickly look away.

In moments of lucidity she would call and berate me for being unkind and neglectful. She would regularly announce she had deleted me from her will only to call the following week to say I had been reinstated. Her frustration at my refusal to allow the will to become a bargaining chip between us did not stop her from echoing previous generations who had used money to bribe their independently minded daughters. Victoria, who had loved her baby daughter with such intensity, who had 'hugged her till she screamed', reached a point when she could no longer manipulate Vita with money or jewellery, and was driven through exasperated jealousy to accuse her of selfishness and ingratitude. My mother's threats that she would cut me off held no power. I had heard them too often. I felt that the umbilical link between us had disintegrated beyond the point of repair. For years I had felt her indifference towards me but I did little to address the problem. I did not know then how to look for the reasons that she drank. Only now do I realise that when a daughter floats outside the perimeters of her mother's experience, even a proud mother can feel a mixture of loss, envy and even anger. Only now do I understand the sense of rivalry that I awoke in her, the fear of her own inadequacy, the fear of acknowledging that her daughter loved her other parent more. Only now do I regret with a pain that twists my heart the irritation and cold impatience with which I treated her insecurity and her emotional fragility.

There had been one unsuccessful medical intervention by her GP into her murky, chaotic existence. Philippa agreed without telling anyone in her family to check into a specialist addiction clinic on the King's Road not far from where we had once lived. All street clothes were removed from those who might try and do a runner and exchanged for hospital gowns, but the clinic had no insurance against the theft of fur coats and my mother had arrived swathed in mink. The coat hung on the hook behind her door until the pub opposite opened its doors and she walked in fur-clad and ordered a double vodka. The following day, having been returned to the clinic by the pub and denied any further access to alcohol, she telephoned Adam, said she was in a prison and asked him to come in a taxi at once to rescue her. He had no idea what had been going on and, worried about her, came at once. The responsibility that, as an adult child, I too felt for her was often difficult to handle, just as Victoria had become a burden to her daughter, a person for whom Vita felt both irritation and affection.

Late one cold December evening in London, James and I heard the muted chuckle-throttle of a taxi engine pausing outside our new home in Fulham. My mother stood on the doorstep in the rain in a tightly belted mackintosh, an expression of apology and fear on her face. She was cold and she was sober. Over the next hour she described the depth of her unhappiness. Alcohol was barely mentioned, but she confirmed that underneath the need to numb herself was the sense that she was wasting her life. She felt trapped and useless. She could see where hope lay. On one side were her children, ready to help the moment she asked, and on the other was her husband, stuck in his ways, irascible, intolerant and uninterested. She had become caught between generations, holding on hard to increasingly invalid claims of youthfulness, dyeing her hair, shortening and lengthening her skirts with the changing fashions, and terrified at the ever steeper tilt into old age. All those past decades, a lifetime of being undervalued, had suddenly become too much. In four years' time she would be sixty years old and she wanted to make some changes before it was too late.

I looked at her face, the deflated skin, drooping like an empty pillowcase on a washing line. She seemed old. And exhausted. And lovable in her courageous desperation. For the second time in my life, I thought I glimpsed the vulnerable young woman who my father had met so long ago, a figure unknowable by her daughter but who had once been as real as this older, sadder version. We drank coffee. We listened to her. And as she sat in the safety of our house, she began to breathe more easily. It was as if by taking off her coat and expecting to brave the chill she had instead found warmth. She had come looking for yet another place of refuge and had at last found one that carried with it no penalties, no conditions. We offered to help. We promised we would do anything we could. We meant it. We were quietly hopeful. The taxi driver had switched off his engine and waited. Two hours later I hugged her goodbye and she returned the embrace with a strength that surprised us both. It was, I realised, a strength gained from her courageous admission of vulnerability, and its consequent, fleeting liberation from fear.

Very early the following morning she telephoned. Anything she had said the night before, she instructed me in a flat voice, was to be forgotten and never mentioned again.

In 1984, James and I moved to New York. He had always been ambitious and had recently landed an impressive new job with Savory Milln stockbrokers. The opportunity to cross the Atlantic was too good to ignore and the prospect of a few years in Manhattan was thrilling to us both. Soon after our arrival, Philippa flew over on Concorde to visit us. She had stopped drinking and there had been an advance call from London from my stepfather, perhaps at Philippa's request, to ensure that there would be no sobriety-splintering drinks in the minibar of her suite at the hotel. We filled our own fridge with orange juice. But abstinence for an alcoholic is a struggle without some sort of support, and willpower is an unreliable chaperone. Since her late-night visit to us in London, Philippa had not asked for any help, or ever acknowledged her problems. But it was clear from her shaky hand and nervous conversation that she was teetering. She had lost the confidence that she believed alcohol gave her. There was none of her usual mimicry of people she had met at the airport, on the plane, in the hotel. She was drained of the energy to camouflage her real feelings. I wanted to talk to her but she was terrified of being left alone with me. She made sure there was always someone in the room with us. I could not reach her.

Shortly after Philippa's return to London she began to drink again. She was powerless to stop. All other attempts to find the elusive magic that would put an end to her unhappiness had failed. And she had tried an array of potential spells. There had been husbands, children, clothes, houses and travel. She had tried food, pills, sex, money, status and a restless, unsustained series of short-lived interests. There had been the tapestry-cushion-making phase, the carriage-driving interlude, the fascination for the iguanas indigenous to the Galapagos Islands, the study of fantail pigeons, the training of two Bernese Oberlanders – giant dogs from Switzerland which were a gift from an admirer – the obsession with llamas, the photography fad, the craze for Lipizzaner horses, racing horses and racing demon, as well as the cooking, gardening and shopping habits that came and went throughout her life. Just as Victoria had brought her total commercial inexperience to the impossible venture of her stationery shop, my mother was ready to try anything once, just in case it solved her unhappiness. But none of these interests lasted, except the fuzzing, nurturing, numbing enemy in disguise, the utterly reliable escape-affording power of alcohol.

Separated from her by the Atlantic I would think about her every day. I dreaded her calls, and I dreaded her silence. I worried about her. I was infuriated by her. Each week I wondered if I should go over to London and try to help her. I knew I was abandoning her and guilt urged me to forgive her every-thing and run to her. I had tried before, but maybe not often enough. Any outright confrontation had been met with denial, the Swiss throat sweets taking the rap yet again. I was split between the adult impulse to look after her and the childlike desire for a mother who would love me like other mothers loved their children, a mother who would once have been waiting for me when I returned home from school. I longed for consistency. It was the unpredictability of her behaviour that I found so difficult.

In May 1987 we fought on the telephone. She hung up on me. A week later she went on a cruise, taking with her a friend who watched horrified as my mother threw lavish nightly parties for the crew, supplying them with unlimited champagne and behaving, according to her lovely conventional friend, 'in a manner inappropriate to her position'. She returned home having done irreversible damage to her liver. Within days her skin turned yellow and within a week she was in the intensive care unit of King Edward VII. Her GP rang me in New York. My mother was aware Mrs Thatcher had won the election the day before, and had smiled when she heard the result, but her mind was becoming hazy. If I wished to see her conscious, the doctor said, I should get on the next aeroplane. I went straight to the airport, the copy of *Anna Karenina* that I was reading when the GP called in my bag. But I was too late. She was already in a coma. As she lay in the hospital bed, she was oblivious to my presence.

I went home to Sissinghurst. That day, as my mother lay dying, was a day of drifting disbelief. My father was uneasy, not trusting himself to be alone with me, all the things he wanted to say unsayable in case they reduced us both to a rubble of regrets. Outside he paced the garden, his nervous affectation, the hiss of his idiosyncratic whistle audible through

the open window while I stood defrosting a chicken in the
kitchen. Tiny flakes of ice burned my fingertips as I put the
cold lump of white flesh on a plate by the window through
which a dark pink, deep-smelling rose was curling its new
shoots. My mother died early the next morning. She was fifty-
eight, exactly the same age as her mother was when she died.

My stepfather regarded funerals as a man's business. Women
were not invited to attend such events in his own family. He
had asked my brother to make arrangements for our mother's
service to take place the following day, giving Adam a budget
for the flowers that Robin wanted sent in his name. I stood
with Adam and Rebecca in the front pew at an occasion that
should have been filled with choirs of angels, but the congregation was sparse. James joined me there, having flown over from
New York. My father came from Sissinghurst, his sense of duty,
guilt and real sadness all prompting his appearance at this final
moment. The chauffeurs from London and Hampshire were
there with the cook and butler from London and three of her
oldest friends. The coffin sat on the conveyor belt in front of
me, like a piece of decorated luggage at an airport, almost
invisible beneath an eiderdown of mimosa, the flower that grows
with such freedom and abandon in the South of France. The
sweet powerful scent hovered at the edge of childhood memories and hit the back of my throat. What a waste, I thought.
She won't see it, she won't smell it. Years earlier Philippa had
made a note of a favourite hymn she wanted sung at her funeral.
The thin small chords of the 1930s organ at the Golders Green
Crematorium accompanied words that celebrated the beauty of

'hill and vale and tree and flower'. I tried to sing, twisting her eternity ring on my finger, the ring she had been wearing when she died, three interlocking circles of gold. But when I came to the lines about the joy of human love for 'brother, sister, parent, child', I could not sing. And I could not weep. I wish I had been able to. She had chosen those lines for us, her three children.

After the service, my father went back to Sissinghurst on the train and we children lunched with my stepfather on roast chicken and lemon mousse in his Mayfair dining room. His usual magnum of Perrier-Jouët was sitting in front of him. It was half empty. He had not been at the funeral and asked us no questions about what had taken place. As we sat down, he announced that he did not wish our mother's name to be mentioned nor did he want any talk about the suddenness of her death or any speculation over its cause. Although he did not say so, I knew that she had disrupted his comfortable life, caused him embarrassment and much inconvenience and the less said about the whole thing the better. For him, her death was shameful but a relief and a release.

As soon as I could I left his house and plunged into the lunchtime cacophony of Oxford Street in a state approaching exhilaration. Never again would I feel the guilt of not going to see her, not answering her telephone calls, wishing she would stop, stop, stop, leave me alone, absolve me from daughter-hood. A friend was having a party the following week and, seeking a distraction from the whirl of my mind, I wandered into the crowded, summer sale-time evening-dress department in Selfridges to look for something suitable to wear for a celebration. But I could not find the energy for dresses. Instead, I looked at the other shoppers around me. I suddenly had a premonition of exactly what their faces would one day look like, as a procession of stretched, smooth-sculpted death masks passed by me. I walked out of the shop and back through the London streets on my way to take the train back down to Sissinghurst, trying to pin Mumma-memories down in my mind. They were not good ones. The recent weeks and months and years had been stained dark by her addictive illness. I wanted to think of her as loving, as lovable, but I could not.

And yet I knew that once she had been those things to me, her daughter. I had not forgotten the brief time after she had left my father when she was free-floating, light as air, unweighted by disappointment, her eyes and smile infused with gaiety, lovely to look at, smelling of roses, fallible, lovely and lovable. There was evidence in that photograph of Adam and me holding her hand as we waited for the ship to dock so many years ago, and in the creased envelope now in my desk drawer, marked 'Juliet aged one', containing one white-blonde curl. I thought of how when I was little she would collect me from school wearing a skirt covered in circus animals because she knew the trumpeting elephants and their trunks made me laugh. Over the skirt she wore a coat with buttons the size of crumpets, the breadth of a child's hand.

If we had been closer, if she had allowed me to help her, if I had not felt so abandoned by her, if I had not been so ruthless in my impatience with her, if she had been proud of me, the infinite ifs, if she had not died, then maybe one day I would have been able to help her. I envied the writer Edna O'Brien her impossible, critical mother who eventually confided to her daughter that she prayed 'we shall both be buried in the same grave'.

In my father's diary I found an admission of his guilt, his deficiency as a husband. 'The prime cause of her leaving me was that I never really loved her,' he wrote, perhaps the saddest thing a child can read about her parents, for it was without love that they lived together for so long and perhaps without love that they made their children. For over thirty years my mother's presence, even during her geographical absences, had dominated my life. And for over thirty years I had wanted to be loved by her. Immediately after her death, the secret I feared uncovering most was the one I had suspected for so long: my poor unloved mother had herself never learned how to love. So I left her alone, not mourning her, and never wishing for her return.

In Vita's biography *Pepita*, she works out her feelings for her mother with a clarity that I would covet. Through writing down her impressions so shortly after Victoria's death, Vita fulfilled that impulse to work out her own position within the mother–daughter relationship. She describes how after Victoria's death she managed to look back on her mother's life and gain a new and, by implication, fairer perspective on her, with 'all the silly little irritations fading and the real quality emerging'. I too felt the urgent need to write something down, to try and work out what I felt about *my* mother. But I could not manage it. I think anger got in the way and stifled me. I wanted to feel for my own mother something of the compassion that Vita had displayed for hers. I could not do it then. All these years later I am trying again.

# 11
# Clemmie and Flora
## Forgiveness

One winter's day, three years after our wedding, I had returned to my office after an appointment with the doctor. Long ago, I had made a secret pact with James that I would quit smoking if I ever became pregnant. That afternoon I telephoned him to say that the moment for abandoning cigarettes had arrived. We did not tell anyone else our news for several months. It was the best secret I had ever known.

The two days on which I gave birth to my daughters remain the most precious of my life. I became a mother for the first time in September 1981 in a south London maternity hospital run by nuns. The holy sisters had made an incongruous choice of profession it seemed to me, given their vow of chastity. But theirs was a wonderful decision for us, the beneficiaries of such professional gentleness. As the time for the birth approached in its predictably unpredictable manner, my bed faced a large window through which the light suddenly sharpened on the sycamore leaves in the way it sometimes does when the autumn sun begins its slow descent to the horizon. During the few weeks before my daughter's arrival, I had felt apprehensive about giving her up to the world. The mysterious and intermittent butterfly flickers of the early months had grown into something more definite as I alone knew when my unborn child stirred or, in that wonderful biblical word, 'quickened' deep inside me. I longed for but also feared her emergence, her first breaths of independent existence, and my subsequent inability to keep her safe in the way I had for nine months. This visceral need to protect was shared by James who, within moments of her birth, announced his role as her chief defender at all times, especially from all future unsuitable boyfriends. I knew he had met the first human being he would willingly die for.

My own emotions were unprecedented. They were untethered, unpredictable, switch-backing from elation to the painful intensity of something I did not recognise, a feeling akin to deep grief and yet nothing to do with grief. I felt like a child who laughs so much that she suddenly weeps. I might in some fanciful, absurd way say that the moon shone more brightly, the birds sang more loudly, or even that some hazy sense of spirituality moved into a sharper focus. But it is both simpler and more inexplicable than that. Scientifically or biologically, the relationship of a mother to her child is founded on the utilitarian requirement to preserve new life. But that prosaic definition will not really do. I have never known a purer feeling than motherhood. Or a profounder one. Or a more complex one. Perhaps I had only experienced the same unarticulated feeling of astonishment once before: at the moment of my own birth.

We called our daughter Clementine, Clemmie for short. With her arrival the role that daughterhood had occupied in my life shifted its emphasis. Until then, other than marriage and, to an extent, my professional life, daughterhood had defined me and identified me. During my parents' lifetimes, whether I was rebelling or seeking their approval, they had both, in their different ways, remained my first point of reference. But with motherhood I reached a point of clarity; my daughter joined my husband as the pivots of my emotional life.

When Flora was born in New York in March 1985, three months after our arrival there, in a hospital two blocks from our apartment, James brought a case of twelve miniature bottles of champagne and a huge bunch of paper-white narcissi smelling of spring, of having come through a harsh winter, of arrival, of beginnings. Clemmie came to visit, the unexpected gift of having her own sister illuminating her three-year-old face. It is an expression that endures, matched by that of Flora herself and one with which I remain profoundly familiar. At the hospital, the new mother in the bed next to me was married to a man who owned a pizza parlour. Breathing in the perfume of the delicate white flowers and the scent of my baby daughter's skin, I shut out the spicy odour of Margherita and pepperoni that suffused our little ward. When I arrived home the following day, I gazed at my baby asleep in her cot, the sight of her so perfectly beautiful, transforming the hard edges of sadness at being far from home. With Flora's arrival, the completing, deepening, blessed sense that motherhood brings and never leaves was re-enforced once again.

As children and adults all settled into the challenge of ex-patriot lives, New York became a tale of two cities. There was Downtown for work and there was Uptown for motherhood. James worked in his high-flying stockbroking office on Wall Street in the shadow of the Twin Towers, I got a job in Union Square at a small, distinguished publishing house, Clemmie went to a school near the river on the Upper East Side and Flora stayed at home in the care of the nanny. Manhattan was in some ways a strange, unsettling, even unsuitable backdrop in which to bring up daughters in the 1980s. Adult society was in turmoil. Alarming articles appeared in the press about the new illness that was ripping through the drug-using and homosexual male communities although New York's gay bathhouses were still operating at full swing. A transvestite club in the meatpacking district carried the innocent symbol of a woman in a ball gown on the door to the ladies' loo. But when the door swung open a bank of urinals confronted you, complete with a line of bare male bottoms, their skirts bunched around their waists. Vietnam vets packed the bar, still twitching and shuddering with post-traumatic stress, chain-smoking and cradling their tumblers of neat Scotch. Listless, gum-chewing taxi drivers waited outside the club, their engines ticking over hoping for a fare. To alleviate the boredom they sometimes became customers themselves, winding down their windows to allow a stilettoed blond, his five o'clock shadow showing through thick foundation, to bend down into the well of the driver's seat, taking half a minute to effect a fleeting pleasure. But the fear and rumours about this rampaging 'plague' that was running through the gay community, and for which there was no known cure, gathered momentum as an increasing number of cases were diagnosed and the notorious bathhouses were closed a year after we arrived. The HIV virus that led to the fatal condition of Aids was transmitted through an exchange of bodily fluids and through virus-carrying drug syringes. Manhattan binmen refused to collect the rubbish for fear of picking up used heroin needles and becoming infected. Restaurants covered their loo seats with disposable cling-film covers. The shared cup containing communion wine was shunned at altar rails. Everyone knew someone who knew someone who had died of the illness but few of the victims' families, or public relations companies representing movie stars like Rock Hudson, would admit it. Homosexuality in heart-throbs was bad for the box office. The physical ravages of Aids were impossible to miss. Skeletal appearances due to weight loss were sudden and dramatic. Talk at the altar rail concluded that mankind had somehow offended his Maker. If sex and heroin had been the infecting culprits, liver cancer and rheumatoid arthritis became the convenient substitutes for denial and shame. The atmosphere and the media coverage of the epidemic fluctuated between censorship and fear until 1986, when a British advertisement showing a granite tombstone engraved with the single word 'Aids' and the strapline 'Don't die of ignorance' promoted awareness of how the virus could be avoided and made international headlines.

The health of the financially successful seemed as precarious as that of the sexually promiscuous. High up in the glittering skyscrapers of Wall Street and behind the portered doorways to Park and Fifth and Madison Avenues' elegant apartment buildings lay riches beyond most people's wildest dreams. At a birthday dinner party on Black Monday in October 1987, a personal butler stood impassively behind each woman's seat. A dozen black-suited bankers craned across their wives to analyse the news of the apocalypse. The world's stock markets had crashed and on that day $500 billion had been lost from the Dow Jones Index. We wives, irrelevant and invisible, emptied our glasses; the butlers leaned forward and refilled them; we drained them yet again. Bread must have accompanied the wine at this last affluent supper, but none of these twelve disciples of the Wall Street ticker tapes nor their wives were conscious of eating. Several hours later, twelve inebriated women swayed precariously from the room as if they too were about to crash to the floor along with the markets.

James and I had been fortunate to find an apartment for our family just a few yards from Central Park, the 843 acres of Midtown Manhattan given over to nature, for so long a source of such pride to the citizens of New York. But the park had begun to lose its green-grassed innocence and acquire sinister associations. In the early morning and late evening, in rain and in sun, the city's population of committed joggers swept past with their fluid movement and toned limbs, running from the beds of their high-achieving, muscle-taut lovers to their office desks beside other high-achieving work-addicted colleagues. In late August 1986, one of these amateur athletes was strangled in the park just behind the huge bulk of the Metropolitan Museum of Art by a former choirboy, the young girl's murder in this safe place shocking the city and putting a nervous acceleration into every runner's step. During the daytime, the open spaces of the park became the resource of the very old and the very young. Old men sat on the benches in groups of two and three, clutching half-bottles of Scotch wrapped in brown paper and discussing unintelligible profundities, while private nurses in immaculate white trouser suits and matching plimsolls slid wheelchairs past them, the frail skull-like faces of the nonagenarian occupants grotesque in misapplied lipstick and blusher. Young children were pushed on the swings by parents and nannies who were warned not to go anywhere near the tame-looking squirrels that reeled their way round the trunks of the chestnut oaks, high on discarded heroin paraphernalia. Near the boating lake, the larger-than-life-size statue of Alice in Wonderland, onto whose bronze lap the children of many decades had climbed, continued to welcome a new generation, among them my daughters, into her comfortable embrace. Alice was a talisman of security in an uncertain world.

But children are infinitely flexible, and if the imagery of my daughters' childhood setting seemed to me at times to resemble a distorted and fantastic Boschian landscape, they took to it in a way I never quite could. My daughters were united in their tolerant familiarity with the eclectic bunch of individuals who populated our urban lives. The brownstone adjoining our apartment was owned by a man with a past. He had once been a respected art dealer and had made a great deal of money. But now he used his prime real estate to house pigeons. There were dozens of them. We could see them through the windows flying around the high-ceilinged rooms as if trapped in a grim fairy tale, and when the man emerged we tried not to stare at the pale grey feathers that clung to his dark, shit-splattered coat. Around the corner, a smiley, bearded, homeless Jamaican with an incongruous, brand-new Mont Blanc pen jotted down poems on a notepad. Complimenting the coiffured, lacquered ladies who emerged from the shiny red door of the Elizabeth Arden salon, he invited rather than implored them to part with a hundred dollars, his charm often proving irresistible.

We had been living in New York far longer than the two years we had originally intended. James was now working for Deutsche Bank and I had been given new responsibilities at the publishing company. My daughters were growing up. They became androgynous New York children, living in jeans and off Chinese take away. They knew the names of baseball stars, collected the all-the-rage miniature felt animals that made up the Sylvanian families, learned about the Native American princess Pocahontas and about Martin Luther King and spoke with American accents. The avenues around us teemed with headline-making personalities. When Woody Allen brought his cameras to film at the bottom of our street he invited a star-struck Clemmie and her friends into his trailer for orange juice and autographs. Flora reported that she had spotted the fugitive writer Salman Rushdie concealed from the fatwa in the shadows of the hotel two doors down. They were both intrigued by the tall dark figure of Claus von Bülow. The notorious former lawyer, recently at liberty after successfully appealing against his conviction for the attempted murder of his heiress wife Sunny, hurried in his modish, mobbish, leather jacket past the little knot of journalists that waited outside his apartment. Every morning, we ate crispy bacon and glazed doughnuts for breakfast in the local diner, before the yellow bus took the girls across the park to their new co-ed school. John McEnroe and his movie-star wife Tatum O' Neal added a frisson of stardust to the morning by turning up to wave their children off at the bus stop. Tom Wolfe's *Bonfire of the Vanities* had lit up the best-seller lists while its author strode the streets around us in his man-for-all-seasons white suit. My daughters knew every slab of pavement between our apartment and the park as well as I had known the London pavements between my own school and home in Chelsea. They considered themselves New Yorkers.

In order to compensate for what felt like the over-sophistication of city living and to give our daughters something of the rural upbringing that James and I had both loved, we found an old brick house in upstate New York, not far from the border with Massachusetts. We made a lovely weekend life there for ourselves, with camps in the woods, makeshift bridges over streams, starry nights under canvas, newborn lambs in the meadows and grey-bearded beavers in their riverside burrows. We were surrounded by fields of high-growing sweetcorn through which a gentle wind swept, sounding like a church congregation rising to its feet. These were all elements that contributed to our idea of what we wanted for their childhood. And despite the paint-blistering heat of the summers and the windowpane-cracking cold of the winters and a cellar where dead bodies had once been laid when the earth was too hard to dig a grave, we some-times felt as if we belonged. My daughters' memories of eating wild blueberries picked from the hedgerows, playing cowboys and Indians, cycling across the cornfields to the nearby lake, exploring the dark and dusty outhouses where 'the chair lady' stacked her second-hand furniture, barbecuing freshly picked ears of corn and catching fireflies at dusk on the bank of the little stream, return them even today to what Flora calls 'the absurd beauty of that place'. The brick house remains a capsule of an American childhood that they both now consider to have been idyllic.

But I did not feel I was getting things right. My determination not to repeat the mistakes that had made parts of my own childhood difficult was not succeeding. I was always leaving my daughters. Just like my mother. When we lived in London I had left the house each morning to go to work, earning enough to pay for Clemmie's nanny, the substitute for my maternal presence. Chugging and swerving along the streets on my moped towards my desk in Covent Garden, I was exhilarated by my office life, but always urged the bike to return faster on the homeward journey. The pattern was repeated in New York; work for the parents, nannies for the children. The nannies themselves were a mixed bunch, some wonderful, a few less so. The arrangement began well with the loving and steady Janet and Linda. After their lamented departures, the turnover became disturbingly rapid. Angela confessed after her short-lived presence in our family that her unexplained exhaustion and the curiously tousled state of my bed when I arrived home on Tuesdays was the result of her weekly lunchtime rendezvous with the dry-cleaning delivery boy. Harriet was no better, tyrannising us all with her icy beauty and superiority, her taste for champagne and banker boyfriends. Jake, an experimental male nanny, admitted within a week that he had a problem with his boyfriend and his haemorrhoids. He left after I informed him that the job did not come with either medical or therapeutic insurance. Finally we found Eglute, a joy of an eccentric eighteen-year-old and a favourite with us all, even though behind my back she taught the girls to swear effortlessly in her native Lithuanian. Old ladies in the park were charmed, unaware that these two little blonde Lithuanian angels were cooing fluent filth over their beloved terriers.

There is little I would not exchange now for the chance to start again, abandon the job, abandon the nannies, and immerse myself for a while in my daughters' young lives. And yet I wanted to work. My sense of myself was that I functioned as a professional woman. I faced a conundrum. I wanted to stay at home and look after the children myself, unlike my mother. And I wanted to go out to work, unlike my mother. In order to try and have everything, I made a bargain with my conscience that I had established a balance that suited us all and which fitted in with the modern way of life. The pay-off for heading Downtown to the office was the reassurance that unlike my own mother I was giving my daughters a blueprint for financial independence, intellectual stimulation, society's respect, an emancipated life, something that they might one day emulate. And yet by leaving my children in the paid care of another, I risked accusations and suffered the guilt of abandonment. And I missed being with them. The choice remained a hard one. I swung between the options with metronomic regularity, reaching one extremity and then being pulled inexorably back to the other. While I rejoiced that professional opportunities for which

Catalina had fought so hard for her daughter had opened up so easily for me, I found the decision about how much time to give to work or home challenging.

The children seemed fine. And they had each other when neither James nor I were around. They were a team, a sisterhood, finding in each other their own best and most secure confidante, sharing a private bond through which parenthood could not permeate. Anxiety was not their burden but mine. I felt that although I could hear my children I was not listening to them: present but at the same time absent. Aunt Pun, the mother of our nanny Shirley, had demonstrated to us years ago how a mother's love should be done. Shirley herself had demonstrated to us how it should be done. I indulged my children but was indulgence the same as love? Being allowed to watch television for as long as they wished, to go to bed at a time of their own choosing, made them feel uneasy and insecure. The extravagant presents I brought back after a two-day work trip and the pizza delivered for supper every night of the week lost the thrill of rarity. Leniency and extravagance were not antidotes to negligence. The father of some friends spoke to his children in the tone of a sergeant major. Clemmie announced she would like to be spoken to in the same way. She craved such a display of discipline. She did not remember ever feeling so envious.

Gradually our marriage lost its footing. James and I had married young and as we grew up and our own separate interests developed we had drifted apart. I was hopeless at feigning interest in the financial world that became increasingly important and absorbing for him. And I allowed my own relationships with my work colleagues to become all-consuming and excluding. There was increasingly little overlap in James's and my social lives. I would take the girls home to England in the holidays as often as I could and I had begun to dread boarding the return plane to America. While the participants who remain in a failing marriage are responsible for sustaining the slow and painful collapse, their children can only watch, bracing themselves for another argument, another door slammed, another edgy meal. Feuding parents invite divided loyalty, often unintentionally, but while carrying an assumption that it is legitimate to ask a child to be their message bearer. Vita had known what that felt like. I had known what that felt like. And now our own children were being submitted to the same experience.

And then I discovered a way to cheer myself up. Alcohol. Although the cause of my mother's death remained raw and salutary, for some inexplicable or cruelly genetic reason, I confused the identical poison with curative medicine. At first I succeeded well in cohabiting with my new habit, certain that I knew how to manage it, adamant that its powerful attraction would not become addictive. And for a while I controlled my intake well enough to hold down my job, but only just. The compulsion to drink became more and more difficult to disguise. There was a sign that I always seemed to end up facing as I strap-hung on the subway on my way to work each morning on the packed rush-hour trains. It had been put up by an alcohol concern charity. 'Alcohol will rob you of your job, your friends, your family, your life,' it warned. I would silently tick off each category on my fingers, relieved that so far all four were intact. At least that is what I told myself.

I have thought a great deal about the wisdom of writing about my struggle with alcoholism, and for many years had decided it was better to keep it private. My grandmother's relationship with another woman was, during her lifetime, hushed up by many and verged on the non-mentionable. And when the decision to publish Vita's confession in *Portrait of a Marriage* was criticised by reviewers, commentators and even friends, Nigel was deeply disturbed by the accusations of disloyalty to his parents. But he never failed to stress that Vita herself had hoped that her memoir might one day help others going through the same emotions as herself, over an issue that society in general found shameful and in some cases illegal. Vita had written that she believed that one day 'such connections will to a very large extent cease to be regarded as merely unnatural and will be understood far better', and that 'the spirit of candour which one hopes will spread with the progress of the world' would lead to recognition, if not quite full acceptance, of both female and male homosexuality. My father also received dozens of letters from people grateful to him for his decision and for having the courage to face up to the criticism. I resolved to write about my own secret only after consulting those who I love most and who had been hurt most by my drinking. It is only with their support and agreement that I do so now. While there are few taboo subjects remaining, several are still misunderstood and fenced in by stigma. If my own experience with one of them offers hope, even to just one individual who might be in despair about this mental and physical dependency, then for me, the decision to write about it will have been justified.

During the weekends at the brick house, my family found

the intrusive, character-changing power of drink increasingly difficult to ignore. And within an alarmingly short time alcohol had become my first resort, my hereditary drug of choice, the default option so frequently chosen by women in my family who had struggled with life. At the brick house escape became the dominant activity. My daughters would escape together to their hideouts, my husband would escape to the garden, to isolation with a book, to visit neighbours, and I would escape to the dubious companionship and numbing comfort of the vodka bottle. And then people at work began to notice that I was frequently late for meetings, that I forgot things, that I was an unreliable employee.

Eventually our daughters, by then aged eleven and eight, with heartbreaking calmness, courage and wisdom, confronted us, their parents, and suggested it was time we stopped fighting. And eventually I too found the courage to ask James if I could take our daughters home to live with me in England. With a generosity of spirit for which I shall always be grateful, he agreed. But even after our return and when our marriage was officially ended in a soulless London courtroom, I continued to struggle. My obsession with drink and continued inability to control it obscured what I wanted to be my main focus: providing a happy home for Clemmie and Flora. It is the period of my life of which I am most ashamed. I felt inadequate, a large-toothed, huge-nosed, divorcee. A long erosion of self-confidence, of never being quite up to the mark, a tendency to give up, of being a Little Miss Can't, finally took its toll. I felt like a failure, just as I now realise my mother had felt. Maybe, especially during the lonely despair of the war, this was how

Vita had felt, how Victoria felt as her own marriage ended and how, in the isolating claustrophobia of Arcachon, Pepita might have felt too. Once I went to a dinner party, determined that a social life of sorts must go on. But I could think of nothing to say to those strangers sitting either side of me, and as they turned away in search of more lively companions, I resorted to counting the petals on the fresias in front of me, staring at dining-room tables all over again.

Much of the time I could not bear to think. To think was to feel and to feel was painful and so I obliterated conscious thought. There were incidents – forgotten dates, humiliating behaviour in front of my daughters' school friends, indiscretions revealed, whispered asides by dismayed friends to restaurant waiters not to top up my glass. And there was an occasion of real embarrassment when, as my father's guest, I interrupted the distinguished speaker at a swanky charity dinner by clinking my spoon on my empty glass, asking the speaker to shut up and let us get on with the party. And then I fell unconscious, awakening with a start as my nose grazed the surface of my soup. The humiliation was almost complete. But still I could not stop drinking.

I used to work out how long I had left to live, conscious that women on my mother's side of the family did not survive beyond the age of fifty-eight. I did not want to die before my father but I knew I would. I wondered which of my friends would be at my funeral. I began to avoid sleeping on my right-hand side. The pressure on my damaged liver was so painful that every twinge confirmed what I already knew. After a doctor's appointment and a blood test for an unrelated complaint, I was told that only 10 per cent of my liver was still functioning. I was tipping over the edge. I did not make any more doctors' appointments. And I continued to drink. My mind and its mental addiction were indivisible from my body and its physical dependency. The whole thing was me. I was a mess. I wondered what the point of me was. I was exhausted by the singing, dancing act that had for so long concealed the truth. Just as my mother's performance as a mimic gave way at the end of her life, so my ability to maintain a charade of normality collapsed. I was attracted by darkness, embarking on a long, slow leave-taking from life, creeping into my bed during daylight hours, closing down, retreating into the embryonic state in which I would be responsible for no one, least of all myself. The act of curling into a physical ball of smallness, once a position of comfort, became one of defence, diminishing my exposure to life.

The guilt that I feel now about putting my children through what I myself had experienced remains sharp-edged whenever my memory rubs up against it. After three years of watching my mental and physical deterioration, and of trying to help in every way they could think of, my brother and sister-in-law had seen enough. Sympathy was not working. I remember the day when Adam told me that he and Sarah, who had been so supportive for so long, no longer cared what I did. The tone of his voice was stern. I could choose to do something about my drinking or I could choose not to. It was up to me. But if I continued to drink, he made it explicit that the authorities would consider my fitness as a mother and without any doubt the custody of my children would be removed from me. My own survival and my relationship with my children depended on making the right choice but I alone could make it. Adam and Sarah hoped, I realise now, that claiming to be indifferent to my behaviour, coupled with the warning of the consequences of my addiction might be the paradoxical solution. My brother still loved me but this was a new sort of love, the tough variety, as tough for him and Sarah as for me. Their courageous decision to concentrate their concern not on me but on my children was painful for them. Friends and relations strongly advised them not to interfere. But unlike Harold, who flunked any such confrontation with Vita when she began to drink excessively, my brother and sister-in-law were undeterred.

Some mothers in my family had not chosen survival. My own mother had given up in middle age. Victoria, a little older, had also eventually retreated to self-pitying and angry isolation. Any urge to fight had left them both. I felt I was genetically woven into repetitive surrender and did not know if I had the courage or the strength to snap the thread and interrupt the pattern. I had arrived at a midway point in my life, tempted to look reassuringly backwards to what I knew, instead of forward towards something different and possibly alarming. But Adam and Sarah had made me see things differently. The importance and fragility of my family had never been clearer, the lessons I had learned from my mother about what *not* to do were all of a sudden invaluable. At the heart of the whole thing were my daughters. At last I realised I did not want to die, not because of me but because of my love for them. How could I abandon them as I once had been abandoned? Adam and Sarah's forever un-repayable act of salvation was in making me understand that there *was* a solution, that help was available but only to those who ask for it, and because of them I made the biggest decision of my life. I asked.

I went to a treatment centre in London where I met Aly. She was a divorcee, like me. And the mother of two daughters, like me. She had become dependent on alcohol, like me. And she wanted to be immersed in the lives of her children whom she loved very much, just like me. Giving each other the courage to try to change, Aly and I had joined a group of wise people who showed us by their own example how to live without alcohol, taking it a day at a time, and leaning on each other for encouragement. Whenever I wobbled, daunted by the task ahead of me, Aly propped me up. And I did the same for her. We have continued that way ever since and I would be lost without her wisdom, friendship and love. With the additional and invaluable advice of Trish, a woman who taught me that, with courage, no personal challenge is insuperable, I discovered that the daily process of deciding not to drink was itself empowering. I knew I could always change my mind tomorrow but each day, as I faced the decision, I chose to stay sober, just for that day. And gradually I felt the stigma of shame at my past behaviour lift as it was replaced with an unfamiliar self-respect.

Sobriety returned me to life. It also brought some other changes of perspective that I had not been prepared for. The first and best thing was seeing how happy it made Clemmie and Flora. They were now aged fifteen and twelve and at last, as my unnerving unpredictability was exchanged for reliability, I began to trust myself not to let them down. I also found that a whole range of experiences, hearing the sound of a cathedral organ, walking through fallen leaves in the autumnal woods at Sissinghurst, did not and probably never had needed the enhancement of a drink to improve them. An ache of sadness in the throat, the draining of saliva at moments of fear, the accelerated heart race of excitement, those times of elation, what Vita called the 'flaring days' of self-confidence, were not only intact but purer and deeper for the lack of any artificial boost. And the absence of shame, of the compulsion to lie, of guilt, of the fear of being caught, brought instead a sense of peace.

I am grateful to be living at a time when much, though not all, of society considers the admission of vulnerability to be courageous. In so many ways I benefit from a kinder, more compassionate society than my mother had done, Vita had done, Pepita had done. I did not tell my father that I had finally addressed my problem. I wanted to be sure that I could sustain my abstinence before I felt confident that my past behaviour was truly in the past. I wanted to make sure that I had allowed the stain of that old behaviour to fade. For five years the subject of drink and the incident at the charity dinner were not mentioned, but one morning when we were having breakfast at the kitchen table, he reached across and put his hand over mine just as he used to do when I was a child. And he left it there. 'I am proud of you,' he said quietly.

Other relationships were readjusted too. Even though James's and my marital storm had blown and gusted for a while, the years after our divorce and my recovery were accompanied by a new and enduring calm. It doesn't prevent me from wishing the unhappiness that preceded it had never happened, but our separation and divorce had a paradoxical effect of reconciliation and of providing a united stability for our daughters. When James married again, he and his wife continued to live abroad. And when eventually they sent their two daughters to boarding school in England, they asked me to act as their daughters' official guardian, an invitation that confirmed the restoration of trust, an invitation that I was honoured to accept.

My daughters would spend part of their holidays with James at the much-loved brick house in America. But when they were in England, Sissinghurst was the place of safety for us all. During these years I loved being my father's daughter, happy that my own children were getting to know him so well. We lived a lot by old habits. 'In the olden days,' he would begin, prompting fake groans. The telephone was still 'a modern miracle' to him, even though his grannyma had discovered its benefits exactly a century earlier. He never went out without a jacket and tie, a blue-biro splodge staining the breast pocket, yesterday's soup in evidence in the middle of his red-and-blue Guards tie. The central heating would be turned off as soon as the spring equinox turned, whatever the temperature outside. On chilly days a terrifying electric fire left over from the war, with grey wire filaments bursting from their springs like an untamed head of curly hair, would be switched on within inches of his already singed trouser turn-ups. If his new book was not going well, his foot would jiggle beneath the desk, brushing against the deep waste-paper basket. The sound of chinking glass betrayed a half-finished bottle of sherry hidden among the discarded pages.

The Ovaltine and Bovril drinks of his schooldays were still considered a bedtime treat. When we had guests, the menus reflected a lifelong wartime nostalgia as my schoolgirl repertoire of macaroni cheese and chocolate mousse was expanded at his request to incorporate steak and kidney pudding and kedgeree. But when we were alone, we would eat curries from a box, the desiccated ingredients packed in little paper envelopes to which you added boiling water. After the girls had gone to bed I would sit with him for hours, trays on our knees, in the room where I had learned the facts of life and where my mother had smoked her golden packets of cigarettes. And we would talk. We talked a lot about love and marriage, and he confided in me his sense of failure and once, with considerable pride, that during his marriage he had slept with a prostitute. He listened to my stories. He was the best listener.

But although he was often sympathetic he could also be unkind. My persistent lack of self-belief and fear of trying anything new infuriated him, and he continued to hurl the childhood accusation that I was a 'Little Miss Can't'. If he thought my current affairs knowledge was hazy, or if I contradicted him about a political issue, he would quote an appropriate line of Shakespeare or Shelley at me that I invariably failed to recognise. Occasionally he would lose his temper when I objected to the many prejudices he had inherited from his parents. There were bursts of anti-Semitism even though his business partner was Jewish. He found any mention of homosexuality between men or women distasteful. He never forgave the Germans. He worshipped John Major. 'Do you not understand that John Major is the greatest prime minister since

Churchill?' he said before the 1997 election as I argued the case for Tony Blair. For all of Nigel's bohemian upbringing and his falling-out with Bournemouth East, he remained a Tory throughout his life. Doors were slammed and mutual sulks followed and I cancelled a non-refundable prepaid joint trip abroad. He undermined me where I felt weakest and most vulnerable, indulging in the old critical misogynistic habits to which he had subjected my mother.

But he never criticised the girls. They could do no wrong. They adored him and he them, the whistle and hum of his favourite songs that had been familiar to me from childhood now part of their own hummable repetoire too. We all knew that the sound of Nigel singing about a bright golden haze on the meadow between mouthfuls of breakfast cornflakes indicated his contentment. Clemmie and Flora began to know and love the house and the garden, and they became as familiar with the paths through the woods, the swing tree, the bronze leaf-dense floor beneath the ancient beeches, and the tiny cemetery devoted to Vita's dogs as I was. They absorbed the historical romance of the Kentish Weald around us, transitory, unselfconscious Orlando figures, wearing flat caps, carrying walking sticks. They too became the beneficiaries of Nigel's particular sort of history-telling. 'Can we go on an expedition?' they would ask and off we would go in his white Mercedes, the successor to the Vanden Plas, bought second-hand in immacu-late condition with a windfall, an acquisition instantly regretted, soon dented and scraped, the seats sticky with barley-sugar wrappers. 'Expeditions' to the nearby fourteenth-century moated castle at Bodiam included shooting arrows through the slits in its four rickety towers. An 'expedition' to the side nave at Canterbury Cathedral involved peering at the ancient stone floor for evidence of the bloodstains of 'poor murdered' Thomas à Becket, searching for the place where in his play T. S. Eliot said that 'good and evil in the end become confounded'. On other days we stood in a Sussex field among munching cows who were quite oblivious, he said, to the fact that the rich grass beneath their feet, freckled with cowslips, owed its deliciousness to the rotting bodies of a thousand soldiers who had lain there since 1066. He encouraged his granddaughters to wince as an imaginary arrow destined for King Harold flew instead straight towards their own eyes, and to shake their heads in sympathy and say 'Poor King Hadji' just as I had once done.

Nigel would come up and visit us in London once we'd settled there, his briefcase with its missing handle carried under his arm like a woman's evening clutch bag. I would watch him from the window walking along the street towards our front door and hear that tuneless whistle, ever-nervous before a social encounter of any kind, even one with a daughter and her children. The girls went to a day school, round the corner from our new home, a little terraced house in Chelsea, and we all began to settle into this new city life. The spirit of our own house depended on this new small unit that had emerged intact after several years of upheaval. The house became the refuge for a dislocated, tightly bonded, even formidable threesome, a house full of daughters. The walls were not pink but some felt they might as well have been. It was a cross-generation household that felt empowered. We had all begun to grow up. I began a new career in journalism, and embarked on writing my first book, with the encouragement of Adam. The girls were happy in their schools. The smell of tobacco seeped out from beneath the closed bathroom door. Music filled the stairwell from the basement to the attic. Bedroom walls were covered in phone numbers and doodles and half-remembered quotes for exams. Boys arrived in our lives. The experience was new and enjoyable, partly because I did not know how to or, more importantly, wish to judge them. Boys were different. They were less critical. They were less focused on the detail. They ate more. They laughed at my jokes. They were all adorable. And then my daughters went away to university and the dishwasher at home would still only be half full at the end of the week. Once I baked a cake and forgot about it, only finding it charred and abandoned in the redundant oven two months later when they returned for the holidays. And then we sold our daughter-house as I moved away to live in the country and they went to share flats in London with girlfriends. I left my daughters that day, the day our home became someone else's home, watching as they disappeared into the Underground and I stood above on the street trying and failing not to show that I knew this was another moment, a parting, and a loosening of the structure of our lives.

After a while I met Charlie, a man who was prepared to put his trust in me, and I discovered how it is possible to learn from the mistakes of the past, blessed to find such a deep and enduring happiness. As my daughters formed adult relationships of their own I hoped we would be able to preserve our mother–daughter closeness while allowing the boundaries necessary for independence to be recognised and respected. I wanted to achieve that balanced state described so perceptively by Susie Orbach as 'a world without the loss of their intimacy and without the burden of the daughter carrying the mother's unmet desires'.

Ten years after we returned to live in England, my active relationship with alcohol hopefully in the past forever and that with my children and Charlie embedded in certainty, I faced the inevitable change that I had dreaded all my adult life. Waking up at Sissinghurst in my attic bedroom, beneath the protection of Vita's golden angel on its plinth above my bed where it had sat since Hadji had given it to me after Vita's death, I would always listen for the sound of my father's radio downstairs, sinking back reassured onto my pillow when I heard the beeps signalling the top of the hour and the news being read. Silence was an aberration I was not yet prepared for. The leukaemia came upon him gradually, a weakness in the knee, a slowness in his walk, a faltering when climbing aboard a boat in Ireland which would previously have set him no challenge. He passed each incident off as arthritis. But this unprecedented fallibility did not yet deter him from continuing to work, to write reviews, to complete an index for a new edition of his father's letters. Articles, bills and receipts were all filed neatly away in the grey cabinets outside his writing room. He was setting things in order. I tried not to think about what all this preparation was for.

And then one February morning his physical strength gave way. After his illness was diagnosed we knew he would not recover. During his last few months, his existence narrowed to a distillation as well as a reflection of the way he had responded to life as various adjustments to his room were made. An abstract painting by Flora, a red-and-blue block of colour, was propped beside his bed, as was a framed print of his favourite old portrait, Gainsborough's *Mr and Mrs Andrews*. The television set was brought from downstairs and took up its position on the chest of drawers. He loved watching television, always marking up the *Radio Times* at the beginning of the week so he could plan his evening viewing. And this was 2004, the year of the Summer Olympics in Athens, and the combination of athletic beauty and a backdrop of his favourite city on earth was his televisual ecstasy.

Although he struggled on for eight months, he never went downstairs again or out into the garden that lay just below his window. Possibly the physical weakness that prevented him from walking there on his own was too distressing to acknowledge. Maybe he chose to save himself from the pain of saying goodbye to a place he had known and loved almost all his life. Or perhaps he could not bear to remember that he was dying in a place so vitally alive. But even though we failed to persuade him to go outside, he welcomed the arrival in his room of a bunch of miniature narcissi, or two or three grape hyacinths in a sherry glass. Early on in those bedridden days the scent of these spring flowers brought for him the promise of new life, and for us, hope. Beside his bed sat a series of tiny vases, the sort that my grandmother used to keep on her writing desk when she wanted to study a single stem for its shape, colour or its perfume. My father's favourites were aquilegia, with their jester caps of every colour, and the creamy Madame Alfred Carrière, the first rose Vita had planted in the garden. As autumn approached he clung to the fading fruits of the summer. Quinces and Kentish cobnuts, blackberries and mushrooms held no appeal for him, but three raspberries popped in the mouth seemed, at least for a day or two, to contain a life-giving elixir. As this almost imperceptible closing-down persisted, I began to believe it would never end. There were still so many signs of a future. Within dying there is still so much living. We talked for hours, the restrictions imposed by the need to meet a train, take a telephone call, catch the post, all lifted by a falsely luxuriant sense of endless time. With this concentration of pleasure came expressions of regret, experiences he would now never have, places he would never visit. And allied with the regrets came a new honesty.

Sex, that most encompassing of all sensory experiences, when the hippocampus, the part of the brain that stores the senses, is provoked into such total response, remained for my father unsatisfyingly mysterious, even somehow shameful. The early embarrassing lessons learned from Olga, the one-off visit to the prostitute, the self-admonishment confided in his diary years later about his inadequate performance with my mother and the whole strange confusion that arose from his parents' physically unorthodox relationship had their consequences. Confined to his single, starchy-sheeted bed, he confessed that he had loved too often but never too well. Even then he continued to be as self-conscious and inhibited as ever, flinching apologetically if someone crossed the line and stroked his hand, yet occasionally ruffling my hair when I bent to kiss him on the cheek as he used to do when I was a child. At the end of his life, he admitted that he had been unable to follow his own advice to me about the three all-consuming passions. This failure took on huge importance for him during those final months; and as he spoke with a new openness, he wept for what might have been, for what should have been, lamenting that he had finally run out of chances to start all over again.

I pitied him, recalling then the urgency of a meeting long ago with someone I loved at a railway station in a small town in the South of France, and a much more recent moonlit swim in the warm waters of the Mediterranean, the start of my new romance. And now, as I remember those days at my father's bedside, when he lamented his lost opportunities, I think how lucky I was not very long ago to walk with my new husband along a pathway of hollyhocks towards pillows of roses and peonies plumped on the window ledges in a country churchyard. I am blessed knowing that I will not share my father's regrets.

During those dying months, the days grew at first warmer and the daylight hours stretched far into the evening, before the autumn cool and shadows took their place. My daughters and I would gather in the corridor outside my father's room, looking out of the window towards the garden, our arms around one another, forming a ring of silent weeping.

Birth and death are the only human experiences that defy a first-hand account. But I knew what the absence of a person could do to those left behind. On my return to London from America I had made friends with a poet, a man formerly much given to reading aloud but who had recently been diagnosed with cancer of the larynx and was desolate about the loss of his voice. He died one evening during the winter, the funeral held on a peculiarly English day when an eiderdown of clouds hung above us like sodden silk. The waiting grave faced the gentle undulation of the South Downs, the bare line of hills interrupted only by three trees, beautiful in their silhouette against the heavy sky. Those of us who had gathered to show our love for this poet stood in silence and at the moment the coffin was lowered into the earth a sudden beam of light arrowed through the cloud. In the silence, and spotlit by the sun, three horses emerged from behind the trees and galloped across the horizon. As they disappeared, the long wintry shadows disappeared too and then the sun vanished behind the clouds. And then I understood the permanence of death.

Julia Samuel, my friend and a woman who understands bereavement better than anyone I know, had suggested that grief, such a small word and yet an iceberg of a word, feels like fear, her perceptiveness helping me through those days. And then in my father's final hours of consciousness something miraculous happened to ease that fear. All of his physical reticence suddenly evaporated and he allowed the old easy fallback of words to be replaced by the enclosing of one hand within another, mine within his. As self-consciousness dissolved, trust and love were condensed and recognised in that simplest of human contact. The greatest eloquence of our relationship lay within that last moment of silence.

Being an orderly man who never went to bed without doing the washing-up even if it was midnight, my father had made detailed arrangements for the time when I would no longer hear the sound of the radio from the floor beneath. A manila folder labelled 'When The Day Comes' lay on the top shelf in his writing room. He used to say the phrase out loud with a little rhythm to the words and accompanied by a rueful smile, his attempt to joke his way out of any difficult death talk.

The relief that follows the death of someone who has suffered a long illness is not just about the ending of suffering for them, but a silent exhilaration at the release from guilt that not enough is being done, not enough visits are being made and from the longing to be let off the caring-for hook. At last the moment arrives when it is permissible to stop fulfilling the all-consuming duties of nurse, shopper, accountant, reader, letter writer, cook, postman, cherisher, brow-soother, grandchild, son, daughter. For a time this new feeling of independence is heady, before the long slow tumble begins, the falling and twisting down through the tunnel where gravity cannot intervene. The loss of a parent can be one of the most foundation-dissolving of adult experiences. Just as Hamlet sees the sky as a caretaker, a 'majestical roof fretted with golden fire', so a parent provides the protecting ceiling above a child's fragility. A parent's death removes the shielding 'overhanging firmament', and in their absence we are left free-floating. For me, orphanhood prompted confusing feelings, the extremes of freedom and of loss, an adrenalin rush that comes from being at the very centre of a drama, followed by the deflation and a sense of 'Is that it?' Adam said that for him the experience was a form of dislocation, as if the limb of his own continued existence had 'come out of its socket'. The comparison is one I recognised for I was no longer sure how to position myself, to balance myself within my own life.

The day after the Day Came we took the buff folder down from the shelf and among The Instructions was a veto on any sort of service to express thankfulness for his life. 'No one will come and it will be embarrassing. Embarrassing for you I mean. I won't be there of course.' When he first became ill my father had begun keeping a list of names in his bedside drawer headed 'People who might come to my funeral' in black biro, underlined twice. When he was feeling buoyant the list increased to as many as fifty, but initial optimism dwindled and by the time the final calculation was made the numbers had sunk to the low twenties; certainly not enough to fill any decent-sized church, let alone anything with grander pretensions. A man of conventions, if not a believer, or even a churchgoer, his helpful notes in the buff file suggested that a small service in the village church would fit the bill. He had typed out his favourite hymns, *Jerusalem* and *I Vow to Thee My Country*, a carefully chosen Bible reading for Rebecca, and a little Post-it note wondering if it would be too much trouble for Adam to make a short address from the pulpit. For me, there was a favourite poem by his mother. The service would be followed by a visit to the crematorium and then burial next to his father and brother in the village churchyard. And that would be that. We held the service in the village church just as he had asked, managing somehow to complete the readings and the address as I steeled myself not to catch the eye of either of my daughters. The poem my father had asked me to read is taken from Vita's long pastoral song called *The Land*. It remains my favourite of all her poetry, encapsulating Sissinghurst and all she felt about it, the beauty of the garden, handed down to us, her lucky, lucky grandchildren and to our own equally fortunate children and grandchildren. And of course it also reminds me of my father and his own love for that place. He had chosen the same reading for Vita's own funeral. The poem begins

> She walks among the loveliness she made,
> Between the apple-blossom and the water –
> She walks among the patterned pied brocade,
> Each flower her son, and every tree her daughter.

But we defied one sentence in The Instructions. His bedside list turned out to be widely off the mark when three months later every seat in a magisterial chapel in London was filled by people who had admired and loved him, and who came to listen to the band of the Grenadier Guards play 'Lily Marlene' and pay tribute to a man who had led a rich and varied life. There were seven short reflections on his life as writer, politician, soldier, publisher, countryman, son and father. There was much left unspoken. We did not speak of his impatience, of his failure to understand women, of his obsession with his parents. There was much talk of what a good innings he had managed. The cliché did not work for me. I preferred another that told me grief is the price you pay for love. A friend wrote to say how she envied me. Her relationship with her father had been devoid of affection and I carried her generosity of sentiment throughout that day. The evening after the service I started a new page in my diary headed 'I am feeling very sad'. The relentlessly creeping awareness that my father was *still* not here and was now definitely not coming back, a truth that I had been turning away from for the past few months, ignoring the impending landslide, suddenly gained pace and clobbered me. It had taken the power of a large gathering of others united in an act of remembrance, expressing their delight in his friendship and tears at his absence, to make me accept the up till now unbelievable.

As the weeks put an increasing wedge between the present and the day my father had died, I thought of the things I would not be able to tell him. His presence seemed to be rushing away from me in reverse, a diminishing of awareness, like an inverted telescope becoming more powerful by the moment, shrinking the past into an ever-receding point. How he would have been horrified by the Boxing Day tsunami, how proud he would have been of my brother's new book, how pleased he would have been by the birth of my sister's second child, and how taken aback and perhaps secretly delighted by the beauty of the memorial service held in his honour. The opportunity to talk about all these things had gone forever. I wondered if I would soon forget the sound of his voice. For a long time I avoided a favourite photograph in which he looked me in the eye as if to say don't be so sad. Religion did not do it for me, although I occasionally lit candles in a church I love, and I knew the concept of the philosopher A. C. Grayling's 'lingering splinter in the mind', the yearning for spiritual reassurance that hope will be resurrected from despair. And I understood what Stevie Smith meant by Tennyson's feeling of 'sea-sad, loamishly-sad', being a hollowness too empty to articulate. But soon I retreated to words to try and understand what had happened, returning to those poets who had always made sense to me, to their eloquence on love, ageing, longing and loss, to Shakespeare, Donne, Herbert, Keats, Hardy, Lawrence, T. S. Eliot, words alive with healing power.

Not long ago, a decade after my father's death, Carol Ann Duffy, the Poet Laureate, stood in a tent in a Sussex meadow in front of a crowd of people and read 'Premonitions', her transformative poem about her mother. Imagining time reversed, she describes a metaphysical world where 'a bee swooned backwards out of a rose' drunk with fertility, the life-power it has ingested, and where the warmth of love returns the dead to those who are still living. She spoke without faltering of the essence of what it is to be 'daughterly', with all the love and affection that state can engender, and despite the private intensity of her words, every person gathered there who had lived through the death of a much-loved parent felt she was addressing them directly, linking our hands with those we had loved and in so doing reuniting us.

During late-September days, the month in which my father died, the unexpectedly strong heat of an autumn sun sometimes feels like the guiding palm of a hand on my back and an illusion lingers that summer has decided just for once to ignore the urgency to leave. The protracted warmth confuses swallows that still swoop in pairs overhead, having delayed their departure longer than is wise, nature's merging of one season with another mirrored by the human cycle of life, death and rebirth. On days like this, I sometimes imagine Dadda coming through the door, whistling silently, clearing his throat, self-conscious, apologetic for having been gone so long. And we would sit at the kitchen table together and catch up. 'How's John Major getting on?' he would begin and we would embark on a consoling, exclaiming marathon, walking round the garden, puzzled that the struggling yew hedge had still not reached its full height, picking a favourite rose to tuck in his buttonhole while I tried not to sadden but to surprise and gladden him about all that had happened.

But I was lucky. Throughout the long, sad year of my father's dying and death I had been sustained by my friends, my family and by Charlie. And throughout that year my daughters, grieving themselves for the loss of a beloved grandfather, did not falter once in their demonstrative love. A short while before my father died I had visited Rome for the first time. The dawn queue to get into the Vatican was so long that as soon as the doors opened I ran through the long corridors and the show rooms, stopping at nothing until I reached the Sistine Chapel. For five minutes I was quite alone. Above me on Michelangelo's ceiling two hands stretched towards each other, almost touching, but holding back at the last moment. The knowledge that a hand is there to guide or to support or to communicate tenderness has been important to me since childhood. During treasured moments in my life, hands have touched across a table at a time of quiet pride, hands were enfolded at the moment of death, hands were held during the blessing of a marriage, and once, on the quay of a London dockyard, a mother had reached down towards her two small children, indicating her love for them as they placed their hands in hers. I know now that the hands of a mother can continue to enclose those of her grown children, offer reassurance without restraint, give them confidence to strive for their dreams, demonstrate her pride in them, their inestimable preciousness to her, her unconditional love for them. And I have learned what it feels like when, with an answering squeeze, a child confirms not only that she loves her parents back but forgives them.

·ᕐᕐᕐ·

## 12

# Imogen
### Love

We are having a picnic on a beach in the south of Harris in
the Hebrides. Imogen is sitting on my knee. She is almost a
year old and the fine almost Caribbean-white sand that I am
trickling through my fingers absorbs her attention. She has
never seen sand before and, for a moment, neither have I.

The day my granddaughter was born felt like the last day of
my youth, my own childbearing years still a vivid memory, the
early years of motherhood illusorily, just a small backward-
reaching gesture away. I knew it was a day of transition as I
hovered on the brink that Sunday afternoon at home in Sussex
when Bean, my son-in-law, rang me, suggesting that it might
be a good idea to take the next train to London. Not long
afterwards, when I walked into the maternity ward of a twenty-
first-century hospital with all its machines and sophistication,
I thought I knew what to expect.

Several months earlier I had been leaning against the thick oak beam that supports our house when Clemmie told me that the baby she and her husband were expecting was a girl. At the hospital Bean greeted me, their first visitor, his face alight, euphoric. And then, there was Clemmie, her five-minute-old baby lying in her arms. She was gazing at her daughter with the same astonishment that I had first looked at Clemmie. As she looked up at me, I returned her gaze, humbled, rejuvenated, astonished too by the intensity of my love for her.

When I left the three of them early the following morning and walked out into the cool London air, dawn was still a lifetime away. Shafts of moonlight were filtering through the clouds and bringing a shimmer to the high overhanging darkness. I went back alone to Clemmie and Bean's house. A half-drunk cup of tea was still on my daughter's bedside table next to a vase of white freesias that they had bought in the Columbia Road Market the afternoon before, an entire existence before. I curled up in bed and slept.

During that first year of my granddaughter's life, I discovered the flexibility of what I had assumed were long-established boundaries of unconditional love. Together Imogen and I have begun to accumulate a layering of memories, none of them yet articulated between us, but all, at least for me, stored forever. Imogen's first summer was backlit by the warmth of the sun and the smell and the sound of the sea, the glitter on a wave, phosphorescent insects dancing in the moonlight above the near stillness of the Mediterranean at night, the shiny wetness of a pebble. French sand is darker and less fine than in the north of Scotland, but if you are a year old the tactile pleasure in digging naked toes into its softness, burrowing for the cold dampness beneath the surface warmth, is just as thrilling now as it was a century and a half ago.

I have watched Imo on her mother's lap spinning round in front of me on an Edwardian merry-go-round, the painted wooden horse scratched by the scuffmarks of generations of children. I have seen her riding high on her father's shoulders while they both sing loud enough to wake sleeping squirrels in the trees around them. I have seen her reach out to be whirled up in the air by Flora. I have watched her discover the pleasure of biting into an apple. I have walked through London parks with her, finding ourselves equally mesmerised by the swans gliding on a pond. I have watched her being bathed in a plastic bucket on a Scottish beach where seals with long whiskers bobbed in the bay and where I last was with my father so many decades before, the black and white of my distant childhood suddenly suffused with colour.

I have sat with Imo on a bench in the beauty of the Green Court at Knole, beside the doorway against which Virginia Woolf once leaned, S-curved, with my ten-year-old father. I have seen her take nascent steps along the path towards the Stone Court down which Vita once wobbled under the watchful eye of a grandparent. I have seen her recognise me and hold her arms out to me. I have marvelled that her first word, and for a while her only word, reflected so accurately her excitement about life. 'Wow,' she exclaimed unvaryingly at the sight of a banana, a bird in the sky, her parents. I have crept into her room in the middle of the night and seen her sleeping, still, silent, peaceful. At the end of a weekend I avoid the sight of an empty wheelbarrow which just hours earlier has contained a small laughing body. I have seen her mother and her father and her Aunt Flora absorb Imo into their own lives as if there had never been a time when she did not exist. And as for me, I have fallen in love with her. Just as I did with my daughters a generation ago. And yet, rather than accentuating my own mortality as I had expected, grandparenthood has deepened the experience of living.

I remember being quite alone with her at Sissinghurst, sitting on a bench in the garden holding her on my knee, engulfed by tenderness, absorbing her stillness, feeling her quiet breaths beneath my hands, as we faced the moat, the covering of duckweed lifted into gentle ridges by the ghost of a wind, noticing her noticing the particles of dust trapped in the sunlight. A moorhen made a dash for the opposite bank, its body cutting a pathway through the green algae; the brilliant May leaves on 500-year-old oaks swayed in the breeze, their branches heavy with the weight of summer growth, dipping down and skimming the surface of the water. Imogen's eyes shone and danced, the reactions on her face changing in quick succession from surprise to comprehension then delight like a speeded-up film sequence of a cloud-filled sky. The only other time I have seen such swift transference of emotion was on my father's face in the days before he died, as if he was trying to fit every feeling in before time ran out.

Last summer I went to Arcachon with my daughters and my granddaughter. We wanted to see where the beginnings of this story had ended. And we wanted to watch Imo feel the warm French sand on her toes just as Pepita's children had done long ago. To our surprise we found a small hotel that had been welcoming guests since Pepita's day. Even better, the hotel was in the same street as Villa Pepa! Walking a little apprehensively in the direction of the casino, Imo in Clemmie's arms and Flora's hand in mine, we were uncertain what we would find. But there, towards the end of Boulevard de la Plage, we suddenly spotted the coronet and the combined initials S&W sitting securely on top of the large metal gates through which Pepita and her tiny kindergarten had swept on their way to the beach some 150 years earlier.

We stared in silence though the gates looking for the house. But the building that Pepita had embellished and made into a lovely place for her young family was no longer there. We gazed instead at the modern white three-storey building that dominated the jungly palm-tree-filled garden, a central archway cut through the white brick to reveal the dancing sea beyond the only redeeming feature of the soulless design.

Just then an elderly couple appeared and put their key into the lock, one of twenty-five couples for whom the apartments at 167 Boulevard de la Plage is now home. Explaining our presence outside the gates, I told them that my great-great-grandmother had once lived at that address. The elegant French woman looked at me closely. '*La grande-fille de Pepita?*' she said. '*Oh non! quel dommage!*' The house had only been pulled down only seventeen years earlier she said, although nowadays new planning laws would not have allowed any such travesty. What a magnificent house it had been! And the pity of us coming all this way and being denied the sight of it! She went into the white building, shaking her head. We watched her until she disappeared, before we turned to each other, smiling through our tears.

I have thought of the great good fortune my granddaughter has in being born into a life where loyalty, respect and equality are all held in the highest regard, where guilt is not a feeling to be encouraged and where the benefits of the imagination are ever-present. If she had been born a boy she would not have been treated any differently. Although the best of childhood experiences and traditions will endure – favourite books, Father Christmas, singing, dancing – Imogen is the beneficiary of a technological age whose advances will remain unknown to all of us born half a century before her. She is also part of a more honest generation, a more communicative generation, hopefully an increasingly tolerant and accepting generation, one that is not afraid to learn from the mistakes of the past and is determined not to repeat them, something I realise that is possibly the entire point of this book.

Hands will be there to steady and guide this precious child, and to loosen their hold when she is ready to make her own way unaided. She will understand that it is laudable to be ambitious. She will be proud and uninhibited to be a woman.

Imogen Flora is the only person in our immediate family to have a middle name, the choice a measure of the love Clemmie and her younger sister, Imogen's aunt, bear for each other. Imogen's first name has its origins in the old Irish dialect, the country where her parents were at university together and where they fell in love. The old Irish meaning of Imogen is beloved daughter.

# Bibliography

Several publications all found in the bowels of the London Library have proved to be essential archive sources including *The Times*, *The Illustrated London News* and that old stalwart of social documentation, *The Lady Magazine*.

In addition to several published histories, biographies and memoirs, I have drawn on many unpublished letters and documents that belong to the Vita Sackville-West, Harold Nicolson and Nigel Nicolson estates, all of them administered by my brother Adam and me. In addition I have consulted several of the many books that have been published by and about the Sackville/Nicolson family.

*Lady Sackville* by Susan Mary Alsop (Weidenfeld & Nicolson 1978)
*The Penguin History of the USA* by Hugh Brogan (Revised edition 1998)

*A Short History of the British Embassy at Washington DC USA* by C. F. M. Browne (June 1930)

*The Civilisation of the Renaissance in Italy* by Jacob Burckhardt (Phaidon 1951)

*Offshore* by Penelope Fitzgerald (Fourth Estate 2009)

*A Hand-book for Travellers in Spain* by Richard Ford (1845)

*Romantic in Spain* by Theophile Gautier (Alfred A Knopf 1926)

*Vita Sackville-West* by Victoria Glendinning (Weidenfeld & Nicolson 1983)

*Wanderings in Spain in 1843* by Martin Haverty (T. C. Newby 1944)

*Spain in 1830* by Henry D Inglis (Whittaker Treacher & Co 1831)

*The Vanished Landscape: A 1930s Childhood in the Potteries* by Paul Johnson (Weidenfeld & Nicolson 2004)

*Virginia Woolf* by Hermione Lee (Chatto & Windus 1996)

*Ammonites and Leaping Fish* by Penelope Lively (Penguin 2013)

*Harold Nicolson: A biography* Volumes 1 (1980) and 2 (1981) by James Lees Milne (Chatto & Windus)

*Spain* (Murray's Handbooks. Part 1 John Murray 1855)

*Sissinghurst* by Adam Nicolson (Harper Press 2008)

*Harold Nicolson Diaries and Letters* edited by Nigel Nicolson (Volume 3 Collins 1968)

*Long Life* by Nigel Nicolson (Weidenfeld & Nicolson 1997)

*Farming on a Battleground* by A Norfolk Woman (Geo. R. Reeve Ltd 1950)

*The Five of Hearts* by Patricia O'Toole (Ballantin Books 1991)

*Tottington: A lost Village in Norfolk* by Hilda and Edmund Perry (Geo. R. Reeve 1999)

*Mujeres Malaguenas en el Flamenco* by Gonzalo Rojo Guerrero (Ediciones Giralda)

*The Disinherited* by Robert Sackville-West (Bloomsbury 2014)

*Inheritance* by Robert Sackville-West (Bloomsbury 2010)

*The Edwardians* by Vita Sackville-West (Hogarth Press 1930; reissued in 2016 by Vintage)

*Knole and the Sackvilles* by Vita Sackville-West (Ernest Benn 1922)

*The Land* by Vita Sackville-West (Heinemann 1926)

*Pepita* by Vita Sackville-West (The Hogarth Press 1937; reissued in 2016 by Vintage)

*Portrait of a Marriage* by Vita Sackville-West and Nigel Nicolson (Weidenfeld & Nicolson 1973)

*The Countryside of East Anglia* by Susanna Wade Martins and Tom Williamson (The Boydell Press 2008)

*The Richard Burton Diaries* edited by Chris Williams (Yale University Press 2013)

*Orlando* by Virginia Woolf (The Hogarth Press 1928)

◇

# Acknowledgements

I owe the idea for this book to a short essay on memoir that I wrote at the invitation of Johnny de Falbe and Dan Fenton at John Sandoe Books. To them and to the gifted Fenella Willis I am grateful to have been given the opportunity to write about the sadnesses and the joys of past days.

The staff of the London Library have as ever been unfailingly helpful to me and to Clemmie Macmillan-Scott, who immersed herself expertly on my behalf in the history of mid nineteenth century flamenco and in the social dance of late nineteenth century Washington DC.

Joan Matthews, and Bronwen Tyler, both local Norfolk historians, have been brilliant in enlightening me about wartime Norfolk and my mother's schooldays in that county. Through them it has been a real pleasure to talk to my mother's old school friends Margaret North and Katherine

Powys, their brother John Walsingham and their niece Katherine Wolstenholme.

Although this is a deeply personal book, I have depended enormously during the writing of it on the encouragement of a group of emotionally generous-spirited people. Among those I would like to thank for their invaluable help, encouragement, thoughts and memories are Catherine Allison, Patricia Anker, Tersh Boasberg, Kildare and Sarah Bourke Borrowes, Annabel Bryant, Caroline Bryant, Jilly Byford, Paul Calkin, Julie Campbell, Jennifer Combe, Margaret Engebretson, Anita Fischel, Alyson Flower, Antonia Fraser, Sophie Ford, David Fyfe-Jameson, Tom Grant, Kathy Hill-Miller, Victoria Hislop, Sam Macambulance, Fiona MacNeil Moss, Virginia Nicholson, William Nicholson, Jennifer Plunket, Shirley Punnett, Gail Rebuck, Diana Reich, Claire Skinner, Nicholas Stafford Deitsche, Tom Stoppard, Monique Wolak and Timothy Young. I am also particularly grateful to Liz Bussey whose amazing wisdom has strengthened me on innumerable occasions. And without the initial and then the sustained encouragement first of all by my brother Adam and then by Joanna Trollope I am not sure the book would have been written at all.

The insights of my dearest friends, all but one of them (though he is equally important too) daughters, have been invaluable, especially those of Belinda Giles, Anne Goldrach, Belinda Harley, Jeremy Hutchinson, Katie Law, Imogen Lycett Green, Julia Samuel, Aly Van Den Berg and Rachel Wyndham.

Nuria Goytre guided me linguistically and expertly through the unravelling of the mysteries of Spanish flamenco. James

Macmillan-Scott has been wonderful about the book from start to finish. Several of my cousins have helped me enormously with facts, photographs, memories and insights among them Joanna Freeman, Mary Philipson, Jo Lascelles and Jeremy Till. Vanessa Nicolson has been unfailingly supportive. It has been a delight to reminisce with Mark Tennyson-d'Eyncourt and my aunt Juanita Tennyson-d'Eyncourt whose knowledge of my mother's family has filled in so many missing gaps. Bridget and Robert Sackville-West have been inexhaustibly hospitable, allowing me to spend fascinating and uninterrupted hours with family albums, papers, stories and treasures contained in the drawers, attics and rooms at Knole.

My agent Ed Victor has, as always, been the greatest enthusiast and confidence-booster that any writer could ever wish for. I would like to thank him for his long and loving friendship and the support of his terrific colleagues Edina Imrik, Hitesh Shah, Maggie Phillips and Linda Vann and William Clark in New York. Cressida Bell has understood the sensibility of the book perfectly and designed a jacket which to me reflects exactly what I have tried to do.

At Chatto I have been immensely fortunate to find myself published by Clara Farmer and Becky Hardie. I am also so grateful to Louise Court, Charlotte Humphery, Penelope Lietchti and Kris Potter for their enthusiastic work on this book's behalf. And any author who finds themselves guided by the exemplary skill of my friend Becky Hardie should consider themselves more than blessed.

The patience and encouragement of my family has sustained me throughout especially that of Bean and of Sarah and Adam.

Beloved Charlie has shown more tolerance and compassion than should be asked of any husband.

Clemmie and Flora have been unwavering in their trust and love. In dedicating this book to them and to miraculous Imo, I thank them for . . . well . . . for everything really.